WOMEN OF WAR

ALSO BY SUZANNE COPE

Power Hungry

WOMEN OF WAR

THE ITALIAN ASSASSINS, SPIES, AND COURIERS WHO FOUGHT THE NAZIS

SUZANNE COPE

DUTTON

DUTTON

An imprint of Penguin Random House LLC
1745 Broadway, New York, NY 10019
penguinrandomhouse.com

Book design by George Towne

LIBRARY OF CONGRESS CATALOGING-IN-PUBLICATION DATA

Names: Cope, Suzanne, 1978– author.
Title: Women of war: the Italian assassins, spies, and
couriers who fought the Nazis / Suzanne Cope.
Other titles: Italian assassins, spies, and couriers who fought the Nazis
Description: [New York, New York]: Dutton, [2025] |
Includes bibliographical references and index.
Identifiers: LCCN 2024057102 (print) | LCCN 2024057103 (ebook) |
ISBN 9780593476000 (hardcover) | ISBN 9780593476017 (ebook)
Subjects: LCSH: World War, 1939–1945—Underground movements—Italy. |
Malavasi, Anita, 1921–2011. | Guidetti Serra, Bianca. | Mattei, Teresa, 1921–2013. |
Capponi, Carla, 1918–2000. | Women guerrillas—Italy—Biography. |
Female assassins—Italy—Biography. | Women spies—Italy—Biography. |
Guerrillas—Italy—Biography. | Assassins—Italy—Biography. | Spies—Italy—Biography.
Classification: LCC D802.I8 C5896 2025 (print) | LCC D802.I8 (ebook) |
DDC 940.54/864509252—dc23/eng/20250207
LC record available at https://lccn.loc.gov/2024057102
LC ebook record available at https://lccn.loc.gov/2024057103

Printed in the United States of America

1st Printing

The authorized representative in the EU for product safety and compliance
is Penguin Random House Ireland, Morrison Chambers, 32 Nassau Street,
Dublin D02 YH68, Ireland, https://eu-contact.penguin.ie.

For Pattra, who never stopped fighting

CONTENTS

Introduction   1

PART 1: War Comes to Italy   7

PART 2: Resistance   85

PART 3: Liberation   291

Acknowledgments   405

Note on Sources   409

Bibliography   413

Archives and Museums   419

Interviews   423

Notes   425

Index   447

delli (53) long ago proved.* The boundaries of this half are clearly marked on the north along the crest of the Apennines, away across to the frontier of France; for the modern prov-

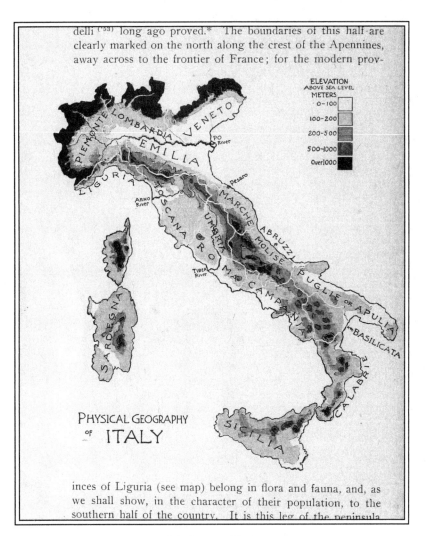

ELEVATION
ABOVE SEA LEVEL
METERS
·0–100
100–200
200–500
500–1000
Over 1000

PO River

Pesaro

ARNO River

TIBER River

PIEMONTE
LOMBARDIA
VENETO
EMILIA
LIGURIA
TOSCANA
UMBRIA
MARCHE
ABRUZZI
e
MOLISE
ROMA
CAMPANIA
PUGLIE OR APULIA
BASILICATA
CALABRIE
SARDEGNA
SICILIA

Physical Geography
of ITALY

inces of Liguria (see map) belong in flora and fauna, and, as we shall show, in the character of their population, to the southern half of the country. It is this leg of the peninsula

A geographical map of Italy, ca. 1899

Anita Malavasi (*far right*),
1921–2011, and unnamed
fellow partisans

COURTESY OF ISTORECO REGGIO EMILIA

Bianca Guidetti Serra, 1919–2014

COURTESY OF FABRIZIO SALMONI

Carla Capponi,
1918–2000

Teresa Mattei, 1921–2013

COURTESY OF ISTITUTO STORICO
TOSCANO DELLA RESISTENZA E
DELL'ETÀ CONTEMPORANEA

WOMEN OF WAR

There are ghosts everywhere. Along Via Cavour in Rome, I imagine watching Carla throw her father's clothes from an open window four stories above, suit pants and collared shirts drifting down to the young Italian soldiers in uniform who need an outfit to blend in among their civilian peers. Now I see souvenir shops and a restaurant selling Chinese-Italian food. Perhaps a half mile away, Cinema Barberini is showing the latest blockbuster while tourists in windbreakers and sneakers take selfies in front of the Triton Fountain, an arc of water from the sea god's conch spraying into the air, refracting the bright sun into rainbows. I stop where Carla stood and watched with horror as her comrade raced down the hill just beyond, toward where the Nazi transport trucks would have parked to ferry the soldiers to and from their barracks.

As I wander the Eternal City, tracing the steps of Carla Capponi, I find myself caught up in a parade of students, its leader holding a metal stick with a purple pom-pom attached to the top; it bounces as she treads the cobblestones. We are all walking toward the Spanish Steps, and the orange of sunset turns violet with twilight as we near. The students dissipate at the top of the steps, above the piazza that gave them their name centuries before, to take pictures of a now-glowing Rome below. But I am thinking of the night during the occupation when Carla and two others crept up these same stairs on a mission for the Resistance—to be caught would have meant arrest or worse. I look to the shadows that would have hidden them from the Fascist night watchmen wandering the city. Couples now pose and groups of friends laugh, leaning against the waist-height wall at the ridge of Pincian Hill, which Carla and her comrades might have crawled beneath as they snuck from the steps to the Villa Medici.

I similarly reanimate the past in Florence, on the dusty streets around the university where Teresa Mattei studied philosophy, the windows of the palazzos, built up close against the sidewalks, shut tight in the heat of a summer afternoon. Or along the mountain paths outside of the small city of Reggio Emilia, where dedicated historians have sought to help others understand the routes walked by *staffette*—a term that translates to "couriers," when in reality, these operatives did so much more than carry messages. Anita Malavasi walked here in the forests that fill the valleys beyond the cities, where so many escaped to save their lives. Still, violence found them here. For some, even death. On a perfect spring day I studied the first crocuses of the season emerging from the verdant green around me and heard the bells from Castelnovo ne'Monti ring out at noon as I walked these same paths, headed steeply uphill, where Anita might have stolen moments to stop and wonder at the beauty around her. But a stick cracking or a rustling of leaves would bring her back to the fear of the unknown. Was today the day she encountered a German hiding among the trees?

In Turin I seek to reconcile the bombed-out street where Bianca Guidetti Serra lived with modern-day *strade* filled with jovial groups speaking multiple languages, waiting in a line that wraps around the block for an animation exhibition at a cinema museum. In a country with such fidelity to blending the past with the present, it is not often easy to tell which buildings were rebuilt since the war, where the old ends and the new begins. Were the roads in the same place? In the Alps, where Bianca traveled with messages or deliveries, they must be: The towns were built right up to their edges, with little room between where the houses end and the mountains begin. They may be paved now, for the most part, but they are still often too narrow for two modern cars to pass comfortably.

In many places, the way that Italy has preserved its past helps these ghosts come alive.

I do not believe we need to be constantly reminded of suffering and war. But I followed these paths to help tell a story almost unknown to English-speaking audiences, to illuminate a past that sometimes feels all too resonant. Over the years that I researched and wrote this book, neo-Fascist politicians were elected around Europe and in the United States. Division and hate—of Jewish people, still, but also of others with different religions or skin colors or heritages who are considered foreigners, unwelcome in their own homes, native or adopted—have intensified around the world. It is my hope that we can learn from the women in these pages, see the story of World War II through new eyes. By centering the experience not on the soldiers, many of whom were compelled to fight by their governments, but on those who chose to enter the war as members of the Resistance, we learn that for Carla, Teresa, Anita, and Bianca, the decision to do nothing was to side with the enemy.

To that end, this is not an exhaustive history of World War II, of the Nazi occupation of Italy, or of the experiences of Italians under Fascism. There are already many excellent tomes on these topics. Rather this is the story of four women within the larger context of their time. Their individual and collective experiences drive this narrative, though I have sought to bolster the larger historical context of these experiences by including facts that we know now. In Italy (and to a varying extent globally), news moved slowly and was incomplete during the war—on the battlefield and in occupied and attacked areas. And there was much that wasn't known until well afterward. The broader stories of war and the historical context provided here are generally more detailed and include more complete information than these women could have had access to at the time. I also strived to give a sense of what they *did* know through Radio London and the clandestine press. I am allowing their experiences to lead this narrative to provide a counterpoint to the many accounts of this time period from other points of view.

I am honored to be able to amplify the stories of these four women and numerous others who were prepared to give their lives for a new future that many could only begin to dream of when the first bombs fell on their imperfect but beloved country. Mussolini's Fascist regime had done its job: An entire generation of young people were brought up largely ignorant of the world beyond their borders. Most, under fear of arrest or violence, had parents who were too scared to share what life was like before Il Duce, or consider what possibilities—for women, in particular—other countries and cultures could provide. These four women, and so many other young Italians, could see a future worth fighting for. And hundreds of thousands of them made the decision to fight against both the Nazi occupiers and their own Fascist countrymen—for themselves, yes, but more so for those who would come after them.

Through these travels, and by listening to and reading many testimonies, I have come to know these women and the terror under Nazi occupation and Fascist oppression, and have sought to recreate their lives based entirely on the details they left behind. And they left behind a lot: Two of the women wrote about their lives in the Resistance through memoirs, all of them gave multiple and detailed testimonies and interviews, and most had fellow partisans—as the Resistance members were known—who also provided testimony about their time together. These stories do represent the breadth of the contributions of the many women (and men) who fought for their freedom during this period, but at the same time I recognize that there are as many unique tales of bravery and persistence as there are women of the Resistance. I do not claim to fully represent the experiences of women during this time.

There are many historians and scholars who came before me who also sought to detail as much as they could from this period, starting in the years soon after the war to help preserve memories that time might soften. Italy also keeps a number of valuable archives—physical and online—of the Resistance, which helped to re-create this history. There are dedicated and knowledgeable librarians who helped me track down rare books and documents, and other journalists and archivists who worked hard to preserve the stories of these women and men in the years before they died. Their work was invaluable to my research. There are also small museums, plaques, and places of interest that note where important moments occurred or hold collections of items and offer further historical details, allowing me to be assured my footsteps matched those I was following.

And yet, there are moments where the testimonies conflict with other accounts, sometimes even with accounts given by the same person, or with the historical record. Further, most of the sources I am working with are in Italian. Most translations are my own, with occasional help, confirmation, or clarification from native speakers. I have strived to note any conflicts or uncertainties in the endnotes, as well as cite my sources. But by and large every scene or word of dialogue is directly taken from, or was implied in the words of, the people who were there, as are details of the women's emotional responses. There are moments when the timing of an action is unclear, and I placed those within the narrative where I believed, from my research, they made the most sense. Please see the note on sources for more details.

These years of research have also allowed me insight into my own Italian heritage. My *nonna*, whom I called Nani, spent her early childhood in Italy and was the exact age of the *partigiane*—female partisans—in this book. If she had not immigrated to the United States, I could imagine her among them. Their road to political activism feels familiar, as I remember my grandmother having progressive newspapers around the county airport office she ran with my *nonno*—whose family were also Italian immigrants—when I was young, of her encouraging me to go to law school and to pursue a career in politics.

I can't help but imagine her as a young bride married to a World War II airman, following the war closely—what letters she might have received from friends and family in Italy, and what news she might have heard of her still-beloved homeland. She died while I was in high school, before I could speak with her in Italian, before I knew to ask her about her childhood under Mussolini, or about her experiences during the war, or stories from so many other parts of her life. For just because one lives through terror or challenges, one need not be defined by it.

While this book is about the experiences of these women under Fascism, they all lived robust, joyful lives in the years after the war. I may only touch upon these in the epilogue, but their acts of public service and activism continued. I am honored to share with you these four women's stories. There were thousands more like them— as there are now, people whose selfless acts deserve a wider audience, to inform and inspire. But here is a start.

PART 1

WAR COMES TO ITALY

CARLA

ROME
JULY 19, 1943

I t was 11:03 A.M. when Carla Capponi heard the explosions. In the nearby neighborhood of San Lorenzo, the first of five hundred American planes had begun dropping more than one thousand tons of bombs on the Eternal City. An hour earlier, in the office at the mining chemical lab where she worked, perhaps she was daydreaming about visiting the beach. Swimming in the cool waters of the Mediterranean just outside the city was one of her favorite things to do on a hot day. From her open window, she had smelled the salt in the breeze. But now she was hiding under her desk. The besieged San Lorenzo neighborhood was adjacent to the railroad freight yard near Termini station—the air raid's target. Within moments the smell of the sea was replaced by waves of dust and the musty stench of crumbled plaster and ancient stones. Carla held her breath as she crawled out from beneath the desk and slammed the window shut before returning to her hiding spot.

Until that morning on July 19, 1943, Romans had believed they might escape the worst of the war that seemed to be happening so far away; they were convinced that the presence of the Vatican and so many works of artistic and historic significance would shield them. An increasing number of Italians had an expectation—a hope—that the Allies would quickly overtake Italy and that the Germans would retreat without much of a fight. This magical thinking persisted despite the frequent drone of bombers overhead. Allied planes had flown over Rome before on bombing raids to northern Italian industrial destinations like Turin and Milan now that they had captured airfields that gave them range to do so. More recently these planes had dropped leaflets warning locals to denounce Fascism and move far from Roman bomb targets like railroads and armories, since precision bombing had not yet been perfected.

Just days before, Allied bomber planes had dropped thousands of fluttering missives over San Lorenzo declaring: TODAY WE CHOOSE TO DROP PAMPHLETS EVEN THOUGH WE NOW CAN CHOOSE TO DROP BOMBS. . . . SEPARATE YOUR DESTINY FROM THE MEN OF THE REGIME.

Like so many Romans, Carla must have seen the leaflets blowing in the hot wind around the city, had stepped on them languishing in puddles among the cobblestones. But few seemed convinced that they might be in danger.

Especially as the Fascists had countered with their own propaganda, such as posters plastered in public piazzas and editorials in the state-run newspapers. A radio address declared: "If the enemy were to be victorious, what fate would await us? The Nation would be torn apart, the people reduced to a breed of servants. . . . Shipped off to work in the mines of the Urals . . . [or] consigned to cultivate flowers for English ladies."

But that day in July, as bombs exploded in their beloved city, the war became real to all Romans at long last. World War II had come to all, not discerning between those who had resisted Fascism and those who had trusted Mussolini's leadership and ties to Hitler and the Axis powers.

The air raid sirens were drowned out by the drone of the next wave of incoming aircraft, and then the high shriek of the dropping bombs and their deafening explosions as they reached the earth. There were a few moments of silence before Carla could hear the hollow rumblings of buildings collapsing. The horns of the rescue workers followed and, finally, the cries and yells of survivors. This cycle repeated as Carla hid, alone in her office, waiting for the piercing sirens to cease.

When Carla felt sure the attack was over, she knew she had to make her way through the citywide chaos to San Lorenzo, still wearing her high heels and dress. On the street she fought the rushing current of people fleeing the destruction in San Lorenzo—although the neighborhood would attract many people like Carla from around the city, compelled to help. Few of Carla's closest friends were politically engaged, but her parents had instilled in her and her older sister a sense of justice and compassion that she had, until then, not known how to act upon. But there was something in this first struggle against the crowd that felt like she finally had a clear direction.

In the bombed neighborhood Carla joined the female aid workers of San Vincenzo who were providing help to survivors. A dense dust permeated the air, making it hard to breathe. Everything was covered in a fine layer of chalky gray. What had been rows of thickly settled stone apartment buildings were now mounds of rubble. It was like the world around her had turned inside out.

"The streets, turned into ruins, were filled with every possible kind of household item, furniture, pots, pans, rags, and shoes," Carla described. "Bodies thrown into the streets were covered with debris and stained with blood. They were lying colorful and unreal among the few signs of former life—household items often completely undamaged, which had somehow escaped the devastation of the houses."

Carla found purpose in this instinctive desire to help—a feeling she had not yet known in her twenty-four years. She stayed in San Lorenzo until the early hours of the morning, working with other volunteers in the near darkness until she was swaying from exhaustion, and then she stumbled home. The next morning she returned and did the same, and then again the morning after that.

NINE DAYS EARLIER, on July 10, the Allied forces had invaded the southern tip of Sicily in the largest amphibious landing of World War II, involving more than three thousand ships that brought more than one hundred and fifty thousand American, British, and Canadian troops to the island, covered by four thousand aircraft. This tactical decision was made to redirect Axis resources from the east, with a goal to establish better-situated air bases and retake control of the Mediterranean corridor. The Allied forces fought against the Germans in olive and orange groves and used barns and homes as shields and safe houses in messy battles with ill-defined front lines. The warring armies scattered families and destroyed entire villages as the Allies made their way in a burning gash across the island toward Messina, the city at the northeastern corner of Sicily that connects most closely to the toe of Italy's boot. Civilians were often caught in the cross fire. Destroyed machinery, land mines, and spent shells would litter the Sicilian countryside for years to come.

On July 19, the Allied forces were still mired in Sicily—a battle that would take them until August 17 to fully win. But they were starting to see results. Adolf Hitler had already diverted troops to Italy from Eastern Europe, aiding the Allied efforts in Russia. In their confidence the Allied leaders decided they would continue their battle on Italy's mainland, marching northward in an attempt to further draw Nazi troops from elsewhere to defend a potential gateway to Germany from the south. British prime minister Winston Churchill was particularly vocal about the strategic need to win Italy, convincing American president Franklin Delano Roosevelt and his generals as well. With this goal in place, and newly won and better-situated Italian air bases from which to fly, the Allied forces orchestrated air raids to bomb key communication and transportation targets. San Lorenzo's rail yards were among their first.

CARLA WORKED FOR six days straight—she helped dig out survivors and bodies by hand or with shovels, cared for the injured in makeshift hospital rooms, and vetted generous Romans who offered places to stay. Perhaps she wore her brother's shirt tucked into her skirt, took her most sensible shoes out from the back of her closet, and pulled her hair up in a scarf. If she had passed one of her friends on the street, they might not have recognized her without her coifed blond hair curled above the collar of her skirt suit.

Each night she made the long trek home in the lonely dark, across her city, which she knew so well, slivers of light barely visible from behind the closed shutters. Government policy dictated that city lights be as limited as possible to deter nighttime bombings. Once home, she climbed the 128 stairs to her family's apartment on Via Cavour, near Trajan's Forum, the ruins of the ancient architectural complex honoring the militaristic emperor of the same name, her feet heavier with each step. And then, inside, she barely had the energy to eat the now cold meal her mother had set out for her, scrounged from increasingly meager food rations, wipe her face with a wet cloth, strip off her dirty clothes, and sink into a deep sleep before rising again just a few hours later. She dared not think about the future in those days, although she understood that her priorities had been reorganized. When her help would no longer be needed at San Lorenzo, she couldn't simply return to her life as it had been.

CHAPTER 1

TERESA

MILAN AND FLORENCE
1929-1938

Teresa Mattei was eight when she slipped behind the curtain of the dark-paneled confessional booth for her First Penance. She knelt and craned her neck upward, directing her girlhood indiscretions through the lattice to the priest waiting behind the curtain on the other side. The layers of thick fabric and rich wood were intended for anonymity between parishioner and priest. To atone for whatever she admitted that day, the priest prescribed three Hail Marys to the Pope.

Teresa responded, *"Ma il Papa e un porco!"*—"But the Pope is a pig!"

The priest jumped out of the confessional booth and pulled back the curtain on the other side.

"Who told you such nonsense?" he demanded of the dark-eyed little girl.

"I don't believe in you," Teresa responded defiantly; she had been taught since she was young about the dangerous friendship of the Pope and Mussolini. "I believe in my father."

PERHAPS IT IS telling that Teresa was born in February 1921—just months before Benito Mussolini first held political office. She was the oldest daughter and middle of seven children, born to a Catholic father and a Jewish mother whose family had escaped a pogrom in Lithuania. Teresa spent most of her earliest childhood in the countryside outside Milan, where her father had helped found one of Italy's first telephone companies. Milan was an industrial hub. It was also the cradle of Fascism, and the Mattei family had a front-row seat to its beginnings.

Her father, Ugo, had felt disdain for Mussolini since those earliest days of his political ambition. Ugo's company was slowly rolling out Italy's first private telephone lines around Milan and received an urgent request for one from Mussolini's newspaper office, declaring a need to be in constant touch with Rome. But Ugo held the position that the newspaper would not be able to jump the line.

One day, Mussolini showed up at Ugo's office in person and demanded special service.

Ugo refused, and Benito's infamous temper flared. He threatened a press campaign against Ugo and his company.

"And I will smash your head," Ugo countered. Calmly, he reached for the inert grenade that he kept on his desk as a personal reminder of the horrors of war, and cocked his arm. Mussolini ran out of Ugo's office, never to return.

Teresa had grown up hearing this tale, and many others. "My father always maintained that Mussolini was a great coward and that a thousand people in Italy would have been enough to chase him away," she said.

Decades earlier, during World War I, Ugo, a decorated naval captain, had an epiphany as he hid under an armored car belonging to the enemy. As he had told the story to Teresa and her siblings, he was trapped there for hours, forced to watch the terror of battle around him. While he, helpless beneath the vehicle, witnessed so many men slaughter one another, he got to know his surroundings well, his senses sharpened, perhaps, by the proximity of death. He noticed for the first time that the tires of this enemy car were made by the Italian company Pirelli. Italian businessmen had supplied both sides of the conflict, profiting double. He had walked away from the battlefield a pacifist, telling Teresa he had come to understand that "wars are only for the convenience of a few." Ugo would spend the following decades using what power he had to resist the oppression of Fascism, and then the threat of war.

UGO HAD FOLLOWED the trajectory of Benito Mussolini since the latter began his career in media. Benito was not much older than Ugo, but his upbringing was far less comfortable. His mother was a schoolteacher and his father a blacksmith and Socialist journalist who often frittered away the family finances. As a young man, Benito became known as an instigator and gifted speaker, and found himself drawn to revolutionary politics, in 1912 landing a job at the helm of Italy's official Socialist newspaper, *Avanti!*, where he quickly doubled its circulation and vociferously opposed war.

While Ugo was having his revelation on the battlefield, Benito gradually came to support the war from behind a desk. Soon, he began writing articles and giving speeches supporting Italy's involvement. Making a name for himself within conservative politics, he was eventually ousted from his role at *Avanti!* and from the Socialist Party. Undaunted, Benito Mussolini founded his own newspaper, *Il Popolo d'Italia,* in Milan in 1914, and then began gathering veterans and like-minded politicians to form the Fascist Party in 1919, the year after the end of the Great War.

Over the next few years he would bring together conservative Italians who were upset at the liberal direction their country was taking. They wanted to elevate Italy's current standing in the world—hence the rallying cry "Bring back the Roman Empire!"—while also keeping wealth and power concentrated among the land and business owners by fearmongering about the ills of Communism and Socialism.

On October 28, 1922, Mussolini's small band of loyalists marched on Rome, demanding that the king hand over control of the government, or they would "take it by force." Within days King Vittorio Emanuele III acquiesced and handed Mussolini the positions of both prime minister and interior minister without a fight.

IN 1933, THE Mattei family moved to the countryside, to a large house in a small town overlooking the city of Florence, after Ugo's partner had squandered the telephone company's profits and run off with a dancer. In Tuscany the family became enmeshed with the local anti-Fascist community, including known writers and intellectuals like Natalia Ginzburg and Carlo Levi, political thinkers like Piero Calamandrei, and left-leaning entrepreneurs such as Adriano Olivetti, whose family made typewriters. The Mattei family often received guests, sometimes quietly arriving in the dark of night to evade the surveillance of Mussolini's black-shirted *squadristi,* his loyalist police force. Teresa came of age hearing political debate and conversation around the dinner table.

As a young teen Teresa helped her family print clandestine newspapers signed by "The Anti-Fascist Front for Peace." They printed them on paper the size of a Florentine bread pan, and Teresa would stack copies in a pan, wrapping it with a towel. And then she set off; few noticed the girl with a basket of bread, delivering her goods to mailboxes around Florence.

By then Mussolini had been in power for more than a decade and had, in effect, invented the concept of "Fascism" to serve his own authoritarian desires. Teresa was brought up to resist this doctrine that states, in Mussolini's own words—but widely considered ghostwritten by Fascist ideologist and philosopher Giovanni Gentile—"Fascism ... believes neither in the possibility nor the utility of perpetual peace.... War alone brings up to its highest tension all human energy and puts the stamp of nobility upon the peoples who have courage to meet it.... Fascism conceives of the State as an absolute, in comparison with which all individuals or groups are relative, only to be conceived of in their relation to the State." A core tenet of the philosophy of Fascism was abject nationalism, with complete trust and loyalty given to Mussolini, the country's ultimate leader. It was a government in charge of all facets of life, shaping the way that citizens lived in and understood the world around them.

Although Mussolini was certainly convinced wealthy land and business owners should be left to their own devices, particularly under the Fascist belief in the "immutable, beneficial, and fruitful inequality of mankind." Fruitful indeed, but only for a select few. Unlike the ideals of Communists, who believed in equal access to commodities, or Socialists, who argued that workers should be compensated according to their effort, labor, and productivity, Mussolini and his totalitarian government—the term was first used to describe his leadership—would decide who were the haves and who were the have-nots. And he worked to build his (relative) popularity with vast public projects—pouring money into buildings, transportation, and other infrastructure, making some people quite rich and impressing many others. These were often designed in the telltale rationalist style—minimalist and chunky design, adorned with Fascist symbolism like the laurel wreath of victory, taken from ancient Roman empire iconography, or the *fasces* from which the party derived its name—which referred to a bundle of sticks tied together with an axe, an ancient symbol of power and authority.

Mussolini loved giving bombastic speeches to large crowds—his favorite stage was a window overlooking the Piazza Venezia in Rome. They were broadcast across the country via radio, his followers dutifully cheering and chanting, *Credere, Obbedire, Combattere*— "Believe, Obey, Fight." And Mussolini was among the first leaders to take advantage of the new media of film, popularized during the 1920s and '30s. He ordered hundreds of hours of propaganda movies that, to this day, are sometimes referenced uncritically as the only representations of life during this time, though they blurred fact with the fictional Italy that Mussolini attempted to portray.

Italians seemed to love Il Duce—"the leader"—or at least this was the expected public response at the many nationalistic events held around the country. Attendance was, if not absolutely required, certainly strongly suggested. Absences were noticed. There was an expectation of complete fidelity to the homeland of Italy. That expectation was reinforced by laws passed with little fanfare or debate, which were upheld by Il Duce's squadristi, who were known to use violence and intimidation to keep detractors in line.

Within a decade, Mussolini had squelched all but the most covert anti-Fascist movements. And he began indoctrinating the youth with his Fascist ideology while ignoring history that illustrated other forms of governing or resistance. Many books that were written by foreigners or offered a different worldview were banned or restricted. Teresa's generation was brought up learning only propaganda-laden curricula at state-run schools and in ubiquitous Fascist social groups. Criticism of the government, for the most part, was only whispered to the most trusted friends and family members, long after the children had gone to bed. Some anti-Fascist sentiment was still tolerated among those with money and social influence—as long as these detractors didn't seem to be getting out of hand.

The Matteis were among those who were known anti-Fascists, and thus were generally kept under close surveillance. Ugo was a member of the Justice and Liberty movement, founded in 1929 with the likes of Carlo Rosselli, who was much more outspoken and had ended up arrested, sent to confinement—where mostly political prisoners were exiled on distant islands for years at a time as punishment—and, eventually, killed for his opposition to Mussolini in the late 1930s. Decades later a defense of Il Duce would be "At least Mussolini never had anyone killed!"—which was certainly not true. But he did prefer aggression, intimidation, and confinement of opponents and, later, Jewish people—to outright murder.

Ugo felt no need to feign acceptance of the Fascist Party, rather bringing up Teresa and her siblings to question authority, critique the church, and think for themselves. When Mussolini had public events nearby, Ugo was often preemptively arrested and then released a few days later, and he was required to periodically check in with the local carabinieri office so they could keep tabs on him. Local Blackshirts, as the squadristi were also known, understood the nuanced dance of keeping someone like Ugo in line. He could speak his mind—to a point—as long as he was not seen as calling people to action.

ON OCTOBER 3, 1935, Italy invaded Ethiopia, known then as Abyssinia, without provocation, in a show of power and a bid for land expansion. This act of aggression came just months after Hitler began bolstering Germany's armed forces, in defiance of World War I treaties, and just weeks after the Third Reich passed the Nuremberg Laws, greatly limiting Jewish people's liberties.

Italy quickly faced economic sanctions from the League of Nations and government leaders began their own propaganda campaign against what they considered an unfair rebuke. Later that autumn in Florence a plaque was installed calling for youths to seek revenge against the League of Nations. Across the city it was widely announced that there was to be a parade of students the next day; instead of regular lessons, they would march by the plaque and consider its message.

Teresa was only fourteen when she and her father and elder brothers snuck into the city from their home just beyond. They moved in the shadows of the cathedrals and palazzos of the dense city center to the plaque that instigated violence. Together, the family smeared it with ink.

The next day the parade was delayed and there was a furious search for the culprits.

AT THE AGE of sixteen Teresa took her first solo trip in service of the resistance. Her father sent her to France to deliver a four-hundred-thousand-lire donation to the anti-Fascists fighting Francisco Franco in the Spanish Civil War. This money—and the involvement of anti-Fascist foreigners—was essential to support the democratically elected Republicans since Mussolini and Hitler provided General Franco with extensive financial support and resources. Democracies like England, France, and the United States made a decision to stay out of the conflict, gun-shy after the death and destruction of the Great War. And yet supporters from Italy and around the world would head to Spain to fight on the side of anti-Fascism, with many others raising money and sending supplies.

Teresa had handed off the money and was on her way home when she was stopped at the Italian border, the reason for her trip under suspicion. She was thrown into jail with women arrested for sex work or petty theft, her first time meeting people whose experiences and upbringing were so vastly different from those of the middle-class intellectuals her family knew. Teresa only shared a few words with them, not wanting to compromise her cover story. But they were kind to her as she sat on the cell bench, fearful but exuding an innate stoicism that would come to serve her well.

In the interrogation room, the Fascist officer barked at her, *Why were you in France? Who were you meeting?* The daughter of a known agitator traveling alone was suspect. *What did your father send you to do?*

"I was just traveling to practice my French," she insisted.

Teresa kept her composure as she was questioned—and her father was able to convince the officers that what she said was true, that he would never send his young daughter to do anything dangerous or illegal. Teresa returned home undaunted. But the women from the jail cell stayed with her as she began to consider her own reasons—and not just her father's—for taking part in these subversive actions.

Only a few months later Teresa sat alone in her high school classroom, in another act of defiance. School administrators had announced that class would end early to celebrate an Italian military victory in Ethiopia. Students were ordered to gather their items and leave to cheer in the streets. As her classmates packed their books and grabbed their coats, Teresa sat as calmly as she had in the cell not long before, ignoring the sharp orders from the teachers when she was the last one seated in the empty room, back rod-straight, staring ahead.

Finally, the classroom was empty and the streets outside the school were filled with noise. She knew what risk she was taking, what obvious message she was sending. But she detested the war and would not be forced into acts of false nationalism.

She stayed in her seat for hours until a janitor came into the room.

"Please, miss, will you kindly leave?" he implored. "I am told I must close up the school properly, but I cannot if any students are still here." So, she reluctantly packed up and went home.

Her act had not gone unnoticed.

IN MAY 1938, Ugo Mattei was arrested again, this time to keep him from instigating any protests while Mussolini played host to someone he considered an important guest. With her father in jail, seventeen-year-old Teresa watched as her hometown of Florence was festooned with flags and banners featuring both the Italian tricolor and Nazi swastikas, as were all the towns and cities along the route. Il Duce met Adolf Hitler's train at the Brenner Pass, an ancient Roman road connecting Austria through the Alps to northern Italy. For weeks workers around the country had been furiously making many long-needed infrastructure improvements to ensure that Italy put on its best face for the Führer. Italians were ordered to cheer at stops all along the route southward.

In Florence, battalions of soldiers and groups of locals had been instructed to gather in orderly, adoring crowds as the two leaders made their way around the ancient city. Early in his reign Adolf had looked to Benito as a mentor, studying his manipulation of the press and methods of threatening local dissenters to learn how to control people. Hitler wanted to emulate this same display of fealty and enthusiasm in the streets, which would then be widely reported in newspapers and on the radio.

And then the pair avoided the hoi polloi on the Ponte Vecchio—the most famous bridge in Florence, lined with shops as it connects the main city with the Oltrarno neighborhood on the opposite side—by strolling through the Vasari Corridor. This passageway runs above the shops and was built as a private walkway for the once-powerful Medici family to travel from one side of the Arno to other. At the apex of the Ponte Vecchio, Mussolini opened the wide windows of the corridor, and the two men gazed outward, toward the centuries-old bridges that crossed the Arno and onto the green hills of Tuscany. The crowds below cheered as journalists took photographs. The friendly duo would also visit the Boboli Gardens and Piazza del Duomo, spending the night in Palazzo Pitti—the decadently decorated palace that had, in the past, been owned by the Medicis and served as the home of the Italian monarchy.

Florence was but one stop on this goodwill trip. They would also visit Naples, Rome, and elsewhere, at each stop the pageantry so ostentatious that the world took notice. Aspects of this visit made headlines around the globe, as much for Italy's splendor as for the ominous message of an Axis alliance. This visit was meant to cement the friendship of these two leaders, who often posed before adoring crowds, giving straight-armed salutes. Little was accomplished as far as official diplomacy. Mussolini had, just weeks earlier, signed a pact with the British that was meant to ensure peace in the Mediterranean. But history would soon show that Mussolini was merely angling for optimal conditions to expand his empire, and that a natural alliance would form between Italy and Germany under these two despots.

With the known anti-Fascists like Ugo detained for the duration of the visit, there were few complications for the Fascist organizers. The most notable protest was by the archbishop of Florence, Cardinal Elia Dalla Costa, who ordered the churches of the city closed for the day and shuttered all the windows of the episcopal palace, located in the large palazzo that faces Brunelleschi's magnificent Duomo, in an unmistakable sign of mourning. This controversial message—by no means shared by all Catholic leadership—showed his distaste for Hitler's racist policies and warmongering, and for the Nazi leader's unwelcome presence in the cardinal's Florentine churches. The archbishop would continue to support the rights and safety of Jewish people during the war. Perhaps he needed not to worry that the two dictators would visit any of the local houses of worship, however. Despite the many beautiful and historic churches along the route, the duo never set foot in a church in Rome or Florence during their visit, in Florence only posing for one photo session outside a cathedral, perhaps to appease the most ardent Catholics.

SHORTLY AFTER HITLER'S visit, the Italian state-supported media began their attack on foreign people of Jewish descent, blaming them for high rent, crime, unemployment, and many other social ills, while erasing their integration in, and contributions to, Italian culture. This racist perspective was nothing new. Mussolini had allowed and encouraged both anti-Semitic Fascists and a small number of Nazis operating in Italy to stir up anti-Jewish sentiment since the early 1930s, in part to win favor with Germany. But Fascism's own oppressive political climate, certainly influenced by the propaganda supporting the Ethiopian conflict, increased racism and xenophobia in Italy during the 1930s as well.

Once the press began to pave the way for discrimination, Fascist think tanks met and composed the *Manifesto of the Racial Scientists*, issued mere months after Hitler's Italian visit, on July 14, 1938, declaring that there existed a "pure Italian race" of which Jewish people were not a part. Mussolini surely recognized how farcical this was—it did not even align with the German definition of an Aryan race. And yet, in August Mussolini created the Office of Demography and Race, which conducted a census of Jewish people in Italy the same month.

Italy passed the first of its increasingly onerous racial laws in September 1938, certainly influenced by Hitler's own persecution of Jewish people. Many believed these laws were inspired by Mussolini's desire to form a bond between Italy and Germany. The first laws stripped citizenship and legal residency from many foreign-born Jewish people. By November laws were passed restricting marriage, work, owning businesses and land, employing non-Jewish people, political participation, and access to education, among other limitations for Jewish Italians. The government was pressured to create many pathways to exemptions, however, in part because of the vast integration and intermarrying of Jewish and non-Jewish people. Additional oppressive edicts would be passed over the next year, barring Jewish people from almost all aspects of society. These were unpopular, even among otherwise apolitical Italians, and historians see them as the beginning of the end of Mussolini's reign. Because so many Italians openly flaunted these laws or found ways to resist or manipulate them to preserve their way of life or that of their neighbor, many Italians began to realize that they could do the same for other rules they didn't agree with but had otherwise been blindly following.

Teresa's family was of Jewish descent, but because her mother had long since converted to Catholicism, these laws did not apply to them. *Yet,* the Matteis must have discussed among themselves and their friends, who included many Jewish people. As Teresa was taught, she would oppose what she believed was unjust, whether or not she felt immediately threatened.

SHORTLY AFTER THE passage of the racial laws in the autumn of 1938, Teresa was seated in science class. She had her notebook out, ready to take notes for the day's lesson. It was her last year of high school, and high marks were essential if she was going to be admitted to university, where barely 20 percent of seats were reserved for women.

Pencil poised, she listened as the teacher began his lecture. *Today we will discuss how Italians are members of the superior Aryan race,* he began. Teresa was well aware of the recent anti-Semitic propaganda but was shocked to hear these abhorrent ideas taught as part of a discipline that relied upon proven theories and time-tested knowledge. She shoved her things back into her bag and stood up.

"I am leaving because I cannot witness this shame," she announced to the class, and pushing her way through the crowded classroom, she left the room.

Soon after, she would be expelled.

CHAPTER 2

BIANCA

TURIN

1938

B ianca Guidetti Serra, nineteen but with blond blunt-cut bangs that made her look younger than her years, was planning her first political action. Forthright among her friends, but not particularly gregarious in larger groups, Bianca was finally noticing the injustice around her and she could no longer stand by. So, she gathered a group of non-Jewish friends whom she knew from her studies at the university and discussed how they could protest the racial laws passed that autumn of 1938.

While Bianca was not Jewish, many of her closest friends were, including her boyfriend, Alberto Salmoni, and good friend, the future author Primo Levi. Bianca saw how these new laws were affecting her inner circle. Primo and Alberto were already in their second year of university, and a clause in the racial laws at that time allowed them to continue as long as they kept their grades in good standing. But Bianca watched with despair as others were denied entrance to school or expelled. Incensed and struck by the seeming indifference and helplessness of so many others around her, she committed herself to doing something—anything—to combat these injustices.

Bianca and her friends met up after dark and together they walked toward one of the busiest commercial streets in Turin, Via Roma, which ran from the main rail station through the city center. Tram cars passed by as they walked, clanging along on tracks embedded in the streets, carrying people around the city.

Along much of Via Roma were long stretches of arched porticoes protecting pedestrians as they went about their errands or moved through the city. Posters aimed at Catholics, declaring Jewish people THE ENEMIES OF THE HOMELAND!, were plastered on shop windows and the walls of buildings. This echoed the anti-Semitic propaganda that had recently begun to fill the state-run newspapers as well, claiming that Jewish people were not truly their countrymen, and therefore not entitled to the same rights.

Bianca and her friends, feeling the relative safety of their small group, walked down Via Roma tearing down the posters, yelling as they went, "We are all Italians!"

The young women were not alone; many took to the streets to protest these laws. While there were some arrests and squabbles between protesters and carabinieri, it seemed, for the time being at least, as if many officers—like many Italians—were also critical of these new laws.

BORN IN 1919, Bianca lived with her parents and younger sister, Carla, in a middle-class neighborhood in the center of Turin. Until this first protest she was, for the most part, ignorant of politics. However, from a young age, experiences were priming Bianca to join the resistance. Her father was a lawyer, but his first love was literature. Their house was full of books and Bianca read voraciously. She was particularly moved by Leon Trotsky's *My Life,* which her father received as a gift when it was translated into Italian in 1934. This was her first encounter with the life and ideas of a revolutionary. She was drawn to this story as a young teen, even if she couldn't articulate why.

Bianca's family was relatively well off, and Bianca and her sister were sent to a school for the children of high-ranking military officers housed in a former palace. Among these privileged families, she learned a love of dance and the opera. One friend's father knew a worker at the theater, and the girls could often get in for free to watch hours-long performances while standing in the back. It was during this time, however, that Bianca became aware of class differences through the school's yearly meeting with the lesser-financed sister school for the children of lower-ranking officers, where students clearly had fewer resources than her own classmates. She understood that her privilege was mere luck of circumstance.

Conscious of their good fortune, Bianca's mother always encouraged her daughters to continue their schooling. She had been forced to apprentice with a seamstress after elementary school and told Bianca and Carla that she would stop and cry outside the upper grade school gates, clutching her box of dresses to tailor, because she had so loved studying, as did Bianca. Despite not being drawn to the work, Bianca's mother and aunt had used their skills to open their own seamstress shop—a rarity for women at that time—and Bianca saw her mother as having relative economic and social freedom in a country that otherwise devalued women's work.

Bianca's political awakening in 1938 coincided with her beloved father's death. His loss made the family's finances more tenuous, and Bianca began to consider a future as a lawyer. Not only did she want to help her Jewish friends, but she was also inspired to help combat the limits on education and hiring for girls and women.

Mussolini had encouraged education for younger students across classes since he came to power, increasing the rate of literacy, but also providing more opportunities for Fascist indoctrination. However, post-primary education for girls was more challenging to secure, especially for working-class families. Depending on the program, boys could attend school at little to no cost, while fees for girls were much higher.

In 1923, the Fascist theorist Giovanni Gentile, who was also considered the mastermind of Fascist ideology, drafted the "Gentile Reform"—a cluster of decrees that served to limit education opportunities for women and further entrench traditional gender roles. Among these decrees was the institution of an unpopular secondary school for girls that provided no path to university and taught courses like domestic science and singing. As Gentile said, feminism was an "egalitarian illusion, a false and ridiculous idea of the woman-man." While this school would be abolished a few years later, these collective efforts resulted in lower rates of education for working-class girls in particular during this time. And for those who were able to gain an education, there were additional barriers to gainful employment.

In 1938 the government also passed a law that women could comprise no more than 10 percent of employees in most professional fields—a decree that codified what had been the norm for hiring anyway. Fascist propaganda had long discouraged women from working if their family could afford for them not to—in 1934, for example, arguing that work was "potentially dangerous" and might induce sterility for women, yet was a source of "great physical and moral virility" for men.

It was in this environment that Bianca finally saw herself as a possible agent for change. She would have to find a job, she knew, to help support her family—but what options were there for her? She did not want to end up like her mother, wishing for a career she wasn't allowed to have. And she felt exhilarated helping to organize her friends to act, wanting to do something more. But aside from tearing down posters, she wasn't sure what else she could do.

CHAPTER 3

ON THE BRINK

I n late March 1939, during the twentieth-anniversary events of the founding of the Fascist Party, Il Duce stood at his usual perch on the balcony high above the Piazza Venezia in Rome, facing a public square packed with people, including many squadristi. In a speech broadcast around the country, Mussolini reasserted his support of Hitler's aggressions against France, declaring that the people of Italy would not back down from the aggressions of other nations but must instead arm themselves.

While the loyalists chanted "Believe! Obey! Fight!," the warmongering talk received relatively tepid applause. By most accounts, even those who still supported Il Duce—those who believed the Fascist party line that England and France were, in fact, the aggressors—had a distaste for Germany as an ally.

TIME SEEMED TO move quickly now, as Italy—and the world—careened toward war.

On March 30, a few days after Mussolini's speech, cities around

Italy from Turin to Rome were draped in flags to celebrate General Franco's victory in Spain.

Despite this celebration of a violent and bloody coup, the state-sanctioned media continued asserting that Germany and Italy only wanted "peace and justice." The stage was being set to blame "the democracies" for acts of war, claiming that the Fascists were acting in self-defense.

This was the propaganda line, even as, that spring, young men were being drafted for Mussolini's campaign to invade Albania, a Balkan country less than fifty miles across the Adriatic Sea from Italy's east coast, already under Italian influence for more than a decade. It was yet another unprovoked military action from a leader purporting to support peace. Women clung to their new husbands, babies in their arms. Mothers, wives, sisters, children wept as their loved ones were shipped out for yet another conflict about which they cared little.

On May 22, 1939, Italy and Germany signed the Pact of Steel, which tied them together politically and militarily. Mussolini's most loyal advisers had emphasized to their leader—and to Germany—that their economy and military would need years to prepare for war, but that seemed to do little to temper Hitler's aggression or Mussolini's promises of support.

Into the summer of 1939 the propaganda campaign continued. Any aggression by "the democracies" would "provoke" Italy into retaliation. Despite the military presence in the Balkans, many Italians seemed to still believe that Il Duce would do what he could to avoid war.

Even as a million and a half troops were called up around Italy. Even as so many worried Italians tuned in to Radio London, as the BBC radio station was called, four or five times a day and bought up every available foreign paper to divine hints of what the state-controlled press refused to report upon.

At the end of August, the government announced a ban on all private motorcars starting in a few days' time in a bid to conserve fuel. These were the restrictions of a country at war. A letter written by a young veteran of the Ethiopian invasion expressed the opinion of many: "Will this war come? I can't believe it. Above all I can't believe that we shall be called upon to fight against people towards whom we have not got the slightest grudge and by the side of people we all despise. I have yet to find a single man who wants to fight on the side of the Germans!"

Of course there were many who bought into the Fascist propaganda, and party loyalists who supported Italy's alliance with Hitler's regime. But by most historical accounts, Mussolini's popularity declined as his warmongering continued. There are anecdotal accounts of groups of seemingly committed Fascist officers wearing the party's laurel wreath pins, who were overheard criticizing or mocking their government when they believed they were safe. This anti-Mussolini sentiment only grew as his government's restrictions tightened.

As summer began to wane, Mussolini outlawed the sale of coffee—in Italy!—in response to an international embargo, just days after reports in the newspapers declared it bad for the nerves. "Wine is far less harmful," the article continued. Italians could do little more than try to make a substitute out of chicory.

Soon meat rationing was introduced, and this new restriction was accompanied by articles about the benefits of vegetarianism.

And then there was a declaration that gas masks were required for certain professions and recommended to all. The Italian people were on edge.

Italians around the country heard the news on September 3,

1939, on the family radio, turned down low. England had declared war on Germany after Hitler refused to leave Poland; France followed suit hours later. It was all Italians could talk about—everyone was worried that it was only a matter of time before they were dragged into Hitler's war, even as many still hoped that Mussolini would keep them neutral.

After weeks of silence, on September 24, most state-run newspapers ran the headline: "The Pilot Has Spoken." Thus was the distillation of a speech Mussolini gave to party leaders: Il Duce is in control. Don't worry. And, more important, the summation included, "Don't speak to the man at the wheel."

The next nine months were more of the same: The Italian state press amplified the German successes and buried any losses. "The democracies" of England and France forced Hitler into this position. There was still a belief, or perhaps a hope, that Mussolini would keep the Italians out of war.

ON JUNE 3, 1940, loudspeakers were installed in public squares around Italy. In the countryside, farm managers were ordered to ensure their workers were ready to attend a public event or tune in to the radio when summoned.

On June 10, all Italians were required to stop work at five P.M. to listen to a speech from Il Duce. Italy had joined the Axis powers and declared war on France and England.

CHAPTER 4

BIANCA

TURIN
1940-1942

B y the autumn of 1940, Bianca was watching the increasing number of young men drafted into the armed forces to fulfill the needs of a country at war. Soon after, quotas on women in public-sector jobs were suspended. So women began to fill more of these roles that had typically been held by men, but almost always at much lower pay. Despite this inequity, any paycheck was better than nothing. A family of women in wartime would have risked starvation if not allowed to work, and companies and factories needed to replace the lost labor as more men left for war.

So Bianca's mother donned her most elegant dress, affixed a matching hat to her head, and made an appointment with the president of the industrial union to ask if he might find a job for her daughter, who was studying law. As a widow, she explained, her eldest daughter's salary was essential.

By that first autumn that Italy was at war, Bianca had been hired to check in on the workers in the nearby factories to which she was assigned, including the Fiat and Nebbiolo Macchine factories, as well as others farther afield, toward the Alpine valleys and elsewhere. She would take her bicycle on the train and then ride miles into the countryside to reach them. There she would assess workers' welfare and assist with sick leave or pensions, or help widows file for benefits after their husbands were killed in the war.

As she started meeting with her clients, she took note of the social problems that they faced—inadequate healthcare and childcare, and wages that still left their families hungry and lacking heating fuel, despite long and often dangerous workdays. If workers missed too many days, they could be sent to the war tribunal for not contributing to the war effort. This, Bianca noted, despite the insufficient rations, or an excessive commute as roads and railways were damaged from the airstrikes. As the airstrikes grew more frequent, more workers would lose their homes as well or move beyond the city because they feared bombings. Eventually there were so many people living far from the factories that dormitories were set up, run by nuns for the women, many of them young and perhaps newly married. They would stay at the factory all week, just going home for a short visit on Sundays.

Often Bianca timed her visits to eat in the canteen with the workers, a free meal being a great benefit during this time of austerity, and sometimes she spent the night in an office in the dormitory as well. As she sat with the workers, many of them her age, she heard stories of their lives and learned more about their struggles and fears, at work and at home. She wanted to help, but there was only so much she could do for them through her job.

THE FACTORIES THEMSELVES were also the targets of bombings—Fiat had devoted more resources to building airplanes to supply the German and Italian air forces and most of the others had also adapted their production to support the war effort. The factories had bomb shelters, but the question was when the workers were allowed to leave their posts to seek safety. An early warning siren could be triggered if planes were spotted, but they sounded before confirmation of a destination. Those in charge, Bianca learned from these women, wanted the employees to keep working through the early sirens, only leaving the line when their factory seemed likely to be the target. This was often a matter of only a few minutes, time the women believed was necessary to ensure their safety—as evidenced by a recent delayed reaction to air raid sirens that had caused mass casualties at a nearby factory. She watched as these women began to discuss their valid complaints with one another, sowing seeds of collective action.

And in fact, whether or not Bianca had recognized what she was seeing at the time, even before the war, female factory workers had whispered plans for resistance. Feelings among the working-class women in Turin, Milan, and elsewhere were rife with discontent, and a few women had even begun to share what clandestine literature they had, discussing ideas late at night in the dormitory, already politically engaged.

Once the war began, Italians around the country were conscripted to work for the war effort, many on assembly lines like at the factories Bianca served, making parts for road vehicles and submarines. It was there that like-minded people found one another and encouraged ideas for sabotage: to improperly cut the lenses of the periscopes so they couldn't focus, creating errors imperceptible until much farther down the assembly process and difficult to trace back to the perpetrators. Others introduced flaws into the axles or made misshapen bearings that would jam. People worked slowly, feigned reasons to leave early or not come in at all, even after managers threatened retribution. And so political leanings were becoming known, and membership in even the most shadowy political groups, like the Communist and Socialist parties, began to slowly grow.

FOR THOSE FIRST long years of war, Bianca visited her factories between classes, doing her homework late into the night. In Bianca's rare free time, she and her new group of university friends had loved to take hikes and ride bicycles into the mountains, and Bianca had loved swimming, dancing, and fencing. But now she was often exhausted, from her long days but also from the meager rations, which, at their worst point during the war, offered less than a thousand calories a day. And she was discontent. She and her most trusted friends discussed their distaste for the war only when they were certain not to be overheard. *What was all of this sacrifice for?* they wondered bitterly.

In Bianca's final year of schooling, starting in autumn 1942, she took part in another small protest. All students and professors typically wore a Fascist uniform to school—either a black shirt or a *sahariana,* a kind of blue safari jacket with large shoulder pads. In defiance, Bianca began to wear whatever she chose to class, nervous at first that it was only she and the eccentric economics professor Luigi Einaudi—who often stood out in a pink shirt—who failed to comply with the implicit dress code. Bianca also stopped paying dues to GUF—Gruppi Universitari Fascisti—the Fascist university youth group that sponsored sports activities, domestic skills workshops, and welfare work, alongside political indoctrination, which had been automatically rolled into university tuition.

"No one said anything," she reflected, "perhaps because we were around the end of Fascism and the climate of war was changing." Or perhaps people were finally realizing that if more people were bold enough to take a stand, change could happen.

———

ON DECEMBER 8, 1942, the air raid siren blared once again, jolting Bianca into action from the kitchen where she was huddled for warmth in the drafty apartment she shared with her mother and sister. Maybe Bianca was reading; perhaps her sister, Carla, was drawing or preparing for one of the art lessons she sometimes gave for a few extra lire. They grabbed the suitcases that they kept by the door, filled with valuables like their grandmother's silverware and other family heirlooms, and headed down the stairs. These suitcases came with them almost everywhere—even to the penny movies, should Bianca's mother decide to splurge—to save them in case their home was bombed when they were out.

The bombings had become so quotidian that they blended together. The sound put Bianca in a state where all thoughts were suspended; the only goal was to find safety with her family. Like so many times before, they hurried to the underground bomb shelters, moving steadily with their neighbors in a well-practiced queue, down steep, dank steps to underground rooms—long and narrow, with benches along each side, more crowded than a tram car. Bianca knew that her proximity to a bunker was lucky—there were far from enough shelters for the entire population of Turin.

The city had been under increasing stress since the declaration of war in 1940. Since then, there had been more than fourteen bombings of Turin and its immediate surroundings—but many more sirens had indicated the presence of planes and the anxiety-inducing possibility of destruction. The Fiat factories, including where Bianca worked, were among the prime targets, but without precision bombing—and despite bombing occurring at night until late 1942 in an Allied effort to limit casualties—there were still many deaths and vast devastation. In November and December

1942 alone, there were five bombings targeting Turin factories, with hundreds of casualties. The bombs were accompanied by Allied propaganda leaflets, which blamed the war—and their need to bomb—on Hitler and Mussolini and encouraged Italians to stop working for the German war effort.

In the underground bunker Bianca, Carla, and their mother sat, helpless, with hundreds of their neighbors. Even from deep beneath the earth they could feel the ground shake and hear the booming of the exploding bombs, rubble raining from the ceiling with each hit. Children cried, women prayed, people clutched their bags of valuables and one another's hands. No one knew what might be left of their lives when they emerged.

Finally, after long minutes of silence, they were given the all clear to return above ground. Bianca's first impulse was always to survey the devastation. Each time she could expect to see new destruction around the dense city center of connected apartments, many once-regal palazzos built of stone. Today, there were new, deep craters in the ground, heavy window shutters from buildings that had been hit were twisted and destroyed, the sellers beneath the porticoes had volumes strewn into the streets. The piles of books were enticing, and Bianca briefly considered picking a few up that she thought might not be salable, their pages now dirty and torn. But she resisted.

And then she heard cries for help. She and her sister joined their neighbors as they ran toward a fire on Via Po. Like they had before, they formed a human chain of buckets and pots, passing water from one person to the next to help stanch the flames. Once the fire was tamed, Bianca made her way up the stairs to the damaged but intact floors above to check for survivors.

In this part of the city there were mostly long, connected multi-story buildings with porticoed sidewalks under the second-floor apartments. Bombs might land on a roof, collapsing the stacked living rooms, breaking through the rounded domes of porticoes onto the walkways below, destroying three or four apartments at once and making the city even more difficult to navigate on foot. Air raids turned some of Turin's tall windows, usually buttoned up with shutters and heavy curtains, into a vista as vast as wide-open French doors, as an explosion might blow out an entire wall of a room, opening it to the elements. Sometimes curtains would be hung as people continued to live inside. The destruction was so extensive that as long as a building was structurally sound—and sometimes even if it wasn't—people often continued to live in destroyed apartments until they were forced to relocate. Soon more than half of Turin's homes would be damaged, gas would be turned off due to the danger of burst lines, and the majority of windows would be blown out around the city.

When Bianca reached the top of the stairs that day, the doorway framed a surreal scene: a solitary elderly woman sat on a chair staring, as if in a trance, at the glowing red stove in front of her. The roof was now open to the sky and the building smoldered around them. From deeper in her destroyed apartment came the sound of a man scolding her, in the local dialect, to *not waste all that heat*. Heating fuel was so precious that Bianca wondered if their warmth was why they had become inured to the sirens, the explosions, the destruction around them. Then she realized that the glowing ember was actually a residual incendiary from the bombing that had landed by chance in their stove. Not for the last time Bianca was reminded of the narrow boundary between life and death.

CHAPTER 5

ANITA

EMILIA-ROMAGNA
MARCH 3, 1943

In early March, in the dark of a late winter night, the sleepy city of Reggio Emilia was awoken by the screech of dropping bombs and flashes of bright lights. The Allied forces were dropping highly flammable incendiary bombs on the local Reggiane aircraft factory and on the power plant in the city. In the daylight when there was better visibility, larger bombers returned to finish the job. Trains were derailed and the main employer of the city was destroyed. Hundreds were killed or injured, both those at the bombing sites and from bombs that missed their targets.

Until that day, war had felt relatively distant from Reggio Emilia, surrounded by farmland toward the plains north and west, and small towns to the south that made their way into the Apennine Mountains. In such a small city, everyone had been affected by the casualties.

Anita Malavasi was seventeen when her family moved to the city of Reggio Emilia to pursue more opportunities than the previous few decades as farmers had allowed. Although, before then, living with her extended family had provided its own kind of education.

When she was a child, once dinner was eaten and the last farm chores were done, Anita and her brothers donned coats and carried blankets to the stable, where they made themselves comfortable among the hay bales. The barn was perhaps chosen to get the children out of their mother's way, who was still cleaning up the kitchen or wanted some quiet time for mending—for a woman's work on the farm was never done. In the wintertime it also was among the warmest places on the property, radiating with the heat of the animals. But it was also likely chosen as a place where they would not receive surprise visitors.

There, among the snorting and baying, her nonno read them classic Russian tales—stories by Dostoyevsky, Tolstoy's *War and Peace* and *Anna Karenina*—books he had enjoyed as a youth, before they were considered transgressive under Mussolini.

Anita's childhood had been spent on this farm in the countryside of Emilia-Romagna, in the plains just beyond the fingers of the Apennine Mountains as the flatlands made their way to Parma, Reggio Emilia, and Bologna. There, she was aware of her standing as a girl, whose ideas and needs were considered inferior to her father's and brothers'. Although she did watch her grandmother read the newspaper every day—which was quite rare for a woman—and she was encouraged by her father to get an education. Despite this, Anita had little sense of her parents' political leanings. However, she did, at an early age, learn firsthand about the personal injustice of the Fascist Party.

When she was around ten years old, Anita won a drawing contest at her school, carefully decorating the Fascist symbol of a laurel wreath and sheaves of wheat, and she was called to attend a ceremony where the local Fascist hierarchy would be in attendance. After the party pomp, her name was finally called as the first-place winner. She climbed the steps and was greeted by a family friend, known because the Malavasis often brought milk to his sickly young children.

"You don't belong to the Piccole Italiane?" he asked her in front of the crowd. This was one of the Fascist children's groups. There were separate groups for boys and girls, split by age, starting barely past toddler and going through young adult. The girls were taught mostly domestic skills, while the boys' groups were athletic and paramilitary. All came with a heavy dose of Fascist political propaganda.

"No," Anita replied. "My father didn't sign me up."

"If that's the case then we can't give you the reward," he responded and sent her back to her seat, disgraced in front of the whole school.

Anita went home crying. She found her mother in the stable doing chores and told her the story between sobs. Then her mother slapped her face. "Now you have something to cry about," she said, and went back to feeding the pigs.

"How can a little girl understand that having a membership card was worth more than her skills or studying ability?" Anita wondered decades later.

It would be years before Anita understood that her mother's seemingly cruel reaction was her way of protecting the family. That as poor farmers, they had to adhere to tradition and ensure their children never breathed a word of their parents' political leanings to teachers or friends. This was why the adults only had their political discussions in the barn, where it was less likely that anyone might overhear them. The act of shielding their children from the Fascist youth groups was risky enough.

WHEN THEY MOVED to Reggio Emilia in 1938, Anita's family took over a restaurant, bar, and bowling alley. There, for the first time, Anita overheard political discussions critical of the Fascist Party.

Their bar became a hangout for Communists and Socialists, and outgoing Anita soon became popular among the patrons. Under conservative Fascist norms, young women generally didn't hang out in bars and cafés, where men gathered to drink coffee or wine, and talk about politics or work or joke around. But her presence as a waitress was socially acceptable—and provided a great opportunity for Anita, who was funny and personable, to befriend people a teen from the countryside might not otherwise meet.

These left-leaning young men started to explain to Anita what she had known only in general terms about the origin and realities of Fascism, and whom it was really serving. In her family's bar they felt safe sharing their own political leanings and discussing the concepts of Communism and Socialism. And she was drawn to these ideas. Sweet-faced and inquisitive, with an unexpected sense of humor, Anita became friends with these men. Some had just returned from Ethiopia, and by 1940 more would be drafted and sent to Russia or France. Anita heard the stories of those who had been on the front lines, and she became the communication hub back home for those newly dispatched. With reports from so many battlefields, Anita started to have a broader view of war, compared to what the state-sanctioned media provided or the dispatches from only a few relatives. Some of the stories from these disparate front lines, Anita said, "made me shiver." And through these accounts she understood "even more deeply the brutality of Fascism." And so, her political education was taking shape.

Compounding these reports from the war front, Anita had been questioning what she had been brought up to believe through her observations of urban life. In the city of Reggio Emilia, she saw women working outside of the home, despite what she began to understand was the male-dominated system that put fathers and husbands and sons in positions of power and control over the women in their lives. Compared to life in the country, women in the city "had more autonomy, more freedom," she noticed. Anita better understood how her mother's hard work and sacrifices on the farm were considered less valuable than a paid worker's. She worked just as hard but wasn't even paid a salary. When they sold the farm, the proceeds were divided only among the men.

In the country, girls could go out and socialize or dance only if a group of older women chaperoned them. It had been just a few years since Anita and her friends would wait for these women in the stable. "Imagine what a beautiful perfume!" she recalled with a laugh. Once at the dance, they could only hope that the chaperones would let them stay out for more than a few songs. These reinforced traditional gender roles, which were even more starkly defined among the less educated and poorer populations of the rural countryside, were all that Anita knew until she moved to Reggio Emilia. In the city, Anita saw that young women could go out with a group of friends or meet up with a boy and no one seemed to care at all.

And she began to see the contradictions of the Fascist regulations around gender and work: that women were expected to deal with all childcare and domestic issues even while many also worked long hours at jobs outside of the home to support the war effort, where they were generally paid significantly less than men for the same work. The Fascist emphasis on a woman's role in the home was a matter of control, Anita realized. This messaging did not keep women from the paid workforce but rather from advancing in roles and pay.

It would take Anita years to fully realize that her parents' move to Reggio Emilia was precisely to counter the social and economic stagnancy they had endured as agricultural workers: lack of educational opportunities, particularly for girls, and limited work beyond the field and the home.

But in the aftermath of the bombing of the Reggiane airplane factory, the city now felt dangerous. Her brother's good friend had died in the bombing, as had her aunt, and her cousin was badly injured. Anita's mother became anxious, running home in fear at the sound of air raid sirens, sometimes simply unable to work. That left Anita to take on greater responsibility as manager of the bar. She worked alone many days, discussing politics with the dwindling number of young men in the city—and her own political leanings became clearer.

ANITA AND HER family lived on Via Dalmazia, a road that ringed Reggio Emilia's small downtown, separating the more densely populated city center from the neighborhoods beyond. One day she answered an insistent knock to find a Fascist carabinieri officer at her door. He wanted to know about her upstairs neighbor, whom she knew as Torelli.

"When does he leave the house? Who does he meet with?" the officer asked.

"I don't know!" Anita answered truthfully, although she knew she would not have divulged any information even had she been paying attention to his comings and goings. Before leaving, the officer demanded that she report any information to the police station.

"You have a very dangerous man living here," the officer told Anita.

That evening, when Torelli came downstairs to drink a glass of wine, she recounted the officer's visit.

"Don't worry," he responded with a seemingly unconcerned smile. But later, in a more private setting, he began to explain about the underground resistance and the alternatives to the Fascists, the sole legal political party. There were people organizing, he told her, and it was more than just revolutionary talk at the bar.

CHAPTER 6

BIANCA

TURIN
SPRING 1943

On Friday, March 5, 1943, a few dozen workers at the Fiat Mirafiori factory, most from the highest-skilled grades, set down their tools when the clock struck ten and walked out of the factory. They had organized with the help of the small, clandestine Communist Party—whose existence in Italy had been illegal since the dawn of Fascism, and whose known leaders had long been arrested or sent to *confino* or otherwise gone into hiding. The Communist Party in Italy and across much of Western Europe was founded on the Marxist ideals of workers' rights and more equal wealth distribution, a counterpoint to the vast inequality and cronyism of Fascism. Communicating through passed notes and quiet whispers, this small group had no idea what might lie in store for them in retribution for this almost unheard-of act of civil disobedience under Mussolini's rule. Their demand was modest: to extend to all twenty thousand workers a wage bonus offered to those who lost their homes in bombings. But they knew this defiant action could have an even more profound political effect.

The courageous workers stood outside the factory holding a sign with their intentions, but otherwise making little noise. Their presence was loud enough. It had been twenty years since workers in Italy dared to defy their bosses or the government. The Fascist leadership had successfully squelched all desire to strike in their first years of rule through violence and painful retribution. Word traveled quickly around the factory and a number of curious and brave observers, including Bianca, her boyfriend, Alberto, and a few other friends, came to see what collective action looked like.

But under Fascism, even gawkers might be punished for giving their tacit approval. Perhaps the group of onlookers walked by slowly, as if they were on their way to somewhere else on the factory campus, which covered vast acres on the southern edge of the city. Nearby was dense worker housing—a number of the plant workers lived at the factory during the week, having been displaced to far beyond the city because of the bombings—but in this part of Turin streets were wider and tree lined, and soon gave way to more open land as the city turned to countryside.

Bianca caught the eye of someone she knew.

"What are you doing here?" he asked, surprised at the interest her presence implied. She realized that to these strikers, she was a naïve young office worker and not one of them.

And then the carabinieri came, roughly rounded them up, and sent them back to work.

At first this strike appeared to accomplish little but endanger those who took part. But news traveled quickly within and among the factories and transportation hubs in Turin, the Piedmont countryside, and beyond, toward Milan. There was one small strike the next day—a Saturday—at another factory in Turin. And then on Monday, galvanized by talk over the weekend, the strikes spread to more factories; railway workers also struck, adding demands beyond the wage bonus, like an increase in their meager food rations, which had caused some workers to lose twenty or more pounds in weight. And these actions inspired further protests and actions like the passing around of hastily printed leaflets at universities, expressing support for the workers, and even a mass peace protest in Rome that caused the Pope to cancel his Easter benediction. Within two weeks of that first strike at Mirafiori, most of the workers' demands had been met by the factory owners to get the war effort back on track. The workers celebrated this win and learned an important lesson. They saw that they could strike without mass arrests or police violence.

Even more potentially dangerous to Mussolini and his administration's grip on power was the implied anti-war and anti-Fascist sentiment in these actions, despite the workers' demands being mostly focused on wages and benefits. History would reveal these strikes to be yet another death knell for Fascism in Italy, showing Mussolini's weakness in capitulating to workers and the increasing willingness of long-cowed Italians to plan mass actions. They were no longer in fear of the squadristi. The years of war deprivation and the fear of bombings were convincing more and more Italians to stop believing, obeying, and fighting.

Bianca's presence that day opened her up to conversations with the workers after the strikes. Perhaps she even talked a little too freely, Bianca later admitted, as she inquired about the workers' politics and expressed her openness to being involved in future actions. But at the time, what had struck Bianca and other young people like her was that resistance was possible. "They gave the signal that you could raise your head and be heard," Bianca realized—both for herself and for so many others around her who had grown increasingly dissatisfied under Mussolini, and with fighting a deeply unpopular war.

BIANCA WAS STARTLED by a knock at her door not long after the March strikes. When she answered, she saw the worker who had noticed her that day. He said to her, perhaps tentatively—it was still spring 1943 after all—"You said you were interested in hearing something about the Communist Party."

"Yes," Bianca breathed. The thought of joining this movement—something she never dared imagine until recent weeks—was a thrill. The surprise visitor began her political education right away, dropping off books and typed pages for Bianca to read. Ever the good student, Bianca consumed everything she was offered, eager for more.

After a month or so, on one of his brief visits, the Communist asked if she might be willing to help them type texts that the party members could then secretly circulate. And so, Bianca spent evenings on her old typewriter, copying pages from Marx and Engels, speeches by Stalin and the like, further learning about Communism through her work for the party. She would keep these documents, carefully wrapped and protected from the elements, hidden under the roof of her house until she could pass them off to her contact.

Later that spring her contact organized a meeting with an older party member, more than fifteen years her senior. When they met, he took Bianca's arm as they started walking through the city, past abandoned apartments and city parks that had been turned into collective gardens. Bianca chafed at the necessity to act like a couple to alleviate suspicion, even as she was excited to learn more. As they strolled, he asked her about her job and family, about her ideas of the Communist Party. He lectured her about politics and current events, like the Nazis' battle against the Soviet Union where "the workers were in power." Bianca answered his questions truthfully: that compared to what she saw in the factories in Turin, what she knew about the Soviet Union seemed like a more just political and social system—"with more rights, more equality—enough with the exploitation by the rich!" Pleased, her companion smiled and gripped her arm as they stepped over rubble in their path.

AS SPRING TURNED toward summer, the same senior party member asked for an appointment in Piazza Vittorio, in the courtyard of the last palazzo on the left, overlooking the Po River. The multistory palazzos, which once spilled cafés out around the square, were now in ruins from bombing raids. From amid the destruction, he emerged, smiling.

"I have some good news for you!" he announced. "You are officially a member of the Communist Party!"

The juxtaposition of the apocalyptic setting and her feeling of happiness was not lost on Bianca. She felt part of a great movement, ready to dedicate herself to this cause. He went on to tell her the rules of the party, including the necessity to keep all party business, and even her membership, a secret. She would adhere to this primary rule with one exception: She told her now fiancé, Alberto. Their relationship had become serious over the past year, their connection strengthened by a similar political zeal, even as he preferred the politics of the more left-center Action Party. She trusted him implicitly. Along with membership, she would be given a *nome di battaglia*—a moniker that ensured her real identity would remain unknown and her family members would be safe from retribution if her name was given by a captured comrade. Bianca was now known within the resistance as "Nerina" for the fight that was certain to come.

CHAPTER 7

CARLA

ROME

JULY AND AUGUST 1943

Carla was walking home from San Lorenzo on the evening of July 25 when she saw women throwing open window shutters. By law, cities were darkened at night to reduce the chance of being seen by bombers flying high above. Warm light unexpectedly spilled onto the street, and she heard cries coming from within. Carla began to steel herself for some terrible news from the war.

Finally, she asked someone what was happening.

"They threw away that scumbag Mussolini. Il Duce is gone!" a woman shouted. After nearly a week of only terror and sorrow, Carla realized what she was hearing were cries of joy. Mussolini's own Grand Council had voted him out of office amid pessimism around the prospect of the Axis powers winning the war. The news said that the king had already had him arrested. People began swarming the streets, cheering, many still in their pajamas.

Carla drifted home, elated. Mussolini had been in power since 1922. She had only really known life under his Fascist regime. Into the night, she and her mother watched the celebrations from their window high above the city while listening to Radio London—for the first time the volume was turned up as loud as they liked, no longer in fear of Fascist laws prohibiting foreign news. They could see small bonfires already burning, fueled by Il Duce posters and propaganda newspapers. Carla knew the next time she went to the movies she wouldn't have to stand and salute while the Fascist anthem played. She hoped women would have more to look forward to than striving for the government bonus they would receive upon the birth of their twelfth child. Of course nothing would change overnight, but for the first time in a long time, she had hope for the future.

CARLA'S EARLIEST YEARS were spent in an apartment overlooking a garden in a less central neighborhood of Rome. What she remembers most about this time was the freedom felt by her and her sister, Flora, a little more than a year older, as they played among the trees and flowers. Her mother homeschooled the girls for years—and later their younger brother as well—teaching them to read and write using the family's own vast library. Her father was a well-regarded mining and geology expert, and he took on the task of instructing his children in science and math. For most of her childhood, politics was rarely discussed in their house, even as her parents' teachings imbued the children with progressive thinking.

Her mother would take Carla and her sister out to buy Socialist newspapers before they were banned, discussing some of the articles she read. And how could Carla forget the time her father refused to take off his hat in the presence of the Fascist flag? He was dragged to the police station by a swarm of squadristi. Although he was released the next day, she could see the fear in his eyes even when he told her that everything was just a misunderstanding. Eventually the girls had to go to school, which was a shock of both ideas and culture.

When Carla was fifteen, her father was asked to join an elite

Fascist group and refused. It was only then that she fully understood his disdain for Fascism, and the hunger for power that undergirded its violence and oppression. As punishment for his disloyalty, her father was sent to Albania, where he was killed soon after in a mining accident. That he had spent his career advocating for mine safety and had bitterly opined that government officials cared more about lining their own pockets than the safety of their workers made his death even more painful. It was that first loss that planted the seed of Carla's political activism.

At school, a British classmate lent Carla a book about Communism—her first exposure to this philosophy. This led Carla to the National Library, where she convinced the librarian to let her read a book about Trotsky, which was intended for serious researchers only. Afterward, Carla tried to quietly inquire about the Communist Party in Rome, but they had retreated far underground and her search was futile.

Despite her nascent hatred of Mussolini's regime, in the summer of 1943 Carla was not yet active in politics. Like so many Italians, she had been quietly hoping to bide her time until the end of the war and the fall of Mussolini. Now Carla wondered what she would do. Il Duce was gone, but the war he'd gotten them into was clearly far from over.

A FEW DAYS later an answer came in the form of a representative of the Catholic Communists who knocked on her door and asked if they could hold meetings at Carla's apartment. Her apartment was likely chosen because of its location on a busy street not far from the Termini train station, where people coming and going wouldn't raise suspicions. The neighborhood's location on one of Rome's seven hills also offered views of the Michelangelo-designed Campidoglio Piazza and Trajan's Column, and was known for housing upper-middle-class rule-abiders and not revolutionary rabble-rousers. In high school Carla had been friendly with some of the group's members, who now also included two known anti-Fascist women leaders—Marisa Cinciari and Sylvia Garrone—who had been released from Rome's Regina Coeli prison on the day Mussolini was deposed. The guards had simply opened the gates and walked away. The fifteen hundred prisoners, nearly a third of them women, made their escape.

Many of these women were political prisoners arrested for their anti-Fascist ideology or protests. Some were leaders of banned Communist or Socialist political parties, while others were arrested merely for defacing images of Mussolini or painting anti-Fascist slogans on city walls. And a significant number of the prisoners had been arrested for obtaining an abortion, in violation of Fascist and Catholic anti-women policies, which carried a typical sentence of five years. Most of these newly freed women went home to see family they had missed in the past months or years, in a desire to live quietly. But a number had been called to revolution, educated and organized by political leaders like Marisa and Sylvia within the prison. They had planned for this very day of freedom and, upon their release, were eager to act. The challenge was how to bring together these disparate groups of longtime anti-Fascists and those who were newly energized for change. Carla's apartment would soon become one of the meeting places to unite these underground political parties and burgeoning women's groups in the following weeks of uncertainty. Carla joined the meetings, but mostly sat quietly, listening, amazed at all she never knew.

EVERY EVENING, CARLA, her mother, and her younger brother sat by the window where the sea breezes might cool the stagnant summer air. With the muted lights of the city as their backdrop, they turned on their radio, listening for both news and guidance from the new Italian leader, General Pietro Badoglio, appointed by the king, as well as from foreign radio reports. General Badoglio had long held influential positions in the Fascist government and was not fully trusted by those with whom Carla and her mother now openly discussed the current state of affairs. Many still saw him as a conservative leader, likely unwilling to work with the left-leaning political groups like the Justice and Liberty movement, or the more centrist Action Party, both of which had core leadership who had quietly stayed together over the previous twenty years, waiting for this moment. And as for the Communists and the Socialists, even the more vocal critics of the Fascist government still considered them radically left. They knew they still had to be careful in this new, more open political landscape. Only a handful of top-level government officials had been deposed alongside Mussolini, so many Fascists decided to lie low, waiting to see what would happen. Mussolini's squadristi still lived freely, and there were plenty of ardent Fascists among the police force. Which laws would they uphold? Mussolini was gone, but his supporters, enforcers, and administrators were still at large. Carla and her companions understood that their release from Mussolini's oppression could be a temporary freedom.

And they were right. Mussolini's deposition had left a vacuum of power that the Germans were quick to fill.

Those who now crowded Carla's apartment on Via Cavour during these meetings might not have known that Badoglio failed to secure the borders, allowing German tanks to stream into the country. Had they spoken to Italians who lived near major railways, they would have learned that trains sped by at all hours, filled with Nazi soldiers. But they did know that there were thousands of German troops already in the country; they saw them on the streets of

Rome and were told of camps not far beyond the city walls. They must have asked among themselves: *What would the soldiers' next order be?* There was much that was uncertain during the tense weeks after Mussolini's fall; Italy was left without a decisive vision for its future, both politically and regarding its role in the war. But what Carla and other emerging members of the resistance understood at this time was that their battle was far from over.

Years later, historians would ask: What if Italian and Allied soldiers were seen fighting side by side starting in July 1943? But for various reasons—Badoglio's hubris, the Allied leadership's long-standing (and understandable) mistrust of Italy after Mussolini's rule, the failure of the Italian government or military to act decisively—this didn't happen. After more than two decades under the isolated and top-down power structure of Mussolini's government, there were few Italians who were prepared to lead. Those who might have recognized the advantages of immediately aligning Italy with the Allied forces didn't trust their own judgment or the strength of their voices. While Mussolini's popularity had waned over the previous few years, even those who had long been detractors had no plan for what to do once he was gone.

The only oblique directive offered by General Badoglio was, "The war would continue." And thus, with dire consequences, it did.

LATER THAT SUMMER, a leader of *L'Unità,* the Communist Party's newspaper, asked Carla and her mother if they, too, might host a meeting at their home. Word had been spreading that Carla's family's apartment was spacious and inconspicuous enough for these clandestine gatherings, and that Carla was sympathetic to the cause. Carla convinced her mother to say yes.

"This must be of the utmost secrecy," *L'Unità*'s editor instructed.

"You play the piano and we will have our meeting in the dining room." They also established a password for entry that would be used throughout the occupation: *arcangelo*—"archangel."

After participants arrived, Carla pausing at every knock to wait for the whispered password, she sat down at the piano. For an hour and a half, she played all of Chopin's nocturnes, muting the voices in the other room with the dreamy and pensive compositions until the meeting ended and the members disappeared like smoke.

"This was the beginning," Carla wrote, "of underground activities that would spread like a wildfire."

CHAPTER 8

TERESA

FLORENCE
SUMMER 1943

Vittoria Giunti, Teresa's math professor, had set up the appointment. She trusted Teresa, whom she knew from Teresa's master's studies in philosophy at the University of Florence. "She's a fellow woman-at-arms," she had told Bruno. "She has always been educated in freedom and has been a part of the youth movement on campus who have been active over the past year." The professor's friend Bruno Sanguinetti, a longtime leftist party leader in his mid-thirties, needed a levelheaded collaborator to connect the anti-Fascist leadership and the student and youth groups who were so eager to get to work. Bruno trusted Vittoria when she told him, "I believe Teresa has what it takes to be a precious collaborator."

Teresa walked with purpose to the Ponte Vecchio and then paused under one of the arches at the center of the curve, gazing out along the Arno, wondering how she would know who Bruno was. Unlike the vast bombings of more industrialized cities like Turin, or the recent destruction of the San Lorenzo neighborhood in Rome, Florence had not yet been touched by this violence. She could not have been able to imagine what a different view this spot would have barely a year later.

Within moments a man wearing a black wide-brimmed hat took her by the arm. He steered her toward the bank on the Oltrarno side of the river, smiling and making small talk as if they were old friends. Teresa had only a moment to study his face before they started walking through the crowds. The first things Teresa noticed were his intense eyes and striking good looks. "He looks like Orson Welles," she thought. Teresa was initially embarrassed by the familiarity of this stranger, more than a decade her senior. She felt like a girl next to him, with her dark bobbed hair and prim schoolgirl dress, and wondered if anyone would be suspicious of their age difference. But his warm demeanor soon put her at ease, and she felt compelled to smile back and lean into him to help their act. It was necessary to stay vigilant, Bruno would later tell her. As a known Communist, he was distrusted even under Badoglio's watch—and he had left home early that day to ensure he wasn't being followed.

The pair walked along the river for a while, Bruno asking Teresa questions, both lighthearted and serious, assessing her personality and dedication to the cause. He explained his need for a trusted go-between.

"We Communists have always been accustomed to secrecy," he told her. "Our rules must still be followed, even now that the situation is so confused." He paused their walking and looked her in the eye. "Is this something you can do?" he asked. Teresa agreed, impressed and excited with their political discussion and easy rapport.

Bruno was satisfied as well, because he then took her to meet another leader, whose reception was much less cordial. This man gave her a warning instead of a greeting: "Look . . . if after ten days one of this formation should be arrested, you end up in the Arno."

Teresa had passed the initial assessment and would be given her first, probationary assignment. But she was only just starting to understand what was at risk.

A few days later Teresa was contacted by telephone and given her orders: She was to deliver documents to her brother Gianfranco at the University of Milan and bring home sensitive documents from him.

Within days she had completed the journey, delivering the documents at a scheduled meeting with Bruno, the two visiting like old friends at a café. And with this package, she won the trust of the Florentine resistance. Bruno knew she would succeed and had come with a gift for her: her nome di battaglia, "Chicchi." There would be more missions to come, he assured her.

NEITHER KNEW THE other then, but a few weeks earlier, on July 25, they had both been in Piazza Vittorio Emanuele II, historically the seat of popular protests in Florence, celebrating the deposition of Mussolini. In the first protests in more than twenty years, Teresa had joined a group of fellow anti-Fascist students who would soon organize into the Fronte della Gioventù—the "Youth Front"—and crowded among the café tables that spilled out from under the porticoes that lined the square. The piazza had long been a meeting place for artists and writers, who might have discussed politics in whispers; today they cheered and chanted, "Long live peace! Long live Italy! Down with Mussolini!"

Noticing the group of young people that Teresa was a part of, Bruno remembered thinking that he wanted to help harness that energy for the cause.

Bruno then found some of his friends, and in a rare feeling of unselfconsciousness—for once he didn't fear surveillance or retribution—he helped organize a group of people to march from the Piazza Vittorio Emanuele II to Le Murate, the prison where the political prisoners were held, to demand their release.

Bruno had come from a wealthy and connected family in the food production industry, and his father was friends with Mussolini. Bruno, however, had aligned himself with left-leaning politics and been a known agitator when he was younger and living in Rome. But now, in his thirties, he was married with children, and had moved from Rome to Florence, where he sought to stay out of trouble for his family's sake. Just days after Mussolini's fall, former colleagues from his politically active days in Rome arrived, wanting him to help them publish a new issue of the Communist paper *Pugno Chiuso*—"Clenched Fist." *The war will soon be over,* they reasoned, trying to convince him to join them again.

"Pay attention," he told them. "This does not necessarily signify peace: The war is just beginning."

AFTER MEETING BRUNO in the summer of 1943, Teresa's anti-Fascist leanings began to focus. In August, Bruno asked her to convene a meeting of the same friends whom he had seen in the piazza on July 25—but insisted that he stay in the shadows. Teresa was never to mention his name, only to use his nome di battaglia if absolutely necessary.

Within days Teresa brought the young men and women together, fellow leader Aldo Braibanti remembering "the sweet gaze of her inflexible eyes." And they began their first initiative, requested by Bruno: to write and distribute a leaflet praising liberty and democracy.

As they talked about their own desires and goals, they also decided to do something more urgent. The group drafted an official request to university authorities to reinstate students and faculty dismissed because of the racial laws. And then they discussed creating a new student committee to replace GUF, the Fascist university group. Soon after, members of the Youth Front would break into the GUF offices, destroying their lists of dissenters and taking what supplies they could use. And so, Teresa and the Youth Front joined the Florentine resistance.

CHAPTER 9

OCCUPATION

On August 18, 1943, Italian general Giuseppe Castellano—who was at one time the youngest general in Italy and the highest-ranking officer involved in the arrest of Mussolini—secretly met with General Dwight Eisenhower's chief of staff in an apartment in Portugal for a long-overdue discussion about the plan for Italian and Allied military cooperation. Badoglio's government had been wasting time for weeks, trying to strategize the most beneficial terms of their surrender. The Americans were rightfully skeptical.

The Allies did not share with the general details about their imminent landing by sea in Salerno, 165 miles south of Rome. But they did negotiate the presence of the U.S. 82nd Airborne Division—over eight thousand five hundred airmen—at an airfield outside Rome to help protect Italy after their announced surrender. The details, in English, were sent back to Badoglio and his team, including requirements to install searchlight beams and amber lights on the airfield, and provide trucks, equipment, and trenches for support. These orders would sit on General Badoglio's desk, ignored and untranslated as the summer continued.

BY LATE AUGUST there were seven well-resourced German divisions in Italy. They had been streaming through the Brenner Pass since the fall of Mussolini, where they also occupied the guardhouses along the border. This Alpine crossing stretches from Austria, which was under German rule, to northern Italy and had been Hitler's gateway to Italy during his 1938 tour with Mussolini.

Earlier in the summer Field Marshal Albert Kesselring, whom Hitler had put in charge of their Italian campaign, had actually asked permission from Badoglio's government to enter the country but had not received an answer. Soon after, Italians throughout the chain of command had raised the alarm that there were many thousands of German soldiers passing through by train and truck. Badoglio ignored these warnings or said it wasn't his jurisdiction. Kesselring decided to just do what he pleased.

CHAPTER 10

CARLA

ROME

AUGUST AND EARLY SEPTEMBER 1943

C arla returned to her secretarial job when her help was no longer needed in San Lorenzo, bringing a new confidence in her abilities, even if the work was not her passion. It was a position she had inherited from her older sister, who left for Umbria when she married a few years earlier, and it was the only income Carla, her mother, and her younger brother had. Over the next few weeks, Carla became more active in the growing political movement, and she sensed a change in herself. While she had once felt shy and uncertain about her capabilities at work, she became bolder in expressing opinions to her superiors. She carried herself with better posture, a surer step. Even her mother had noticed. Carla had always been comfortable in social situations among her peers, but as she became more politically educated and began taking part in discussions during the meetings held at her apartment, she found security in her intellectual abilities as well. Despite needing the money, more and more often Carla would skip work or leave early to attend meetings or wander the city, feeling like she was seeing the world with new eyes.

On one hot day in late August, Carla decided to ride her bicycle to the beach for a swim, the sea breezes calling to her as they had the morning before the San Lorenzo bombing. She had not been past the city walls since. There had been many sightings of Germans outside Rome, and they and the Italians seemed to have brokered a quiet truce. Still, as she rode into the countryside, there was a sense of foreboding. Houses and fields appeared abandoned and bare, "as if there, too, signs of the war threatened the peace of the landscape," Carla thought.

Carla felt uneasy when she arrived and found only the lifeguard and a pair of young Nazi soldiers guarding the entrance to the otherwise empty beach. She walked past the gate and dropped the entrance fee into the slot on top of the sealed box.

"Can't I swim?" she asked the frowning lifeguard on the other side of the gate.

"It's reserved for *them*," he responded.

"Well, I paid and I intend to take a dip," she told him, and continued walking toward the changing area, where she put on her suit and swim cap.

When she emerged, the elder soldier came up to her. *Verboten,* he said. *Swimming prohibited.* Resigned, she took off her cap and turned back toward the changing room.

Then the younger soldier called to her, seemingly more friendly. "You can go in."

Carla returned his smile, put her cap back on, and took off running toward the beach, the crashing of waves drowning out the pounding of her feet on the hot sand. It burned her skin, but she didn't care. All she wanted was the freedom the sea could offer her. She leapt into the waves and swam out past the break. The sound of the sea filled her ears, made her forget the tension of the past weeks, the smell of lingering dust and smoke that had hung over Rome since the bombing. She dove under the waves again, considering that maybe this small concession of humanity offered by the soldier was a sign that the Germans might simply return home, that war on the streets was not imminent after all.

Then she heard a *pop pop pop pop pop*. Carla spun around in the water, looking for the source of this noise, of the unnatural splashing of the water around her.

The Germans were shooting at her.

Carla swam underwater farther out and came up for air, shaking. She could see one soldier with his legs spread apart, helmet askew, aiming a heavy mounted machine gun at her. More popping and splashing and she ducked underwater again, the waves rough this far out. When she emerged, the young soldier was gesturing for her to come ashore.

They would let her live that day, finding glee in her fear. Back at Via Cavour, Carla told her new friends that she now understood: War was coming to Rome.

BY THE END of August Carla was participating in all of the women's meetings, which were growing weekly in size. This was where Carla received, as she described, her first "real political and historical education about the rise of Fascism to power, the defeat of the working classes . . . the ideals of our fights and the rules of underground life and activities." She was ashamed that she hadn't been more critical of the relatively broad support Mussolini had leading up to the start of World War II, even as he began fraternizing with Hitler, who had been widely disliked in Italy from the start. Her new revolutionary meetings taught her to identify the propaganda the Fascists had employed in speeches and articles, pitting "rich" aristocratic nations like England and France against "hardworking" Italy—a Populist narrative embraced by many Italians, especially as it was presented in the state-controlled press.

Even as she recalled her mother scoffing at the posters in the shop windows that declared IL DUCE IS ALWAYS RIGHT!, Carla had felt some pride at the way she and her friends had made the best of the war rationing starting in 1939, when driving private cars became illegal and restaurants were allowed to only offer one meal of meat or fish daily. Carla remembered relishing the wilted greens her mother brought home, the scant bread they had to share, feeling like she was helping a worthy cause. She realized now that even as she had hated Mussolini for what the Fascists did to her father, she, too, had naively trusted that he would keep the country out of the war.

It seemed to Carla that everyone she knew had been against the war from its start, all praying for the same outcome—the end of war and the fall of Mussolini—even if they had no idea what they could do to help achieve either end. What she hadn't known at the time was that there had long been people—like the women in her home right now—who had been fighting for this very thing.

Resistance proliferated in Rome and among like-minded Italians around the country. For every uttered password in the Eternal City, there were people meeting in rural barns or basements using a secret knock. Political pamphlets were printed again at surprising rates, passed from handbags and fruit carts. Some who had grown disillusioned or fearful in the last years—and there were many—now felt emboldened to speak of their discontent in voices louder than a whisper. Those who had been long active in small, furtive groups brought more people into the fold. Now they had to decide how to work together to fight back.

ON ANY GIVEN night, Carla's apartment on Via Cavour swarmed with people. There would be groups of women—Carla, her mother, and perhaps members of the women's group—sitting by the windows in the evening, listening to the news reports in the only breeze that cut the stifling heat of late summer. They were together on September 3 when they heard the reports that the Allied forces finally landed in mainland Italy, near Calabria.

And so began the reports that the Allies would be in Rome soon. Italians not directly impacted by the fighting went on with their lives the best they could. In Sicily, people were rebuilding after weeks of brutal fighting. The Allied victory would be swift, they believed. During the evening *passeggiata,* as families took walks together around the neighborhood, they would greet one another with the hopeful call of *Two weeks!,* even as that empty promise would stay the same week after week.

In reality, no one in Via Cavour believed that war would end so soon. As the Fascist loyalists kept quietly out of sight, the once-hidden anti-Fascists started to come out of the woodwork. Those who had continued to anonymously publish Socialist or Communist newspapers, worker organizers, and an increasing number of people like Carla, young and old, began meeting and recruiting others in groups with specific interests such as women's groups, or with a focus like writing educational pamphlets. They knew that the Fascists next door wouldn't give up their black shirts without a fight—that there were more Germans than ever in their country. Around Italy, like in Rome, people were preparing to fight for the future of their country.

CHAPTER 11

SEPTEMBER 7, 1943

On September 7, Allied and Italian generals met in Rome. A written report from the meeting notes that there were now "12,000 Germans . . . in the valley of the Tiber, who have heavy equipment including 100 pieces of artillery. . . . The Panzer Grenadier Division had been raised to an effective strength of 24,000 men with 50 light and 150 heavy tanks."

The Americans were shocked to learn that the plans to secure the airfields near Rome had not been executed, having sat on Badoglio's desk for weeks. The Italians begged for a delay in the official announcements of their surrender, arguing, not incorrectly, that "the only result of an immediate armistice would be a German-supported Fascist government in Rome." But the Americans were unmoved by this late attempt at negotiation.

When Eisenhower got word that there had been no Italian action to prepare for the planned arrival of the 82nd Airborne, he called off the air support—some airplanes had already taken off and had to be rerouted midair. Anyone in Rome who wanted to resist the growing German presence was alone.

CHAPTER 12

BIANCA

TURIN
SEPTEMBER 8, 1943

Bianca had joined the Communists under Mussolini's rule, but for five weeks during that summer of 1943, starting with the fall of Il Duce, these clandestine parties began to emerge from secrecy. Meetings were held a bit more freely, with more people joining as the weeks went on, even as they still practiced caution.

As August turned to September, Bianca had been invited to be a part of the confederation that was working to plan Italy's next government, uniting the disparate political groups under one coalition. Utilizing her experience as a social worker, Bianca was asked to help set up their new office, which would be housed on the third floor of a municipal building. There was hope that even the most progressive political parties might be able to operate with full transparency in a new era of Italian political freedom.

When the day came, Bianca traveled there in the afternoon, after her work at the factories. She had stacks of once-hidden papers in hand, the result of her months spent at the typewriter. But when she arrived, the office was vacant. Doors were open, desk drawers were ajar, barely a scrap of paper remained. There was nothing.

Bianca returned home, fearing the reason for her comrades'

return underground. By the evening broadcast of Radio London she would know why.

It was September 8, exactly forty-five days after Mussolini was deposed and the day that everything changed. Later this period would be known as "the Forty-Five Days."

CHAPTER 13

CARLA

ROME
SEPTEMBER 8–9, 1943

On the night of September 8, Carla had stayed up late with her mother, watching the artillery light the sky from their fifth-floor window, listening to Radio London as usual. The day had felt ominous from the start. Her new comrades had stayed uncharacteristically quiet, and she had the sense that they knew something that she did not. She and her mother had been listening to the radio all day, switching between the official Italian station and Radio London, hoping for answers as to why the city felt on edge.

Finally, at six-thirty P.M., American general Eisenhower had announced that Italy had surrendered to the Allied forces unconditionally.

He intoned:

The armistice was signed by my representative and the representative of Marshal Badoglio and becomes effective this instant. Hostilities between the armed forces of the United Nations and those of Italy terminate at once. All Italians who now act to help eject the German aggressor from Italian soil will have the assistance and support of the United Nations.

After a few uneasy weeks, this news was thrilling. But what Carla had realized that day at the beach, what was most often predicted in the meetings she had been attending for weeks, was that war on the streets of Rome was all but imminent.

From her window, Carla could see and hear the firefights that broke out mere minutes after the announcement. She understood now what her friends had known. The remaining Italian soldiers and others who had been eyeing the German interlopers on the edge of the city were preparing to defend what was left of their country.

Hitler had been waiting for this announcement. Incensed at this perceived betrayal, he immediately commanded his soldiers to surround Rome and many other Italian cities, to prepare for occupation at daybreak.

There were plenty of Italian forces near Rome, and strong enough that they could defend the city against the incoming Germans. But King Vittorio Emanuele, General Badoglio, and their entourage decided to escape Rome rather than defend it. In a half-mile-long convoy of black cars, they fled east. The general ordered many of the nearby troops to retreat to Tivoli, to protect their escape route. The Eternal City was abandoned and leaderless.

Those who remained sent word into Rome's labyrinthian streets for backup. Hundreds of miles away, even more German forces streamed over Italy's northern border, toward Turin and Verona. The few who had argued that this was the end of Italy's involvement in the war were silenced.

This was the moment that the political action groups that had been meeting and planning for the past forty-five days turned into *la Resistenza*—"the Resistance."

ON SEPTEMBER 10, Carla awoke to the sounds of men hurrying to the edge of the city to help hold back the Germans. Many were armed with old rifles, and they were calling into the open windows, asking for more men to join them. It had been little more than a day since Italy had surrendered and already a new phase of the war was beginning. Despite her mother's protests, Carla ran down the stairs, following the same instincts that had carried her to San Lorenzo weeks before. She and the men ran toward the sounds of the guns, south to the city gate of Porta San Paolo.

Those who were armed—with weapons pulled from basement stashes, guns from World War I, or even rifles taken from smashed display cases at museums—joined the remaining Italian troops trying to stop the Germans from entering the city. Without a gun, Carla first ran to help the women and men dragging disabled vehicles and rubble to block the roads leading to the gate, which was one of the only entrances to the center of the still-walled city. An ancient fortress surrounded Rome, with stone walls more than thirty feet high and eleven feet thick that had withstood attacks for nearly two thousand years. The Nazis would have to enter through one of the arched gates that could, in theory, still be defended as they had been for millennia. The Pyramid of Caius Cestius stood in front of Porta San Paolo—an imposing 119-foot-high monument erected in the first century BC from slabs of white marble.

Fighting had already occurred beyond the city between the remaining Italian soldiers and the advancing Germans. But now the battle approached the city walls, where civilians began to take a stand. The Germans had greater numbers and firepower, but few places to take shelter. The Italians took aim at them from the shadow of the pyramid, with the Germans firing back. Stray bullets bounced off the pyramid's surface, chips of marble raining down. Italian tanks flanked the ad hoc army, helping to keep at bay the Germans who made it past their roadblocks.

Amid the firefight Carla moved to help evacuate and care for the wounded at makeshift triage tents on Aventine Hill, just inside the city gate. But within hours, discouraging news came from the front line. German Tigers—formidable sixty-eight-ton tanks—had arrived and made quick work of their barricade, forcing the much smaller Italian tanks into retreat. Behind the Tigers came flame-throwers and heavy artillery.

By the afternoon, half of the Roman force had been killed, wounded, or captured or had fled. There were nearly six hundred casualties, including more than two dozen women. The battle ended with streams of Nazi trucks and tanks entering through the gate, their sheer number and firepower far superior to the outdated armory of the Romans. The Germans threatened mass bombings if the resistance didn't cease. Not wanting to risk more casualties, most resisters turned back on foot, Carla included.

As Carla neared the Colosseum on her own solitary walk home, she paused at the sight of a row of German tanks facing off against a single Italian tank known as a "sardine can." These tanks were so tiny that only smaller-statured Italians could fit inside to operate them. She watched, unnoticed behind a row of flowering oleander trees, as the Italian tank began to retreat toward Via dei Fiori Imperiali, the wide avenue that ran northward from the Colosseum toward Trajan's Column. It was the route where Mussolini loved to stage his grandest nationalist parades—and the only path to freedom. She was shaking, as if a movie were being played out in front of her, and then she jumped when a Tiger broadsided the smaller tank and blew the driver partway out of the hatch. Without thinking she ran toward him. Only when she had emerged from her hiding place behind the oleander did she realize how far away the man was—and how potentially foolish her decision. In a moment she could feel the crosshairs of the German guns turn upon her. Now that she'd been spotted she knew she couldn't turn back.

Dodging fire, she ran toward the tank and pulled the delirious soldier from the hatch, dragging him toward safety, bullets and shells crisscrossing just above their heads as the German tanks engaged with retreating Italian tanks near the ruins of the Circus Maximus. The soldier had a bleeding wound, and once they were hidden again behind the oleander, she bound it with a tourniquet torn from the hem of her dress. Then she pulled the soldier onto her back and stumbled forward once more, past the ruins of the ornate Temple of Venus, considering the irony that she was in the middle of a battle taking place in an open-air museum where ancient Romans had honored the goddess of beauty and love.

As the two made their way to her apartment a few hundred yards away, Carla knew that there was no turning back to her previous life where she would stare out the window, waiting for the war to end. Instead, she would be on the front lines, fighting for her beloved city and a different, free future.

THAT NIGHT, AS the soldier whom Carla had saved rested in a makeshift bedroom in their pantry, Carla watched from her window as fighters retreated, many shedding their Italian military uniforms, which they feared would make them targets for the new occupiers. It had become common in the past six weeks to see groups of Italian soldiers abandoning their posts in droves, walking toward a distant home. Many changed into civilian clothes—some stolen off clothes-lines, others given by helpful women who might also offer a bit of food or a place to stay for the night. These mothers and sisters and wives understood that these men had family members who wanted them home, just as they waited for their men to come back. But Carla knew her father would never return. She now realized that he had taught her that it was up to her to forge her own path. From her window, she dropped her father's clothes down onto the street below in hopes that they would have a new life, too.

PART 2

RESISTANCE

CHAPTER 14

SURRENDER

On the first day of Italy's announced surrender, General Bado-glio had merely instructed his soldiers to "resist attacks from wherever they come." The same day, German officers went to Italian army headquarters across the north, where they now had thousands of soldiers, and demanded cooperation or surrender within an hour, or else they would open fire. They cut telephone wires and disseminated misleading propaganda, all to isolate and confuse the Italian troops.

A day later, on September 9, Badoglio's administration told Italian troops "not to take the initiative in attacking the Germans." Those who had defended Rome at Porta San Paolo had risked their lives of their own volition.

It wasn't until September 11 that the war office told Italian troops to "treat the Germans as enemies," although Italy would not declare war against them for another month. By then, 80 percent of Italy was occupied by the Germans and most army headquarters had been taken over or shut down.

After the war, military analysts would piece together that in those first days of the occupation, the Italian army that had remained outside Rome had fought gallantly against the Germans. Had many not been called east to Tivoli to protect the escaping Italian leaders, historians believe they would have held their own against the invading Germans. Certainly, they could have defended Rome for the four days needed for the airfields to be secured and the 82nd Airborne to arrive.

CHAPTER 15

ANITA

REGGIO EMILIA
SEPTEMBER 1943

Twenty-two-year-old Anita Malavasi heard the air raid sirens yet again. Reggio Emilia had woefully inadequate bomb shelters and was still marred by deep scars from the Reggiane factory bombing six months earlier. So, Anita and her friends had taken to riding out into the countryside to escape likely bomb targets, adrenaline helping them pump their legs fast even in the sweltering afternoon heat.

Usually, with the recent sirens activated at even a distant sighting, the young women would ride toward the foothills of the Apennine Mountains just beyond the city, where they waited for the dreaded drone of airplanes.

But that day no bombers were seen, and then the far-off blaring ceased. So the friends returned to the city, each young woman only separating from the safety of their group at the turn for her own street.

They might not have known yet of the battle that happened in Rome, but by that second week of September, they had already seen Italian soldiers being taken prisoner by the increasing number of Nazi troops who were occupying the town. The growing German presence prompted the elders to retell stories of the concentration and POW camps of the First World War, where prisoners died of hunger, stoking fear. Anita's father had begun insisting she feed her brother more, helping to insulate him against the worst they could imagine should he be captured.

When Anita reached her house on Via Dalmazia, she stopped short at the sight of German SS soldiers blocking her way.

"*Halt, raus!*" a soldier commanded.

Her round cheeks flushing, Anita insisted, "It's my house! Mine! I have to fix dinner!"

This time the soldier pointed his gun at her. "*Raus. Schnell. Schnell!*"

Anger rose within Anita, along with fear, as she considered protesting more. She was not a young woman who could keep her words to herself. But facing the gun, common sense prompted her to turn around and retrace her path, where she soon met up with her friend Maria Montanari, who reported a similar situation.

"It's not the fear of the gun, you see," Anita reflected decades later. "It's realizing that you were absolutely nothing to them. . . . You were less than a bug."

CHAPTER 16

DVX

On September 11, Field Marshal Kesselring made it clear to Italians who was in control. He announced that it was forbidden to carry arms, and anyone caught with munitions or "organizing strikes or sabotage . . . will be shot immediately. . . . Private correspondence is suspended. All telephone conversations should be as brief as possible. They will be strictly monitored."

In a blow to worker morale in the north, Italians were forced to hand over row after row of tanks and armored cars, fresh off the Fiat and Lancia assembly lines, for the Germans to use against the Allies.

The next day, a German airlift liberated Benito Mussolini from his cell in a hotel on a remote mountain plateau, nearly a mile above sea level in the Gran Sasso Mountains in central Italy. The hotel was one of three planned by Mussolini, intended to be built in the shape of the letters *D, V,* and *X*—Latin for "leader" and from whence his nickname "Il Duce" derived. He was held in the hotel shaped like a letter D—the only one ever built. Ten gliders, each with ten men, took off via their pull-plane from an airfield near Rome. Less than an hour later they arrived on the mountain, this dangerous and dramatic rescue ordered directly by Hitler. Other officers and soldiers arrived via funicular and small plane—which could have been a less dangerous, if also less theatrical, way for the soldiers to arrive. After the extraction, Mussolini would be in Vienna by nightfall, meeting with Hitler in his "Wolf's Lair," as he called his main bunker, a few days later.

The Germans made a show of rescuing Mussolini likely because he was supposed to be handed over to the Allies as part of the armistice agreement. But General Badoglio was so focused on his own escape that he had given Mussolini an opportunity for the same. Yet while Mussolini was grateful for his freedom, he also knew that it came at a price: He would forever be under Hitler's thumb. His own diaries speak to his reluctance to return to rule, but he had little choice but to obey the man who had freed him.

On September 18, the newly reinstalled Mussolini broadcast to the Italian people on Radio Munich that there was a new Italian Fascist state in German-occupied Italy—and that Italy would fight "alongside Germany" and take "revenge" on those who betrayed him after July 25.

This new neo-Fascist puppet government was called the Italian Social Republic of Salò, named after the town on the shores of Lake Garda where it was based. Mussolini was its de facto—albeit nearly powerless—head. There, Il Duce was under constant surveillance—an Italian-speaking German officer even lived in his house—and any effort he made to shield his country from the ravages of Germany could be thwarted.

Around occupied Italy, Fascist soldiers and Italian police began to work with the Germans—ostensibly they were independent entities of the new Republic of Salò, but in reality they answered to the occupiers. The police were expected to keep order and prosecute non-political crimes, although where the line was drawn was blurry. Often there were both German and Republic soldiers working together at roadblocks that had been hastily built with makeshift walls spanning most of the width of a major thoroughfare. Together they guarded prisons or initiated mass arrests. The Koch and Carità gangs were also deputized as mercenaries for the Nazis. They were not trained soldiers and were known to be extremely violent and merciless, volunteering for this role in many cases to exercise their darkest tendencies with impunity. Among this varied group, what was clear was that the Germans were ultimately in charge, and they were all united in their focus to eliminate the Resistance.

AT THE SAME time, the leaders of the various anti-Fascist parties were organizing as well. Despite their sometimes conflicting viewpoints, the political parties that had reasserted their influence during the Forty-Five Days understood the need to collaborate against what was turning into a dual war: the civil war against the Italian Fascist government and the war against Germany. They also wanted to show a united front to the Allied forces, so they would take them seriously as an ally during—and after—the war. General Badoglio was still the official leader of non-occupied Italy, although he held little influence. The Committee of National Liberation (CLN) was officially formed by leaders of the various left and centrist political parties following the armistice, intended to be the central united leadership of the Resistance. CLN organized quickly, installing regional committees around occupied Italy that began connecting with local Resistance groups. For many Italians, eager for change, this was the government they now recognized as their own, and they were willing to die defending it.

CHAPTER 17

BIANCA

TURIN
SEPTEMBER 1943

Bianca's desperation to find her way back to her revolutionary friends was soon replaced by her fear at the prospect of continued war. German tanks arrived in Turin, bringing with them the same violence and mercilessness they had shown the rest of Italy. There were reports of people being beaten in the streets, and friends of Bianca who were openly involved in politics during the Forty-Five Days were afraid of arrest. At least twenty people—many of them Jewish—had converged on Bianca's home that first night of the occupation, most sleeping on the floor. Some would leave the next morning, others stayed for a few days. Bianca's comrades with the Communist Party found her soon afterward, having returned underground to organize. They had a role in mind for her in CLN's nascent government.

ON SEPTEMBER 15, Mussolini, under authority "from Hitler's headquarters for the constitution of the Italian Social Republic," announced his return to leadership and ordered "all military, administrative, and scholastic authorities . . . to immediately re-sume their posts." The Nazi-Fascists wanted to form a new army under the Italian Social Republic of Salò. But few would heed this order. Therefore, Germany demanded that sixty thousand able-bodied men report to the local *questura*. Again, that call was largely ignored. German commander Kesselring was furious and made an-other demand for thirty thousand more.

Those north of Turin could watch the fleeing soldiers from a dis-tance. In each of the valleys—which included the inhabited area from the foothills to the ridges below the imposing snowcapped Al-pine peaks, just a few dozen miles north of Turin—there was often a single main road. Small towns had been built amid steep elevation changes as the narrow thoroughfare made its way through the craggy ridges. Young men with backpacks headed north toward the Swiss border, fleeing through the more independent-minded val-leys, where small towns had long had to fend for themselves and many had thus resisted Fascist ideology. Once they neared the Nazi-occupied Italian border crossings they had to forge their own way over the peaks toward Switzerland. Even in the last days of summer there was snow on the glaciers of Monte Rosa—the com-pact mountain group on the border. Deserters could be seen from far away, like ants on white cotton. Once on the other side, they could only be heard, tossing their hand grenades down into the ra-vines before they reached neutral land.

SOME, THOUGH, CHOSE a different route. During the Forty-Five Days, there had been factory workers who began organizing like-minded people in early Resistance groups. Others coalesced under political parties, or just began talking more freely with friends.

Some of these groups went around their cities or towns with a hammer and chisel to chip off Fascist symbols from public buildings. Others decided to collect munitions instead of destroying them.

When, after September 8, the German occupation moved quickly, so, too, did the young Resistance. Some helped Jewish families from the now-occupied cities hide in small towns and villages beyond. Anti-Fascists found one another, like a group of workers from the Olivetti typewriter factory outside Turin, who rounded up arms or stole them from unguarded barracks and hid them, all too aware that they might soon be needed for a different kind of war. Those who had begun writing political pamphlets continued, surreptitiously passing them from hand to hand, or placing them in mailboxes under cover of darkness. World War II had not ended for the Italians, as many had hoped. Instead, the front line had come to them. But this was a new war—one in which Italians had to choose sides in a civil war as well. Every Italian would have to decide whether they would cast their lot with the Fascists or the partisans. To fail to choose would be a choice in itself.

BIANCA'S FIANCÉ, ALBERTO, knew he had to flee the city—he was Jewish as well as a young man of fighting age. Bianca would lead him to safety—and she wanted a way to indicate to him if there was danger. So, he and Bianca devised a plan. They rode their bicycles into the countryside, Bianca ahead of Alberto, singing loudly as she pedaled. If she went silent, he should prepare to hide himself. She would only begin singing again when she was sure the way was safe.

Beyond Turin the snowcapped Alps were a distant vista that grew larger as they made their way closer. The pair was the most exposed for those first miles across the vast farmland to the foothills, which quickly steepened. There the few roads built into the treacherous terrain crossed through the middle of towns, buildings built next to the roads, their windows buttoned up tight. Alberto found safety among the growing members of the Resistance in the Alpine towns, joining a group of men camping in an abandoned mine barracks. Bianca would make the same trip again, leading two former classmates to safety on foot, singing her way from the city to the mountains.

Likewise, other women would do the same for friends and strangers, as hordes of men fled to the countryside in fear of the increasing Nazi scrutiny in the cities and towns.

Their friend Primo Levi left for the mountains as well. Along with his mother and sister, he escaped the city in the days after the occupation, finding lodging in a hotel in a small Alpine town called Amay, with vistas of the low peaks below. Soon after, Primo met with some other Jewish friends who were also in hiding nearby. The group debated whether to hire *passeurs*—border smugglers, who were now charging thousands of lire (more than five thousand dollars today) to lead people into Switzerland. Not everyone had that kind of money, and there were stories of the guides abandoning their charges or even turning them over to the Nazi-Fascists for rewards. The group did not come to a decision. But as the young men considered what to do, at least they had one another.

CHAPTER 18

CARLA

ROME

SEPTEMBER AND OCTOBER 1943

In Rome the Nazis declared buying or selling on the ubiquitous black market punishable by death, as was listening to enemy radio, harboring a fugitive, and possessing propaganda, among many other common actions. Carla and her mother had already liquidated most of the valuables in their apartment, selling artwork and Etruscan vases for food and necessities in the years since her father had died. But they knew they would continue to mine their possessions for goods they might sell or trade. And they would listen to the radio and read whatever news they could. They, like most Romans, just laughed at these new laws. Everyone did these things! Were the Nazis going to kill the entire city?

Additionally all arms, ammunitions, and bombs were to be handed in to the German authorities. The punishment for resistance was death. Dead partisans would soon be found, splayed out on the ground, with a sign hung on them: WHOEVER IS FOUND CARRYING WEAPONS WILL SUFFER THE SAME FATE.

Then the roundups started. Men might show up at Carla's door, breathless, telling of their escape from Nazis swarming city blocks, looking for those of working age to force into joining the new Italian army or send to Germany to toil for the war effort. People who didn't comply willingly would be deported to concentration camps or killed.

German soldiers and re-emboldened Fascists searched apartments, taking whatever they wanted; they drove tanks down ancient narrow streets, pointing their guns at women and children. Some apartments stood empty as their former inhabitants went into hiding. Other homes held multiple families who thought this new space was safer than their last. If Germans requisitioned any rooms in a building, many remaining inhabitants would leave the next day, fearing their proximity.

Nobody was safe. Germany made the claim that Rome was an "open city"—a term that meant that the city was neither occupied nor defended by a military force and should not be attacked, and its inhabitants were not to be treated as enemies. This declaration was supported by the Pope, who hoped that the central location of the neutral Vatican City, and the presence of so many priceless works of art and architecture, might convince the Germans to leave Rome untouched by war. But it was far from an open city in practice. By international law this should have meant that no acts of war were occurring within its borders by either side, and that the city would be peaceably occupied. Instead, the Nazis considered themselves the ultimate authority, with the local Fascist police and military operating under their control. Any apartment could be deemed compromised by the Resistance, and its inhabitants terrorized or arrested. The streets were not safe, either. Those caught out after curfew could be arrested, and were often beaten as well. Contrary to international law, the Germans used Rome's streets for military transport and activities, and hunted for anyone they considered a threat. For its inhabitants, Rome certainly felt like a city at war.

Carla and her mother's apartment became a respite in this new battle zone. They would take in whoever came to their door, whether for a day as they prepared their escape to the hills beyond the city, or for longer to help with the growing Resistance in Rome. If you knew the password.

ADELE BEI WAS told of the safety the password *arcangelo* provided soon after the start of the Nazi occupation. She was among the many political prisoners released in June 1943, and had been imprisoned since 1933 for serving as a courier for anti-Fascist groups and disseminating anti-Fascist literature. She had spent years in Rome's Regina Coeli prison, but more recently had been held in confino on an island off the coast. She had arrived in Rome, after a decade away, to continue the work she had started to empower women in what she hoped would soon be the new Italian republic.

When Adele arrived at Carla's for the first time, she checked out the apartment like a picky tenant, deciding on the dining room as the place where she would hold her meetings. Adele called the furnishings "too elegant" but later relented, calling them appropriate if the meeting would be regarded "as invitations to play canasta and drink tea." Despite her brusque first impression, Adele would soon warm up, giving Carla and her mother a wide smile, showing her beautiful white teeth. Adele apologized, blaming her time in confinement for her lack of manners.

It would be Adele who introduced Carla to local partisan leaders who were planning more aggressive action. Carla started accompanying Adele on missions where being a woman was a particular asset, as they could move around the city with less scrutiny. They would sometimes visit the Imperial Movie Theater, where comrades still worked the bar and where a huge cache of arms was hidden under the stage. Carla and Adele helped transport the weapons to partisans around the city, tucking guns into handbags or under trench coats.

One day, Adele took Carla along on a mission to a drugstore in a nearby neighborhood. When they arrived, Adele and the pharmacist chatted like old friends, but Carla could tell he was sizing her up while they spoke. He finally asked Adele, "Who's your friend?"

"This is Elena," Adele said, telling Carla later that the name was inspired by Helen of Troy: "a woman they fought a war over." This would become Carla's *nome di battaglia* when she soon joined the pharmacist's new guerrilla fighting group—the reason Adele had brought her there.

Carla's newness was an asset, as she was yet unknown to the Fascist *squadristi* who had now resumed their patrols, helping Germans to target known resisters, and generally keep the Roman population in fear. Many of the student activists under suspicion by the Nazis and Fascists were from working-class homes, and few suspected revolutionaries would be in her more monied neighborhood, where residents had benefited from Fascist policies. At any time of day or night Carla or her mother or younger brother might hear a knock at the door, their hearts beating violently until they heard the password whispered. Their secret was still safe.

CHAPTER 19

ANITA

REGGIO EMILIA
SEPTEMBER AND OCTOBER 1943

A nita pulled on her brother's pants over her dress, buttoning his shirt over the top. Always careful with her appearance, she must have fussed with the shirt to fit as smoothly under the trousers as possible, trying to make the look natural. She pinned her hair on top of her head and pulled a hat down as low as she could, hoping to hide her big eyes and soft, girlish features. Maybe she practiced walking, stepping heavier, like a man.

And then she and her brother went to the local army barracks on the edge of the city. She nodded as her brother explained they were there to visit some friends. Once inside, they found a dark corner where Anita stripped off her brother's clothes, handing them to a soldier who wanted to desert. She fluffed the skirt of her dress and took down her hair. And out of the barracks Anita strolled with the soldier turned civilian on her arm. Her step was lighter, his joyous, too, perhaps, happy to be headed out for a free afternoon.

ANITA AND HER closest group of friends, which included Maria Montanari and Anita's cousin Sandra, stayed vigilant as they moved around the city, whether they were going to work or doing the shopping for their families. They might notice a young man moving furtively down the alleyways in the tightly built Reggio Emilia downtown. Or perhaps Anita's brother would ask if they could help a friend.

They devised a plan of action. One woman went ahead as a lookout for German or Fascist officers or roadblocks, while the other stayed with the man, helping to find places to hide if needed. Anita and her friends guided the men until they were well beyond the city, headed toward where other young men were rumored to be camping out or squatting, in abandoned barns or cottages on the plains, or in growing camps or stone huts in the ridges and valleys of the rugged Apennines, all trying to figure out their next move.

The number of Italian soldiers dwindled and the Nazi demands to report for service resulted in few new soldiers and workers. The Germans passed another decree: Anyone caught helping these men escape would be sent to concentration camps or executed. Anita and her group continued their work, undeterred.

BY THAT SECOND month of the occupation, Anita's upstairs neighbor Torelli, whom the Fascists had already made clear they had under surveillance, had come down after work as he often did. Anita poured him a glass of the dark wine made from local Sangiovese grapes that her father was known for fermenting in large vats in their basement, to share and to sell. When the nights were warm and the windows were open, the talk stayed more neutral—even with a few feet of space between the houses here, voices could carry. More than ever, now was the time that people were deciding how they and their families would survive the war. But as autumn continued, the temperature dropped, sashes were closed, and soon evening fires would be lit. Conversation could be a bit more critical of the occupying forces and might include speculation of which Fascists had aligned themselves with the Germans and were to be especially feared. Anita's brothers did not hide their support of the burgeoning Resistance—her older brother had already gone south to volunteer with the Allied forces while her younger brother still lived with her and their parents and was a member of the local Resistance.

But still, Torelli knew that some things were to be kept secret for now. He waited for a brief moment when he and Anita were alone and leaned toward her to whisper, "The things you're doing are very important; we are quite surprised by you."

She was pleased her work had been noticed. She assured him she and her friends would do what they could to help.

"Good," Torelli responded, and explained to her that a partisan army was being formed in the mountains, made up of the men she was helping to escape the clutches of the Nazis. "You must try to collect everything that a clandestine army might need," he told her.

And so, Anita and her group began gathering clothes and food and arms, and taking them to the growing army beyond the city. Before that conversation with Torelli, Anita acted mostly, she said, "for humanitarian principles: As a woman, you saved another woman's son." But after that day she realized that her work in the Resistance "had to be something conscious." Anita was part of something bigger now, she realized. And she was all in.

CHAPTER 20

CARLA

ROME
AUTUMN 1943

The tenor of the meetings hosted at Via Cavour began changing, and the safe house gained its own name as well: *Foro Traiano.* Those in the Resistance knew they had to do more than talk and plan. They had to act. With Carla's permission, Adele invited members of the pharmacist's newly formed guerrilla fighters, the Gruppi d'Azione Patriottica—or GAP—to meet at Foro Traiano one evening, and introduced Carla to Rosario Bentivegna, one of the group's leaders. The *gappisti* believed that the Germans were becoming too comfortable in their beloved city—using machine guns to terrorize families going about their errands, parking their vehicles in the shadow of the Pantheon.

Carla learned that the GAP was modeled after similar groups in the French Resistance, who had begun their fight against the Nazis when France was first occupied in 1940. The gappisti were in the process of setting up three-to-six-person squads; there would be direct communication only within each discrete group, but different squads might work together on larger missions. The idea was that they would be nimble, able to make decisions quickly, and relatively insulated from one another should a squad be captured. They needed men and women who could blend in on the streets, who were committed and loyal. Adele thought this was a perfect role for Carla.

It would be months until Rosario told Carla that he had been prepared to dislike her before they even met. He had been working his way through medical school when the war began, and the bombs that fell on San Lorenzo had torn through the hospital he had just left after an overnight shift. Like Carla, he had run toward the destruction, wanting to be useful—and cementing his festering anti-Fascist beliefs, stoking "an anger against those who had brought my country and my city to ruin," as he described it.

In the first few weeks of the occupation Rosario had met a number of people who were only now joining the Resistance from a place of privilege, having been relatively insulated from the tyranny of the Fascists for decades. He thought that they couldn't fully understand what the gappisti and other members of the movement were truly fighting for. What Adele had told him of Carla, with her fashionable apartment and recent interest, fit Rosario's assumptions. He had wondered if he would be able to trust someone like Carla with his life.

The night Rosario first came to Foro Traiano, he whispered the password at the door and was led to the study where the informal meeting was taking place. He was skeptical of what the night would bring, and he narrowed his eyes, assessing the people in the room.

At the sound of someone entering the room, Carla looked up and noticed the serious-looking, dark-featured stranger and smiled, her blond hair falling over one eye. She was sitting among their comrades, smoking the tobacco dregs of her cigarettes in her father's old pipe. Rosario would later admit that in that moment she seemed to him like a young woman just looking for adventure—not truly invested in the struggle as he was.

But as they played cards that night, he was drawn in by her easy laughter. And, later, when they discussed politics, Rosario could see her conviction to the same anti-Fascist principles he held. He was intrigued by this fellow revolutionary.

CHAPTER 21

BIANCA

PIEDMONT REGION
AUTUMN 1943

V al Germanasca—one of the valleys that snakes its way between ridges from the foothills near Turin, running deep into the Alps—would soon be known as Valley of the Partisans. Encampments around the valley were growing in number, with strong leadership helping to organize the young men who sought to do more than hide.

Ten miles from the closest train station, up switchbacks on the steep, pitted road that led from the valley toward the first ridge, partisans took over the former barracks of the abandoned La Gianna talc mine. Built into the side of the mountain near the ridge, the barracks could provide relatively comfortable housing for dozens, and with only one easily patrolled road in and out, this encampment and the nearby homes were completely controlled by the Resistance. It was here that Bianca's fiancé, Alberto, found refuge.

Their first arrival there in September must have given Bianca a reminder of the freedoms that she was fighting for in the cities. Women and men, young and old, had welcomed the young men into the safety they provided. There seemed to be little need for secrecy—armed partisans roamed the area openly, and the windows to the barracks were thrown open, letting in the sun and breeze. At night they even sang and danced along to the accordion.

In those first months of the occupation, the Nazis and Fascists did not focus their attention on rooting out these men hiding in the mountains, although there were sporadic patrols and arrests, and one could never be too careful. And while some groups in the Piedmont mountains were organizing themselves in battalions, like Alberto's band, others were merely camping out in small groups, whiling away their days. It was still relatively easy to buy food in the small towns or barter chopping wood or household chores for basic necessities.

But as their numbers grew, so did their boldness. From early that autumn, leaders in the valleys beyond Turin gathered weapons and searched for nearby Nazi-Fascist patrols or encampments, no matter how small, which they raided for munitions and supplies. When they managed to secure explosives, they began scouting the best places for sabotage. The primary targets were bridges and electric and communication towers and poles, which connected the few soldiers in the mountains to occupied France on one side and the Nazi leadership in Turin on the other.

The groups of young men would assess the target and ensure there was an escape plan—from both the explosion and the inevitable patrols who would come in response. Despite their lack of resources, the partisans had advantages over the Nazi-Fascists. There were many among them who knew the valleys well and could navigate the densely wooded valleys between their target and safety. And they had the support of the hardy mountain folk. Relatively isolated in small, often self-sufficient mountain towns, many had long trusted one another for survival.

Once the partisans decided upon a target, they needed a bomb with adequate power and a long enough fuse. These were often cobbled together using what elements they could find or steal, or what visitors from the city, like Bianca, might bring to them. They weren't all successful. But, when they were, it could be spectacular. As one partisan described it, "When the high-tension poles explode, it is like a fireworks spectacle. You should see the magnificent circles of light—yellow, blue, and green—a marvel!"

MEANWHILE, BACK IN Turin, the Resistance began to organize themselves under the leadership of CLN. The city was divided into five sectors, and Bianca was asked to serve with sector five—the city center—as they furtively sought to create order and plan actions. One tenet of the Resistance was focused on communication and education. Since July 1943, underground newspapers had come roaring back, with many burgeoning Resistance groups creating their own publications. In an attempt to centralize some of these efforts and communications, each sector was asked to create their own *giornalino*—a two-sided newspaper meant to help educate and share information among their neighbors. Bianca was in charge of her local publication.

These publications were especially important to the Italian Resistance. While there were other clandestine newspapers and manifestos published by the Resistance around Europe, they were uniting groups who were fighting for a return to a life they had known before the war. Italy was different. Their numerous publications were meant to articulate—to themselves as much as to their fellow Italians—the reasons for their resistance to a Fascist past that they wanted to leave behind as well as their new political understanding and goals. There would be more than six hundred different publications around occupied Italy over the course of the war.

By October, underground publishing became a life-threatening operation. Across occupied Italy, Germans issued terrifying local edicts. One read: "Anyone who is discovered compiling, printing, distributing, and spreading anti-German propaganda will be punished with immediate execution by firing squad." Still, Bianca and many others continued.

Once Bianca and her team had written a flyer or pamphlet, their next challenge was to find a safe place to print it. Bianca had access to an old mimeograph machine, which was messy and loud. But the growing Resistance had many allies who showed themselves willing to help. A sympathetic *latteria*—dairy shop—allowed them to store items, and the concierge of an apartment building meant to help house people displaced by bombings gave them keys to an empty room to set up their print shop.

The women had already spent a busy few days writing and revising their first missive, passing drafts around by the fire late into the night, perhaps reading sections out loud and then scratching out sections to be rewritten before they drifted off into a fitful sleep until they could move about the city again once the daily curfew was lifted. When they were ready to print, they moved quickly.

At the latteria, women talked in low voices, maybe sharing warnings about the occupying soldiers who had requisitioned some of the few damage-free apartments in their neighborhood, or news from loved ones who had left the city for the mountains. In the shop's back room, Bianca, strong and sturdy from her years of bicycle riding and mountain hiking, hoisted up the heavy machine and practiced carrying it nonchalantly, as if it were the day's washing. The women she worked with carried the papers and other necessities. As they hoped, the shop's customers let the young women pass by without scrutiny, worried more about being overheard themselves.

Despite Bianca's awkward load, few people paid them any mind as they moved about the city. On the tram, yawning riders on their way to work or mothers clutching young ones' hands scanned the streets for new roadblocks as they clanged by, holding their breath at every stop, willing the tram to move again before a Fascist officer got on, demanding to see everyone's papers.

At the building of their new print shop, the concierge led them toward their room as if the women were new tenants. Anyone who saw them in the halls would have thought their baggage was their belongings. Finally, behind the closed door, they put down their heavy load with a sigh of relief.

Next, they went about setting up their machine in the space. The printer was reassembled, and then they set the type. This could all be done quietly, but the women thought it was safer to do the printing late at night and into the early morning hours, hoping the thumping of the machine might be missed while people slumbered.

Finally Bianca took her first shift at turning the crank of the printer, which would spin the papers past the fragile netting that another comrade had spread with ink, imprinting the typeset letters onto the paper helped by the weight of a heavy drum. What emerged were words that could have gotten them killed:

"Like perhaps the majority of men," one publication read, "women in Italy have woken up to political life. . . . We fight so that women's work does not continue to be an object of exploitation."

THAT AUTUMN BIANCA was walking with another member of the Resistance who pointed out Ada Gobetti—a petite, dark-haired woman walking briskly across the street. Ada was the forty-one-year-old widow of the early anti-Fascist writer Piero Gobetti. He had been severely beaten by squadristi in 1925, dying in exile soon after, leaving Ada and an infant son, Paolo. Paolo was now seventeen years old and had begun going on missions with the partisans in the Alpine foothills near their country house in the small town of Meana, just beyond Turin. Ada was known as an anti-Fascist thinker in her own right and was now taking on a leadership role in the Resistance. Bianca admitted then that she had never heard of the name Gobetti. But she soon familiarized herself with Piero and Ada's work, borrowing illicit copies of their work from friends and devouring their words. Soon, Ada would seek out Bianca's help to connect to the factory workers she knew so well.

This friendship would become a turning point in Bianca's political education. The two women, despite their nearly twenty-year age difference, would forge a close friendship, staying up late by the fire, writing articles, discussing politics, or fretting over the latest news from the Resistance, because of the curfew needing to stay together until the first light of day.

CHAPTER 22

CARLA

ROME
OCTOBER 16, 1943

E arly that morning Carla left her apartment with copies of the first issue of the Catholic Communist underground newspaper *Voce Operaia*—"The Worker's Voice." Along with the two-sided sheet's call for action and manifesto of beliefs, it explains the "Revolutionary Organization" of the Resistance. "The condition in which we find ourselves living our political battle is still that of illegality," an article starts. It continues to explain that members of the Resistance "must be carefully and strictly disciplined," and details their shared goals of mobilizing the masses in "revolutionary struggle."

Carla had read these articles many times in the two weeks since the issue had been published and felt pride that she was among the dedicated group of revolutionaries helping to educate the masses. The gappisti had started to discuss plans but had thus far done little in the way of dramatic actions. Sharing this newspaper would have been enough to justify her death in the eyes of the Nazis, but she seemed to be able to walk through her city without arousing suspicion, so for now her role was focused on spreading information and connecting with like-minded Italians. Despite the newly posted edicts and intimidation of the Nazi-Fascists, it had seemed that for many who remained in Rome, life might go on, albeit tenuously, like normal.

The first stop on her route was to pass off copies of the newspaper to fellow members of the Resistance who would quietly disseminate them in their designated neighborhoods around the city. She was to hand out copies in Trastevere, a longtime Jewish neighborhood with rows of modest centuries-old homes winding along narrow cobblestone roads across the river from central Rome. Their meeting place was in the basement of the Santa Cecilia church—a space that Resistance members had discovered early in the occupation was kept unlocked. It was there that Carla's contact told her of the massive roundup of Jewish people that had occurred just hours before—and that the area was crawling with German military.

At five-thirty that morning, the SS had besieged Trastevere, where about a third of the city's Jewish population lived. Nazi soldiers had surrounded the neighborhood and then began firing their weapons indiscriminately while officers pounded on doors. Once inside, they cut phone lines before ordering everyone onto the street. Children cried and elderly people nearing collapse waited in the rain and cold for trucks to take them away. In all, the Germans arrested 1,259 people, more than 1,000 of whom would be sent to concentration camps, and almost none of whom would survive the war.

Hearing this news, Carla hurried off. Her next appointment was with Rosario near the Teatro Argentina, just blocks from one of the largest synagogues in Rome and close to Ponte Garibaldi, the main bridge that crosses the Tiber River to connect central Rome to Trastevere. She was fearful of him being found alone amid the heavy Nazi presence, and of what this roundup might mean for her Jewish friends and neighbors.

It had only been a short time since Carla had first met Rosario and learned about the new GAP organization. She wanted to be involved, even if she was still on the perimeter. In the first few weeks she helped transport packages for them, although she didn't yet know what was inside or how their contents were being used. Other times, she brought news and orders from other women doing delivery work around the city, just as she was that morning. She would soon find out that the gappisti were making plans for their first major action, using the intel that she and other members of the Resistance were helping to gather about the comings and goings of Nazi and Fascist commanders. Their goal, a GAP Central member noted, was to make the Germans "understand that they were not the masters of Rome, that they had a hostile population on their hands." The question was what to do first. Carla had already been asked to help as a "cover" for Resistance members who might arouse suspicion if hanging around in a piazza alone as they gathered intel. With Carla or another young woman, they could linger for hours as they pretended to be lovers, perhaps sitting closely on a bench, whispering nursery rhymes to each other to keep up the ruse, while they noted the routines of the occupiers or possible places to hide explosives.

CARLA LEANED AGAINST the ancient wall of the connected storefronts along the narrow street, scanning the crowds for Rosario. If he were to be targeted, there would be few places to hide. There were German trucks with soldiers in front of the temple, but people seemed to be passing freely over the bridge. Suddenly Rosario appeared and whispered, "Turn around slowly." Carla tried to move casually until she could see what he was indicating. Nazis were looting a glove shop, carrying box after box out the front door, the owner distraught and trying to pick herself up from where she had been thrown to the ground by the soldiers.

"Are you armed?" Rosario asked Carla. She wasn't. GAP leadership hadn't allowed her to have her own gun yet, despite sometimes being asked to carry one for the men, who were more likely to be searched. Being caught with one would mean arrest, or worse.

"Me neither," he said.

Together they ran toward the woman, snatching her away from the soldiers who were now telling her in terse German-inflected Italian that they intended to take what they wanted.

"There's nothing you can do," Carla whispered as she gripped the shopkeeper's arm. She was beginning to understand the true nature of Rome's occupation.

But the shopkeeper resisted Carla's and Rosario's efforts to protect her and ran back toward the truck, begging the soldiers to stop.

Carla and Rosario understood they had to leave her. In that moment they felt helpless—unable to aid the shopkeeper, their Jewish neighbors, or any other fellow Roman. Carla later reflected, "We had the feeling that we could no longer do anything useful without putting ourselves at risk." Rosario would go back to the gappisti and tell them what he and Carla saw at the shop and report the news about the tragedy that had happened at Trastevere. These events only compounded the recent murder of six young draft dodgers by Nazi soldiers.

Rosario told his comrades, *The time to act is now.*

CHAPTER 23

TERESA

ROME AND FLORENCE
OCTOBER 15, 1943

The day before the Trastevere roundup, Teresa was standing on the Termini train station platform in Rome with her brother Gianfranco, waiting for their mother. The growing Nazi presence in Florence had made their mother anxious and she had decided to join her husband in hiding. Once she arrived, Teresa and Gianfranco would take her to an apartment owned by the author Italo Calvino, a safe haven arranged with the help of Bruno Sanguinetti.

Her father, Ugo, was the head of a large workers' union and had called for his members to defend their factories and tools on September 8 so they would not end up in German hands. With Bruno, he had also written a manifesto that declared Italian workers the enemy of the Germans, signing his name. This had prompted a bounty of two million lire on his head, forcing him underground. Rome had seemed a wise place to hide. It was a bigger city where he was not well-known. And his son Gianfranco was there as well; he had left his job at the university in Milan to establish himself as head bomb maker for the Resistance.

Around them, Termini station was in a partial state of ruin and rebuilding, an apt metaphor for the state of their young country.

The original station, built in 1867, had been demolished a few years earlier, with an intention for it to be rebuilt for the World's Fair in 1942—which was then canceled because of the war. Work had finally begun for reconstruction in early 1943, but had been halted, along with many other infrastructure projects, at Mussolini's fall and the subsequent occupation.

As the siblings waited on the platform, they heard the "mournful sound of the iron footsteps of the SS," Teresa later remembered, as the soldiers marched through the vast station. The large Nazi presence felt ominous, even as Teresa and Gianfranco had little inkling of the terror those soldiers were about to unleash on the Trastevere neighborhood the following dawn.

Gianfranco hugged Teresa tight and bent his tall frame low. "You know," he whispered in her ear, "one of us isn't going to get out of this war alive."

WITHIN DAYS OF the occupation, the Germans had begun rounding up "foreigners," which included Jewish Italians who had lost their citizenship with the passage of the racial laws a few years earlier. In some areas there were announcements posted ordering Jews to surrender by the following day or face "immediate death," and local Jewish leaders were being asked by the Nazis to provide names and addresses of their synagogue members. This prompted many Jewish people in Italy to seek safety elsewhere, some moving to new towns and managing to register as Catholics, others seeking shelter in monasteries or convents or with sympathetic Catholic friends. Others, like Primo Levi's family, found a room in a small town where they hoped they might be ignored. Those who acted early were the most likely to survive. But not everyone would or could leave their neighborhoods.

Despite the press being highly controlled, as was movement and communication throughout cities, some local Jewish and Resistance leadership had sounded the alarm, often at the behest of Jewish refugees who had already escaped Nazi roundups in France, Poland, and elsewhere. The Italians had a reputation for protecting Jewish people in the areas they controlled—they had refused to round up or deport people in areas they occupied, despite the demands of their German allies, sometimes even defying Nazi orders outright, other times conveniently losing lists of names. Relatively few Italians shared the extreme anti-Semitic beliefs of the Nazis. But this protection was clearly over. The Italians were no longer in control of their own country, despite the front of Mussolini's Republic of Salò.

The roundup in Rome was a wake-up call for many Italians, Jewish and otherwise, who believed that Jewish people were safe in their country. Italy had been serving as a relative safe haven for many displaced religious refugees from all around war-torn Europe. When news of the Trastevere roundup reached Florence, the city's chief rabbi, Nathan Cassuto, went door to door encouraging Jewish families to move, hide, or change their names. He helped connect them with people who could house them or provide false papers—and would be credited with saving many who might not have understood what danger they were in.

The vast majority—by some accounts 80 percent—of those who had gone into hiding by the start of the occupation would survive the war. Many small towns and families took in Jewish children and refugees, in some cases keeping them completely concealed during the remainder of the war. More often they allowed them to hide in plain sight, referring to them as displaced family. These generous Italians could have been outed to local Fascists by neighbors—

small towns would certainly have reason to notice these new residents and suspect their cover stories. But many stayed silent, despite knowing that their presence could endanger them all. It was not unheard of for Nazis to shoot an entire family if they were known to be housing a Jewish child, for example, and entire neighborhoods were firebombed by Nazis for even unfounded suspicion of helping to hide partisans or Jewish people. Yet while these tragedies could and did happen, many Italians still risked their lives to help Jewish people hide during the occupation.

NOVEMBER 6, 1943

BY THE TIME SS officers began targeting Jewish people in Teresa's hometown of Florence in early November, many had already gone into hiding or left town. But a few still remained. There had been some stories of German atrocities against Jewish people during World War I that had turned out to be untrue, which caused skepticism of the reports of roundups and concentration camps. Many believed these rumors to be Allied propaganda.

In Florence the roundups of Jewish people began on Saturday, November 6, 1943, when German troops surrounded the ornate Synagogue of Florence, arresting the few people they found inside. (The Germans would soon requisition the building and turn it into a stable for their horses.) Those abducted would be forced onto the trains carrying others from Siena and Bologna.

News of this first roundup of Florentine Jews traveled quickly among the local Resistance, and Teresa remembered watching the train head down the track and out of the city. She had friends on that train, she knew. She thought of Lascan, with whom she had gone all through school and who had been arrested with her family. And Uzielli, who "looked like an angel" and had a beautiful singing voice to match.

There were five hundred Jewish people deported from Florence, three hundred of whom were crammed into wagons of that train bound for Auschwitz, which departed from platform 16 at the Santa Maria Novella station. One hundred and ninety-three were immediately killed in the gas chambers. Eight of them were children.

They "turned to dust," Teresa would later remember, although she could not have known then what their fate would be, "like so many other comrades for whom no tombstone will remain."

CHAPTER 24

CARLA

ROME
NOVEMBER 7–8, 1943

On a chilly autumn evening in Rome, more than a dozen women gathered at Foro Traiano for a political discussion led by Adele Bei and Egle Gualdi. Egle, a woman of about forty who wore a handkerchief on her head and walked with a slight limp, had recently arrived in town. The two women spoke to the *ragazze* gathered before them about the meaning of the Russian Revolution, particularly for women. This political educational meeting had been disguised as a social gathering for ladies, where they could play cards and drink tea and gossip. Female members from various other Resistance groups had been invited as well.

The impetus for the lesson that night was the news from the war front that the Russians had liberated Kiev from the Nazis, likely heard as breaking news on Radio London. Listening to foreign radio was now illegal and punishable by arrest.

Adele and Egle told the women about the contributions of Rosa Luxemburg, the feminist Jewish revolutionary who—along with Clara Zetkin and Anna Kuliscioff—was active in the Russian Revolution in which workers overthrew their oppressive imperialist government. The revolution, they were taught, was first instigated by a strike of female workers on International Women's Day on March 8, 1917, and would result in greater workers' rights and suffrage for women in Russia. For those women, their victory would not be lasting. All three were persecuted for being Russian revolutionaries, Adele and Egle told the gathered women. Few, if any, of those gathered that night had heard their names before, having all been taught only Fascist-approved curricula in school.

After the political education gathering ended, Carla and a few others remained to discuss that night's action. Small groups were assigned to different zones around the city with a plan to paint graffiti: calls for revolution and messages to the occupiers indicating that the Resistance was present. Carla, Rosario, and another Resistance member named Rodolfo were assigned to the center, starting with iconic monuments near Foro Traiano. When she had first heard of the plan, Carla had some hesitation for marring what beauty remained in the city she loved, but understood that it was even more important to do what they could to prevent the war from enduring.

Around eleven P.M.—past curfew—Carla and the others hid paint buckets inside shopping bags and set out to their assigned neighborhoods around the city. The trio's first target was the Vittoriano—the huge white marble structure in the center of Rome, with ornate columns and statues of winged chariots representing victory in battle. Carla had hated this ostentatious monument for blocking her view of the beautiful roofs beyond; it seemed to emerge incongruously from the midst of an ancient residential neighborhood. She was ready to take revenge against what she saw an as "absurd presence" that represented the power of Italy's monarchy.

The sky was cloudless, and the moonlight lent a magical glow to the streets as the three made their way through the city center, paint and brush in hand. Hidden by the ruins of the Roman villa that had stood on the left side of the Vittoriano, Carla held the bucket while Rosario and Rodolfo took turns spelling out DEATH TO FASCISM and NOVEMBER 7 in red paint on the white wall. The date was a reference to the Allied victory in Kiev just a day before the anniversary of the Russian Revolution.

The next target was near the Palazzo Montecitorio, the large palace that once housed Italy's Chamber of Deputies, which had recently been replaced by the Chamber of Fasces and Corporations, a figurehead group with nominal power. Hiding in the shadows of the building's imposing, medieval-like towers, the trio began to write when they heard the footsteps of a German reconnaissance patrol. They slunk back into the darkness and waited until the streets were once again silent before they crossed the Via del Corso and headed through the alleys toward Piazza di Spagna.

The three regarded the Spanish Steps from the shadows across the narrow piazza. Assessing the 135 stairs that gracefully make their way up two levels to the church of the Trinità dei Monti, they considered where they might make their mark. The trio would have to be quick and decisive—the stairs were wide and exposed, and if they were spotted, there would be nowhere to hide. After pausing to listen for patrols, they scaled the first level, where they decided to stop and paint a large hammer and sickle on the wall that divides the grand staircase into two more narrow ones that rise on either side toward the church. In the morning, when the city was again full of people, this would be unmissable from the piazza below.

They painted quickly and then ran up the left-side stairs, at the top ducking behind the trees that line the walkway leading from the church toward Villa Medici. For a moment the three could pause, safely obscured from possible patrols. Below them lay the silent rooftops of Rome, illuminated by the moon. This was the city

Carla loved and wanted to protect, even as she was defacing it. Carla was well aware of the risk they were taking. Their clothes were covered in paint splatters, and Rodolfo and Rosario were armed. If stopped, they would not make it through the night alive. But she also felt privileged in the moment, crossing the city she was fighting for on silent cat feet, with two people as dedicated to the quest for freedom as she. In the silence and vastness, Carla felt a great joy as she tasted the freedom for which she and the others were risking everything.

Wordlessly, Rosario pulled Carla away from her thoughts and toward Villa Medici, which sat on the edge of a tree-filled park they could traverse in relative safety. They took a moment to listen for patrols again at the top of the stairs that led them down to Piazza del Popolo—the "People's Square," long considered significant as a symbol of welcome for travelers, and, until the 1800s, a site of executions. They moved as a group toward the hundred-foot-tall ancient granite Flaminio Obelisk, large and exposed in the center of the square. Carla slipped off her shoes and Rodolfo helped her climb onto Rosario's shoulders, from which she painted another large hammer and sickle high upon the spire, with the goal to make it more difficult to erase in the morning—and visible from farther away. In their haste, more red paint splashed on Rodolfo's hat.

Once finished, Carla slipped her shoes back on and impulsively ran toward the line of trucks parked along the edge of the piazza, which was also a section of the wall that surrounded the city. She thought back to their discussion about the Russian Revolution, and the message they wanted to send to the Germans. She drew a hammer and sickle and wrote W ROSA LUXEMBURG and W KARL LIEBKNECHT—the W meaning "long live," followed by the names of murdered revolutionary leaders, unknown to most of their fellow

Italians but likely imbued with meaning for the Germans. Their paint cans empty, the three left the buckets and brushes on the ground and made their way back toward Foro Traiano before first light.

Rodolfo was the first to ascend the stairs at their safe house, with Carla and Rosario entering behind him. In the dim light of the stairwell, Rosario pulled Carla toward him and kissed her. Her first reaction was surprise. But then she kissed him back.

DAWN WAS CREEPING in through the windows of Foro Traiano, which had a clear view of the hated Vittoriano. Along with Carla's mother, who was awake and straining to hear Radio London for any news of the war, the trio, wide-awake and joyous at their safe return, decided to stay up and watch the discovery of their work from their top-floor vantage point.

As the city stirred, Carla made them all a breakfast of orzo with toasted stale bread, a feast from their meager rations, and a favorite comfort food since her childhood. And they watched as passersby began to notice the graffiti—first pausing to gape, and then, in fear, hurrying on. Eventually the workers came to try to clean it off, their anger obvious, even from a distance.

RODOLFO LEFT FOR Trastevere not long after the curfew was lifted for the day, wanting to check in with other groups. Rosario would soon leave, too. Carla also had an appointment that morning, to meet up with another Resistance member to share news of the evening's activities and help transport and disseminate propaganda. She would hear descriptions of other successful actions—graffiti was prominent around the city, and no one had been caught. In one of the most audacious acts, a group of Socialist comrades were even able to fly a red flag from the Campidoglio Tower.

After her meeting, she walked toward the Spanish Steps, where she saw there had been an attempt to cover their hammer and sickle in white paint, only making it stand out more as the red bled through. As she milled among the gawkers in the busy piazza, Carla wondered how many Romans knew the significance of this symbol, herself having only recently learned the history of the Russian Revolution that had been erased from Italian history books by Mussolini's regime. She knew, however, that it didn't matter. These messages were to the Nazis and Fascists: a signal that Rome was not a place of refuge for them but rather the front line of war.

Carla walked the few blocks north toward Piazza del Popolo, a young woman on the city streets lined with apartments and shops, anonymous among the many Romans running errands or going to work. There was no need to hide in the shadows during the day. She walked toward the obelisk, where a group of people were standing around, gazing up at the marks she had made just a few hours earlier. Carla couldn't help herself and asked someone what had happened. The man, dressed as a doorman, replied, "But can't you see it yourself? Someone's played a joke and now they're pissed off!" The two shared a knowing smile.

CHAPTER 25

RULES OF PARTISAN WARFARE

As more men escaped drafts and roundups in Italian cities and towns, and others joined the Resistance for ideological reasons, the hidden army of partisans in the hills and mountains around central and northern Italy grew into the tens of thousands during that first autumn of the occupation. With the help of former military members, some recently defected from the Italian army, they organized themselves in battalions of a few hundred soldiers consisting of multiple detachments of not more than a few dozen. The relatively small size of these units made the most sense considering the current landscape of war. Not only did they need to be mobile and able to hide but the logistics of feeding and housing a large army would be too difficult if they were all stationed together. And so this unique partisan army was born.

Units were particularly robust in the Apennines and the Alps, where they found shelter in abandoned buildings, or built elaborate camps hidden in caves or under a canopy of trees. Good relations with the local populations were essential, not only to keep their presence a secret but also to help with procuring the basics needed for survival. What they couldn't buy, barter, or ask from the local peasant population would have to be supplied by their female family members and supporters. These *staffette* would visit frequently with food, medicine, clothes, and munitions, as well as to share intel, orders, and other communications from the CLN leadership. Over that first autumn, the organization and rules of the Resistance army were established and codified.

Soon, the printed "Rules of Partisan Warfare" were handed down from the new collective of anti-Fascist leaders. They began to shape the actions of these roughshod groups of, mostly, men hiding in small towns or mountain camps or urban basements.

"The essential principles of partisan warfare: MOBILITY, SURPRISE, AUDACITY!" Edicts such as this had been informed by the organization and work of other partisans thus far in the war. In places like France and Yugoslavia they had been refining a style of warfare that was proving successful for ragtag armies facing much larger and better resourced militias. These rules went on to demand discipline, with a focus on acts like sabotage and surprise armed ambushes, executed by small groups. "These are all actions you can do with scarce means at your disposal," the directive encouraged.

CHAPTER 26

TERESA

FLORENCE
AUTUMN 1943

M any messages were written on small pieces of paper that could be rolled up and hidden in bicycle frames or sewn into clothing. These were the strategies of the staffette. But Teresa did not want to take any chances. She took the note that Bruno had given her, the slip of paper inconspicuously passed under the table as they were leaving the café, and waited until she was alone to read it. She read it through once, then twice, and then closed her eyes to commit the words to memory. Perhaps she tore the paper into tiny pieces and threw them into a puddle, making the paper disintegrate as she rubbed it with the toe of her shoe. Then she got on her bicycle and started riding.

In her role as a staffetta, Teresa preferred to memorize the information she had to deliver, singing it to herself like a song as she rode the streets she knew so well, past the Romanesque palazzos—their shutters almost always closed tightly—to the basements or safe houses where partisans hid. Often her orders took her beyond the city and into the countryside, to partisan camps in abandoned buildings or barns or thickets of trees.

Already connected to and trusted by the anti-Fascist leadership because of her familial ties, many of whom were friends of her family or knew her from her years of work at school, Teresa was entrusted with some of the most sensitive messages. And as one of the few people who knew Bruno's true role in the Resistance, she was the main connection between him and the Youth Front and partisan brigades.

Staffette were essential to the Resistance. Because women were assumed to have no political interest, that first autumn of the occupation they were rarely searched. And even if they were, their wisely hidden or memorized messages would likely go undetected. As German calls for volunteer soldiers and workers went unheeded, it became more dangerous for men to move around the city. It was up to the staffette to transport everything from documents and maps to munitions to underground newspapers—and more.

The Germans, working with the local Fascist police, had placed blockades to ensure that anyone who traveled across or out of Florence—or around occupied Italy—would be stopped and required to show their identification papers to pass. These papers listed the birth date, address, physical characteristics, occupation, and other information and would trigger suspicion if someone was far from home or of draft age. To travel, a person was safest with a letter from the local questura, typed on letterhead with a stamp, indicating permission and a reason, although this wasn't required by law. And while there were reports of even pregnant women or small children being searched to create terror or confiscate black market goods, there was little real suspicion of widespread political action among women.

Teresa knew, from her own experience and the stories of her female comrades, that women were not taken seriously as possible members of the Resistance. Women were simply expected to travel from the city to the countryside and back again, to check on family members or deliver food and items, among other activities. Some who had to cross through roadblocks regularly learned that a smile and a greeting helped them get through quickly. There was the tale of the staffetta who, when asked by the SS officer at a roadblock what was in her bags, responded truthfully, "Bombs." They shared a laugh, and she was on her way, her bags unsearched.

Teresa slowed her bicycle when she saw the roadblock ahead. The message was safe within the confines of her memory, and she held nothing else on her that might be suspicious. She was just a young woman on her way to visit family on the outskirts of the city. While her heart beat faster, she didn't smile and she wasn't afraid.

The teenager Teresa had been when she was first stopped and searched at the French border years before had long been replaced by a knowing young woman with a steely gaze who approached the checkpoints with cool indifference. The song of her message echoed in her head while the officer checked her papers and let her pass.

CHAPTER 27

ANITA

EMILIA-ROMAGNA
AUTUMN 1943

Anita helped her father move the heavy dresser in her family's kitchen a few feet to the left, then watched as he removed the loose tiles that were now exposed and stacked them quietly, working quickly, perhaps glancing toward the door at the sound of any distant noise. Beneath the tiles was the family's stash of guns and ammunition, hidden in an empty space between the floor and the vaulted ceiling below.

Anita's younger brother had recently joined the Resistance, headed to the mountains to join a partisan detachment—and now her father was using their home as a way station for munitions. By late autumn, the young men who had camped or hid in groups beyond the cities were organizing. They had been collecting weapons and gathering what they could to supply an army and survive the impending winter. Her father wanted to support them in what ways he could.

As a known winemaker, her father would hide bullets or other contraband in compartments inside wine crates or bottles, then deliver his goods around the city, many making their way to the partisans—his son or the sons of his neighbors—beyond. But even as Anita watched him hide and transport these items, she didn't share that she was a member of the Resistance as well.

Perhaps she didn't tell her parents because she was afraid they would forbid her to help—her mother was already fearful of the daily reports of violence outside the door, and her brothers and other family members were already risking their lives to help the cause. Maybe she relished having something that was hers alone. This was an act of finding her agency, of forging her own path without asking any of the authority figures in her life for permission. And perhaps, also, she was all too wary of the limited view most people had about the difference a woman could make in this war. No matter the reason, she was among the tens of thousands of young women who were supporting the more than one hundred thousand men who would eventually take up arms against the Nazis and Italian Fascists.

SHE HAD STARTED small—with salt. That autumn Anita had been traveling to visit her boyfriend's mother in Ceresola, a small town about fifteen miles outside Reggio Emilia, when she'd met some partisans who asked if she might bring them something from the city. Perhaps a few young men couldn't resist calling out to a solo young woman their age who liked to wear outfits that accentuated her curves. Good at small talk from her job at the bar and always curious, Anita struck up a conversation about what life was like for them in the hills. It wasn't a stretch for them to ask her to bring them something the next time she might be back this way.

And Anita often made her way to Ceresola. She adored her boyfriend's mother and had visited often while her boyfriend was away at war. Anita had met her boyfriend years earlier, before he had been deployed. For years they had known each other primarily through letters, and now that he had returned, Anita thought they felt like strangers. The couple had already had disagreements about their vision of the future. Anita had told him, "I don't feel like bringing a family into this reality," during one of their serious discussions not long before July 25 changed their daily lives. And since the occupation, she believed this even more fervently. But still, Anita had little concept of her choices then, as women were expected to marry by their early twenties, and she was already twenty-two years old.

Anita's boyfriend's mother told her during one of their many visits, "Take a moment to think about it . . . because if he makes you lead the life his father made me lead, it's not a life that is worth living." Anita was doubting their suitability, but she believed she had no choice but to marry him. Still, she knew better than to tell him of her work in the Resistance. And no matter how she felt about her boyfriend, she knew and cared for his mother, and would continue her visits, now with even more reason to do so.

Anita came to know the roadblocks on the way to Ceresola well. She would smile and chat with the soldiers as they checked her papers, and it felt so easy, her work so satisfying, when she delivered her packet of salt to the thankful men. So next she brought publications, hiding them among the gifts she was bringing to her boyfriend's mother, joking with the officers she started to recognize, perhaps flirting a little as well. She began choosing her outfits with her job in mind, wearing low-cut dresses to distract the SS from searching her further when contraband was hidden elsewhere. Her connections in Reggio Emilia and the mountains grew, and she was asked to transport more challenging items as she proved herself—and the need increased. To move guns safely, Anita strapped them to her body beneath her dress, or sometimes hid them in her ample cleavage. And then she would hop on her bicycle and ride to wherever her contact had instructed her.

Her new orders took her farther, beyond the suburbs of Reggio Emilia. Bands of men were now gathering in greater numbers deeper in the valleys of the low Apennine Mountains, where she might have to take her bicycle onto the train, riding up steep narrow roads once she disembarked. Once in the mountains she passed off her goods, and sometimes received something else—messages or a gun needed by the Reggio Emilia gappisti—to deliver back to the city in return. Anita, often traveling with her cousin Sandra or friend Maria, was soon known as a reliable staffetta, regularly sent on missions both in and beyond the city.

This work was dangerous, Anita knew. As autumn continued, she heard almost daily reports of local GAP or partisan actions, of sabotage or raids, and the resulting retribution of partisans arrested, tortured, or killed by the Nazis and Fascists. Some known Fascist supporters from before the occupation had seemed to switch sides, perhaps handing off donations to the staffette or even joining the army in the mountains. Others who had not been known as Mussolini loyalists entrenched themselves with the occupiers. One teacher, Professor Lazzorini, was believed to be someone a nearby partisan detachment could trust. The professor had been friendly with some of the young men as they hid in a camp near her home.

One day Anita ran into a member of the detachment she had helped and saw that he had a haunted look about him. She implored him to tell her what was wrong. He told her the story of how the teacher had informed on the young men, telling the Nazi-Fascists where they were hiding. As the soldiers advanced upon them, opening fire, the older partisans hid this boy, only seventeen, under a pile of sticks. The men fought until they ran out of ammunition, and then the anti-partisan team assassinated them one by one.

"Only I had seen them," he told Anita. "Some of them were shot in the mouth and some were shot in the back of the head." He escaped hours later, when he was sure the soldiers had left, and was still in shock from what he had witnessed. Hearing about this betrayal, Anita realized she would have to be more careful whom she trusted.

ANITA WAS RIDING her bicycle down the pitted streets that led from Reggio Emilia to the countryside beyond. Perhaps the leaves were beginning to change, and there was a chill in the air. On each of her handlebars she had a bag swinging like a pendulum, its bottom heavy and the strap too long. Today's transport was a load of bombs hidden inside small table lamps. Her heart raced whenever she couldn't avoid one of the many bumps in the pocked roadways, fearing the swinging bags would hit her bike frame and explode. But she rode on.

ANOTHER EVENING, ANITA was racing home to beat curfew, then typically set around ten P.M., although this could change by location and at the whim of the local Nazi-Fascist leadership. She and another staffetta were returning from the mountains with three guns between them. Anita had one strapped around her waist and another stuffed between her breasts.

They approached a roadblock, hoping their smiles might let them pass without question. But it was late: *What are you doing out at this time, two young women alone?*

Anita had her cover story down, but her usual confidence turned to dread as she felt her bra unhook and one of the guns start to slip beneath her dress. It was the first time she felt truly scared in this initial season of the occupation.

Thinking fast, Anita began to feign sickness. "I need to rest!" she cried, leaning on the other staffetta, hoping if anything dropped, she might notice it before the soldiers.

Her acting was good—the soldiers offered to take her to their medic with genuine concern.

"No, no," Anita insisted. Her nonna was near, she said, she would go to her and be treated. She and her companion limped out of sight, escaping with their lives.

AS AUTUMN TURNED toward winter in the foothills of the Apennines, Anita continued to keep her missions for the Resistance a secret from her parents and fiancé, even as they took more and more of her free time. Those working for the Resistance, under the scrutiny of the Nazi occupiers, learned to be careful with their words, and often knew only a handful of trusted contacts from whom they took orders or to whom they handed off goods.

But with each successful transport, each message that made its destination, the web of contacts widened, and the Resistance grew. Anita and her fellow staffette brought guns and bombs and munitions from the cities into the hills and back again, providing or hiding weapons used in specific actions against Nazi and Fascist soldiers. They shared maps of enemy encampments and orders for actions. They brought food and blankets and the heavier winter clothing the soldiers would soon be needing.

Now Anita had another task—to choose her nome di battaglia. Anita would become Laila, the name of an Aztec princess who took her husband's place in battle after he was killed.

CHAPTER 28

BIANCA

PIEDMONT

NOVEMBER AND DECEMBER 1943

In November, the Committee of National Liberation of Northern Italy (CLNAI)—the regional arm of the Resistance CLN government—issued a CALL TO ITALIANS!

It read:

> Italians! Hitlerian Germany has menaced our country, revealing itself under its true guise as a greedy pillager.... Men and women, old and young, everyone must consider themselves to be mobilized for the great common cause.... For our civilization, for the future of our children, let us resist the bullying of a tyranny that has already been condemned by history.

A group of like-minded women responded to this call to action by meeting in Milan later that month. There they formed what would become the *Gruppi di Difesa della Donna e per l'Assistenza ai Combattenti della Libertà*—"Groups for the Defense of Women and Assistance to the Freedom Fighters," abbreviated GDD. They acknowledged the CLN coalition as their government, committing themselves to the Resistance. Their written response noted, "Italian women who have always opposed Fascism . . . cannot remain inactive at this grave moment. . . . We cannot give in. We must fight for liberation."

And then these women returned to their home cities and got to work. Ada Gobetti was an early founding member of the GDD in Turin, and her new friend Bianca began working with her immediately. Ada was well connected to the anti-Fascist leadership around the city and was growing her web of young staffette to help write and deliver flyers and pamphlets communicating news, political lessons, and messages of resistance. Bianca, she knew, could share these flyers at some of Turin's biggest factories.

How revolutionary, this organization of women! To have gone from almost no political knowledge or engagement over the previous twenty years to regular political education classes and mobilization against the regime that had taught them they were worth little beyond their roles as mother and wife. They finally had a way to take action against this devaluing, as many supported their families and the war through their work on farms and in small businesses and factories, where they were paid significantly less than their male counterparts, if anything at all. Ada and Bianca got to work creating political education pamphlets, using Bianca's growing network of allies to help publish and deliver them, at great risk, to the workers and housewives around Turin.

These early pamphlets urged women who rarely interacted with one another to work together on causes common to all. They encouraged women to talk about politics and consider ways they could support the Resistance. An early PROGRAM OF ACTION from November 1943 read:

Women of all social classes: farmers, workers, employees, intellectuals, and peasants gather together by the need to read and by the love of their country. Born of every religious faith, of every political tendency, women without parties unite for the common need that there be bread, peace, and freedom.

Others were instructions on creating small chapters of the GDD. Women began meeting in cemeteries and attics, where they discussed the pamphlets they received about what the group stood for and how they could make a difference in ways big and small: "Collect money, food, clothing for the freedom fighters with information. . . . Organize resistance to the Germans, . . . sabotage production, . . . prepare women to fight."

Bianca quietly shared these publications with the women she met at the factories where she worked, or through her connections in the Communist Party. She gathered women together in small groups at her apartment, perhaps, or at another safe space closer to the factories. The women would take up every chair in the sparse room, and sit attentively as Bianca, decades younger than some of them, explained that they had power if they worked together. She passed around reading—restricted books by Marx and Engels, or others found hidden at one of the sellers with stacks of books that spilled out under the porticoes of Turin—and gave lessons on workers' unions and the concept of Socialism.

Some of her first meetings were of just a few women, no more than five. Bianca described them as "mostly simple women, not very cultured, as indeed I was a bit, too." Often, she was sharing ideas from texts she had just read herself.

"I don't know how much we got out of it," Bianca later said, "but there was still the effort to understand together."

Bianca continued recruiting while visiting factories for her job. Perhaps over their meager shared meals when Bianca ate with the women in the Fiat cantina or as she helped them fill out their paperwork for survivor benefits, Bianca planted the idea that even small actions might make a difference. Later, in more private spaces, she might meet with larger groups and share with them the political lessons she had only begun to learn herself over the past year: These women had the power to come together to create change—for themselves and for all women. She understood that it was also about feeling a sense of community and belonging; meeting together to discuss what was important to them was novel and empowering after a lifetime under Fascism's thumb.

These groups spread from Turin and Milan southward to Florence and Reggio Emilia and Bologna and Rome, and by early 1944 to all corners of occupied Italy, into the small towns and countryside as well. For the first time in Italy, working-class and middle-class women came together to discuss their shared struggles—while also learning about the issues unique to each woman as they strived to provide for their families and themselves during the perils and deprivations of war, increasingly without a man's help.

The GDD quickly coalesced, outlining their demands: pay equal to men's, the right to vote, maternity leave, sufficient rations, and safe housing for those displaced by the bombings, among other essential issues. They also called for a representative in every Committee of Agitation, a male-dominated CLN initiative to encourage action against the Germans and slow the war effort across industries. Bianca became the representative in Piedmont, helping to secure demands including that women responsible for children or elders should receive head of household status, which was considered great progress in the effort toward worker equality.

THE EMERGENCE OF the GDD came around the same time as the first military draft for the new Salò Republic army. As women were being called to arms metaphorically, they now had reason to resist their husbands, brothers, and sons being called to fight for the other side. The first military draft had happened in the first week of November, ordering young men born between 1923 and 1925 to report for duty. Few did so—and many fled to the hills, mountains, and plains, joining friends who had gone before them, or seeking out the small bands they had heard were hiding there. Although in the weeks after, some would return and enlist in fear of Fascist punishments, such as arresting draft dodgers' family members. The Republican National Guard—the new Italian Fascist army—would soon have adequate numbers, even if many of their soldiers were less than enthusiastic to be serving.

Ada's son, Paolo, would turn eighteen the following month, born days before the end of 1925. To Ada, and many others active in the Resistance, there was no question that Paolo would evade the draft. Yet, employed by the state as a teacher, she and her colleagues were told to report to the headmaster if they had a son of draft age who had not presented himself. Ada would have to do as she was told.

"Where is he now?" the headmaster asked.

"I don't know," she answered truthfully. He had gone on a mission into the countryside that morning. He could be anywhere, although the fact that she expected him home in the next day or so, she didn't say. Ada stared at the headmaster until he lowered his eyes.

"Indeed," the headmaster finally responded. "It will be necessary to say something to the superintendent. We could say, for example, that your son was in southern Italy when it was invaded and that you have not heard anything more about him."

"Certainly," Ada responded. "Say it just like that. Thanks."

And so, the numbers in the mountains grew.

THE ANTI-FASCISTS WERE also actively recruiting. In some cases, like in the Alpine region around Turin, those with the means offered draft dodgers money and supplies to join them. The money came from various donations, such as from the left-leaning factory owner Camillo Olivetti, who donated more than ten thousand lire to the cause. Local bands supported by this money could offer new recruits warm military jackets, food, and munitions.

Then on November 30, under Nazi pressure, Mussolini's Social Republic of Salò issued Police Directive Number 5, by some accounts allowing word to spread quietly in advance to facilitate escape. This directive called for the arrest and internment of all Jewish people in occupied Italy. While there had been numerous roundups, this was the first explicit law criminalizing the freedom of Jewish people. The Jewish people in hiding around the country could no longer believe that Mussolini's previous lukewarm embrace of extreme Nazi anti-Semitism might save them. For the many Jewish people who had escaped the cities for the mountains, like Primo Levi's family, hoping their out-of-the-way rentals might be a safe haven, this law meant that they had to go deeper into hiding. Primo's mother and sister found a new refuge closer to the city, where they would be able to live quietly, without using their Jewish name. Primo elected to stay in the mountains.

For young Jewish men, joining the military was not an option— it was only hide or fight. Primo, like many others, chose to fight. "Really, we knew nothing," Primo would say much later. "We had to invent the Resistance."

Primo connected with a few other men who had spied one another around town, and, like so many other small groups doing the same around Piedmont and occupied Italy, began to make a kind of plan. First finding a suitable home base—in boardinghouses or barns or abandoned barracks, or even setting up camp in the elements. And then they went out to find weapons—perhaps asking sympathetic local farmers to donate to the cause or searching in barns and haylofts and helping themselves. They recruited others, trying out a tentative trust. After every draft notice or roundup, their numbers grew.

However, as the weather in the Alps turned colder, this growing army would have starved or frozen, or sat idle with bullet-less guns—or no guns at all—were it not for the GDD. While both the local population and an increasing number of staffette were supporting the partisans, their sheer numbers meant that a wider web of support was needed. While these groups of women quickly undertook political education and organization, one of their first acts had been to gather to support the partisan army. They now supplemented and organized much of what loved ones had gathered for their men in hiding, and the staffette had begun to deliver with greater efficiency. More and more groups of women began forming their own small chapters around occupied Italy. With the help of the GDD, they began coordinating donations for what was needed by these growing partisan bands, while also recruiting and educating others about the cause. This organized group of women was the reason these bands could turn themselves into the army of the Resistance.

ON DECEMBER 13, one of Bianca's friends from the university, Luciana Nissim, was awoken at dawn by the sounds of dogs barking. She, along with mutual friends Vanda Maestro, Primo Levi, and a handful of others, were hiding at the Hotel Ristoro—a rustic inn they thought might be safe from roundups, as it could be accessed only via a long hike on a snowy forest path. Here they hoped they could continue their work with the Resistance, having connected with a small group of partisans nearby.

Hotel Ristoro was now surrounded by Fascist militia, who swiftly fanned out through the building, arresting everyone. Luciana just had time to hide anti-Fascist leaflets in the toilet before getting dressed in her ski clothes as she awaited certain capture. Primo was able to hide his mother of pearl–inlaid gun—"a weapon that in any case I was not sure I knew how to use . . . the kind used in movies by ladies desperately intent on committing suicide," as he described it, before being forced outside. For both, these moments allowed them to be captured as Jewish people, not partisans. The latter distinction could have carried an immediate death sentence.

Once rounded up, the prisoners were marched along the snowy trail through the forest that led to the town of Brusson—the closest with a road. As they trudged in the cold, Primo assessed what he had in the pockets of his hastily donned coat and realized what danger they could present. He pretended to cough and slipped a false identity card into his mouth, which he slowly chewed and swallowed as they walked. Then he watched for a snowbank close to the path to pretend to stumble, enabling him to hide a notebook full of addresses of Jewish and anti-Fascist friends.

Once they arrived in Brusson, waiting to be loaded onto a bus that would take them down the mountain, a small group of locals gathered to watch. "I saw friendly faces as well as some who looked indifferent," Primo later wrote. "One bunch of them was congratulating the militia men. 'These people should be eliminated,' I heard them say."

From there, the Jewish prisoners were sent to Fossoli, Italy's only internment camp for Jews.

THAT DECEMBER, BIANCA was approached by a member of the Resistance.

"How much do you earn a month?" the representative asked her. It wasn't much, maybe seven hundred lire.

"Do you want to work only for the party?" he asked, offering a similar salary. Bianca took a moment to consider this offer. She had no one to support her and also contributed to her family's meager finances. While she was spending more and more time doing work for the Resistance, her government job provided the permit card that enabled her to travel around the region without question.

After some thought Bianca accepted the offer. Her work in the Resistance was the most important thing, she understood. But before she quit, Bianca snuck into the administrative office and stole as many circulation permit cards—called *personalausweis*—as she could carry, all pre-signed by a Volkbrinkel—the German officer who issued them to workers who had a sanctioned reason to move around the city, like Bianca. These would be disseminated to the Resistance and provide safe passage for many in the coming months.

CHAPTER 29

THE FIRST WINTER
AT WAR

The cold rains of that first winter of occupation made transporting troops and munitions difficult, and washed away temporary bridges and roads, stalling fighting between the Allied and Axis forces. In the last weeks of 1943, the Germans held their positions at the Winter Line—one of a series of German-controlled military reinforcements spanning Italy in various strategic locations south of Rome, compounding difficult terrain with treacherous weather. The Allied forces had faced stiff opposition in the push northward from Salerno, gaining only a few dozen miles by mid-autumn when the rain started in earnest. Plagued as the Allies were, not only by the weather but also by waffling directives and leadership, it was clear that the early promise of "two weeks"—and the private hope of a mid-October arrival in the Eternal City—would be unrealized. The dreams of a quick liberation were now forgotten, as partisans across the country accepted that little would change until the spring at the earliest.

Despite the lack of progress, Allied forces kept pressure on the German fortifications, knowing that keeping them engaged in Italy would draw resources away from campaigns elsewhere. But still, the Allied and Axis forces traded military defeats at battlefields around the world. November saw heavy bombings of Berlin and other Allied victories in battle, even as the Germans held them at bay in central Italy.

Amid this pessimism and mud there was debate about whether to shift focus from Italy toward other theaters of war. It was Churchill who argued for the continued push toward Rome. In part because of a broader fear that Italy, after decades of working-class oppression and with the left-leaning anti-Fascists already forming the basis of a new government, would turn toward Communism, which these economic powers worried would hurt Italy as a trading partner and foment anti-capitalist feeling. This fear would also temper the relationship between the Allies and the Resistance forces and would even be a factor in the Catholic Church insisting on staying neutral on the topic of the Nazi occupation of Italy.

Then the leaders of the United States, Great Britain, and the Soviet Union began planning one of the grandest operations of the war. Operation Overlord, as it was code-named, was the invasion of Normandy, scheduled for June 6, 1944—more than six months from then. France, the United States argued, should be the focus of the European offensive, and the Soviets agreed. With fighting in Italy stagnant, the Americans were happy to turn their attention—and resources—elsewhere. But it was Prime Minister Churchill who convinced the Allies to also stay the course in Italy. He saw Italy as a linchpin in the defense of the Balkans, which he hoped would become allies in the defense against the expansion of Soviet Communism post war. He advocated for a beach landing closer to Rome, to connect with the Allied forces that—they hoped—would break through the Nazi line and meet up with them to help take Rome from the east and push the Germans farther north. And he dangled Rome as a prize—who wouldn't want to be the commanding officer who liberated the Eternal City? The compromise the Allies reached was that they would continue their quest for Rome, but with fewer resources. Americans acquiesced in contributing arms and men for an invasion at Anzio in January, as long as enough of the big ships needed for Operation Overlord were available soon after.

Even if the partisans had known this top secret landing was imminent, this information would be of little help to those far away from the front lines of the Allied–Axis war. As the bands in the mountains organized under the leadership of the CLN, they also began more coordinated attacks on Nazi-Fascist camps and sabotage of railway lines and communication systems. And the Nazi-Fascists retaliated. Soldiers were ordered to root out opposition—and they became increasingly tyrannical in their methods. Partisan actions, like ambushing Nazi-Fascist soldiers, might result in the arrest or execution of innocent locals. Nazis torched entire neighborhoods—sometimes in retaliation for one family harboring a partisan, foreign soldier, or Jewish person; sometimes for no reason at all. The goal was to pit neighbors against one another, to induce a state of constant fear and a willingness to give up anti-Fascist friends to save oneself.

CHAPTER 30

CARLA

ROME
DECEMBER 1943

Carla and Rosario strolled arm in arm toward the Teatro Reale dell'Opera in Rome. The streets were silent and dark, a stark contrast to what the pair knew was happening inside the theater on that cold December evening. They had intel that a number of Nazi commanders and soldiers were attending the opera, dressed in their formal wear among the four tiers of box seats, designed more than sixty years prior to maximize acoustics beneath its ornate dome. Under Mussolini's watch, the theater had been updated to include, among other changes, a thirty-foot-wide chandelier comprised of twenty-seven thousand crystal drops.

Earlier in the day, one of the gappisti's explosives experts had dropped off a package at Foro Traiano, instructing Carla to use the utmost care in storing and transporting it. She knew little about how the bomb worked, but she wrapped it carefully for her appointment to meet Rosario that evening just a few blocks from her apartment. Carla wanted to prove herself. She had been helping to organize a local chapter of the GDD and establish collaborative relationships and exchanges of information among other Resistance groups at the request of Luciano Lusana, a GAP leader. But Carla had recently asked if she could be more involved and been rebuffed. She hoped that her work tonight would prove that she was ready to join the gappisti while still taking part in the other initiatives.

Rosario had asked Carla to join him as his cover, the pair meeting up at a dinner celebrating yet another successful GAP mission. The gappisti, which included small detachments like Rosario's based in neighborhoods around Rome, had been particularly active in the prior month, with more than thirty successful actions, including bombings and sabotage. As a result, the Nazi occupiers walked a bit more carefully in the streets, no longer assuming the "open city" could be traversed with impunity. But along with these successes came increased security and surveillance, Rosario knew. They couldn't let down their guard, so he hoped that Carla's presence would disguise them as a couple, strolling the streets in the waning moments before curfew.

Now, in the early darkness of December, Carla and Rosario wandered among the vehicles parked outside the theater; their drivers and the Nazi commanders they transported still watching the spectacle within. To keep up their ruse, they whispered to each other in low voices, like two people in love. They didn't know each other well, and that kiss from weeks prior had not been repeated. But they had discovered that, besides a shared passion for politics, they also both loved poetry. Rosario whispered the words he had memorized from a recent book by Eugenio Montale.

He murmured, "Esterina, turning twenty threatens you / gray-rosy cloud / which little by little closes you in itself. / You understand this and do not fear. / Submerged we will see you / in the smoke that the wind / torn or thickened, violent."

Carla's heartbeat quickened. She noticed the drivers exiting the theater, signaling the end of the show was near, and it was time for them to act. Staying in the shadows, the pair approached the rounded gas tank of a troop transport truck parked on the street above the sunken piazza of the theater, and placed one of their packages on it. Rosario showed Carla how to free half of the fuse from the paper and then attach the other half, the first step in arming the bomb. Her hands shook, and she was afraid she wouldn't have the nerve to complete the connection. Rosario would do the same on the gas tank of another truck they had chosen, and then return to light the fuses.

Staying in the shadows of the perimeter of the small plaza, they ran down a darkened block away from the theater. Together, from a distance, they heard a single explosion—whether the bombs had exploded simultaneously, or one had failed to ignite, they had no way of knowing.

They slowed to a walk as they headed toward Foro Traiano, saying little as they listened to the wail of sirens from the Nazi police headquarters as they sent help.

Rosario came inside when they arrived, knowing it was too dangerous to be out alone, especially as curfew neared. Leaving him in the living room, Carla found her mother sitting on the well-worn sofa in her father's office where Carla slept, reading. Carla joined her.

"What were you doing tonight?" her mother asked as Carla settled in. She offered no response.

"Who is that boy who's staying with us?" her mother tried again. She must have heard the sirens, and perhaps the sound of an explosion as well.

But Carla refused to answer, as were the rules of the underground.

A MAJOR PART of the recent success of the Roman gappisti was their new and improved *santabarbara*—their bomb-making cache—the name originated from Saint Barbara, the patron saint of artillerymen and bomb makers. To help support this front line of urban resistance, Teresa's brother Gianfranco had ensconced himself in a secret bomb-making lab on Via Giulia with Giorgio Labò, who had been an architecture student before the war. Just off a busy street in the center of the city, they hoped their comings and goings would be masked by the crowds. They were responsible for the bombs Carla and Rosario used outside the opera and also many others that fellow gappisti placed in similar actions around the city.

The gappisti also began using the four-pointed nail. Inspired by an ancient Roman weapon meant to hobble horses, the nail head was crafted with four opposing points to similarly halt a convoy of Nazi vehicles. Simply thrown on the ground by the handful, they punctured tires, often catching a number of vehicles by surprise, or creating a great pileup, especially when used on a downhill. Ideally this would stop troop movements in their tracks, providing sitting targets for Allied bombers or partisans' grenades.

DAYS LATER CARLA walked tentatively into the back room of a dairy shop wondering if this might be the time she would finally make a connection with the Bandiera Rossa—the "Red Flag"—a clandestine military group similar to the gappisti from whom she was charged with getting essential information about a collaborator. GAP leader Luciano had reluctantly given her this mission after the successful bombing a few days earlier. Carla had already missed two previous connections with this elusive group through no fault of her own. She knew that, as a woman, she was granted less grace for errors than the men of the GAP and she wanted them to take her seriously.

As soon as Carla stepped into the room, two men pointed pistols into her rib cage, one on each side.

"What's the password?" one demanded. Carla took a breath. It was a complicated exchange she had to perform perfectly.

"*A quanto le metti?*" she asked, as if she was buying cigarettes on the black market. A man answered, only with his hands, motioning five. "The price is right," she responded.

A third man arrived and, initially placated, looked her over before asking, "Do you know how to keep an address in mind? Can you then forget it when necessary?"

"I believe so," Carla responded evenly.

"You *believe*?" he exploded. "You must be sure!"

Carla, suddenly incensed with an anger that surprised even herself, responded, "Comrade, we take risks here every day. If I hadn't been capable they would have chosen someone else, but instead they chose me. Isn't it because I'm a woman that you don't trust me?"

The man laughed. Her moxie convinced him, and he gave her the information she needed.

THE ROMAN RESISTANCE had been watching a German colonel who was staying at the Hotel Majestic, located in an area with hotels filled with Nazis. They noted that this man, who was always seen carrying a bulging briefcase of presumably important documents, would take a daily walk from his hotel to the Ministry of War, a few blocks away, feeling a sense of safety under the watchful eyes of so many fellow Nazis. But the gappisti also saw that this route was adjacent to a busy piazza, which might allow them to intercept him with a possibility of cover and a chance for escape.

Rosario and Carla had shown themselves to be an effective team. For their next action, at lunchtime in mid-December, two couples—Carla and Rosario, joined by Giovanni and Maria, who were a romantic couple as well as a GAP team—sat on the benches under the trees in front of the hotel. On schedule, the colonel strode out of the hotel and started walking down Via XXIII Marzo, so named in honor of the birth of Fascism on March 23, 1919. The couples casually stood up and followed a few yards behind him, each arm in arm.

Carla was wearing a trench coat, which was the fashion of the day and also a kind of uniform adopted by many gappisti, all the better to obscure weapons big and small. On that day, it was also appropriate cover for the cold and damp weather, and she blended in among those walking along at midday. She gripped her revolver in her right jacket pocket, the hammer cocked with a round in the chamber.

As Carla and Rosario approached the street crossing, which was their signal, Rosario whispered to her, "It's your turn to shoot. You'll do it as soon as you get off the sidewalk." They stepped into the road, their target not yet across the street.

"Now," Rosario said.

Carla pulled out her revolver and fired. The man collapsed to the ground, screaming in German—Maria, their cover, who had paused nearby, ready to create a diversion if necessary, would later translate his words, *My God, I'm dying. Help me!*

Carla stood, immobile, as Rosario grabbed the briefcase and then her arm, steering her toward the crowd in Piazza Barberini. She touched her face, numb, realizing that she was wet from the insistent rain.

Rosario had just opened his umbrella when a group of uniformed Fascists appeared, demanding to know what had happened.

"Someone was shooting on Via XXIII Marzo," Rosario told them, and they ran off in the direction from which Rosario and

Carla had come. Only then did Rosario see that Carla was still clutching her gun, walking down the street as if in a trance. In their rush, the Fascists hadn't even noticed.

"Rosario understood that I was upset, that I had made a great effort and was in the grip of anguish," Carla later recalled. He walked her toward the Galleria Colonna, which was also used as a bomb shelter. "Perhaps because in the confines of that immense environment I could give vent to my emotions, at least talk about it with him, as I did, the rain and my tears commingling on my cheeks." She understood that she had killed someone, and nothing would ever be the same.

The documents gained from this assassination would prove extremely useful. They contained maps and blueprints of German power and communication grids as well as antiaircraft placements in and around Rome. These would be given to CLN, who would order that all the German assets be destroyed by partisans. The first of them—antiaircraft guns hidden in a Trastevere train station—would be blown up two weeks later by Rosario and Carla, their partnership now solidified. By then, Carla understood that death was a necessary part of war—and she wouldn't let remorse or shock get in the way of her fight against the Nazi-Fascists again.

AS A GAP leader, Luciano Lusana was more likely to have food and supplies, and Carla never passed up an offer to meet at his house, where she might be asked to share a meal. She still acted as a staffetta, sent to various points in the city to gather or share intel, sometimes also bombs or munitions. A few days after the colonel's murder, she was sent to Luciano's to hear news of the previous night's action.

His sister Rina, who also worked as a staffetta, was roasting fat sausages in a pan when she arrived. "Do you want a cup of coffee?" she asked. The answer would always be yes—coffee was still only available on the black market. As she cooked, a staffetta appeared as scheduled, with news that fellow gappisti had successfully bombed a favorite trattoria where Nazis and collaborators liked to eat their meals and relax. Six Germans were killed, and more were injured.

The small group rejoiced that the power of the Resistance forces was being felt around the city.

ON THE EVENING of December 18, the Roman air was cold and crisp, leaving Carla and Rosario shivering just uphill from Cinema Barberini, pretending to flirt while they waited for German soldiers to exit the theater. Nestled at the base of the Quirinal Hill, one of the seven hills of Rome, the theater sat across the way from Piazza Barberini, which hosted Bernini's Triton Fountain. It depicted Triton, god of the sea, supported by dolphins, blowing a conch, carved in travertine. When first erected in the 1600s, the Triton Fountain created an effect of the god rising from a watery deluge—puddles surrounded the earthen ground around it, emphasizing, as scholars interpret, a show of a new Italy emerging from the depths, after the end of the War of Castro. Once a popular source of clean water in the city, this fountain, like most around the city, had run dry—and like most major statues, it was covered in cloth or boxed in wood to protect it against the devastation of war.

A special show had been planned that night for the occupying forces, and large trucks were waiting in the piazza below to bring them back to their barracks at its end. Carla's job was to provide cover for Rosario before he executed a bombing, with Maria and Giovanni placed elsewhere in the piazza to help provide a diversion if needed. Carla and Rosario were now quite comfortable with each other as they stood watch, waiting until the cinema exits opened and the soldiers flowed into the square. But despite Carla's recent reconciliation with the necessity of killing the enemy, as the doors opened and warm light illuminated young men her age, joking with their friends as they spilled into the night, she still felt a great sadness for the lives that were about to be changed or ended. She had a brief longing to leave them be—to return to a simpler time when she went to the theater for fun, not to kill.

"I'm going," Rosario announced, pulling her back to the moment, and he jumped onto the saddle of his bicycle. In his pocket was the bomb delivered to him earlier—small but powerful. He kicked off and started racing down the short downhill stretch toward the crowd exiting the cinema.

Carla held her breath as she watched him stop within attacking distance from the crowd. It was her job to intervene if she sensed he was in danger, but she couldn't figure out what was causing him to pause, one foot on the ground, holding his bicycle up like a tripod as he seemed to struggle with his jacket. She would later learn that the igniter had gotten tangled in his pocket after he had lit it, and he was afraid he would have to act as a human bomb.

A few yards from Rosario, soldiers were climbing into their trucks, their laughter drifting up the hill, pleased with their night of entertainment. Finally, he pulled something out of his pocket and launched it into the crowd. He gripped his bicycle and began riding away, but Carla could see he was spotted by Fascist police, who began shooting and were now in pursuit. He pedaled faster, the American-style wide-brimmed hat he had been wearing to obscure his face blowing off his head as he rode. Carla willed herself to turn her back on the square and walk briskly up the street where she was to meet with Maria. Giovanni was to return to their safe house, where he would meet Rosario afterward.

A moment later Carla heard the explosion behind her, followed by a moment of silence, and then shouts and screams drowning out the noise of the running engines of the waiting trucks.

She reached Maria at the next corner, and they finally looked back. Illuminated by the truck headlights they could see the wounded being helped by their fellow soldiers, a scene of carnage and chaos replacing the revelry of a minute earlier.

Carla did not have to feign fear and horror as she turned back around and came face-to-face with a high-ranking Nazi officer, an elegant and grim-faced woman at his side.

"Ask them, 'What are you doing here?'" he commanded his companion in German, and she began to repeat the question in Italian to Carla and Maria. But Maria knew perfect German, having grown up in northern Italy along the border of Austria.

"We met up with two German soldiers for the show," she explained in German with a forced sympathetic smile. "A tragedy," she added, nodding down the hill. The officer dismissed her with a contemptuous wave, muttering to his companion that they were "nothing but prostitutes." The two women walked on, and when they reached the safety of an air raid tunnel they embraced, relief at their escape tempered by horror at the casualties.

THE NEXT DAY, GAP comrades placed bombs on the ground floor windowsills of Hotel Flora. They had received intel that the hotel had been serving as the secret headquarters for the German high war command and hastily put this plan into action. Two of the four bombs exploded, causing apparent damage and casualties. This action received little coverage in the German-sanctioned news, as German leadership downplayed another successful partisan attack—but their immediate punitive response was a new curfew restriction of seven P.M., with bicycles prohibited after five P.M.

REFUSING TO EASE the pressure, the gappisti planned another action for a few days after Christmas. Two staffette had recently been sent to stand in line with the families and friends waiting at Regina Coeli prison for news of their loved ones, to gather information about the timing of the changing of the guards. This infamous prison now held many newly arrested suspected partisans who had been caught during the increased patrols implemented because of the rash of attacks.

With this knowledge in hand, Central GAP planned a bombing of the trucks of Nazi-Fascist soldiers arriving for and leaving their guard shift.

It had been Carla's role to carry a bomb close to the prison, and then pass it off to fellow gappisto Giovanni, who was supposed to light the fuse and drop it into the back of the large soldier transport truck, beneath the tent covering the seats in its rear. Afterward, he would escape on a bicycle.

Carla watched from a distance as Giovanni changed the plan. He lit the bomb and began racing his bicycle at high speed toward twenty guards who were exiting a truck outside the prison, throwing a double-sized *spezzone,* which exploded among the crowd, causing a dozen casualties immediately.

To escape, Giovanni turned his bicycle around and sped toward a gang of Fascists, who dove for cover when the Germans pursuing him continued their spray of bullets. Head down, Giovanni miraculously made it out alive.

Within days Fascist philosopher Giovanni Gentile would answer this attack in an article published in the state-sponsored newspaper, rallying Italians to support the Fascists, calling the partisans "sadistic rebels."

The Germans had a response as well. A new edict was posted: No bicycles were allowed in Rome at all.

CHAPTER 31

TERESA

FLORENCE
DECEMBER 1943

Teresa and Bruno were at one of the usual meeting places, in front of the public baths near Piazza Santo Spirito. Teresa was now a vital link between the Resistance leadership and local action groups, and with her growing confidence, their conversation became more natural and intense. Despite the chill in the air, they could lose an hour discussing history and politics in quiet voices, perhaps talking about one of the banned books Bruno would bring Teresa, like *The Communist Manifesto,* which she had quickly slipped into her bag the last time they had met.

Perhaps they started in low tones, Teresa passing on information about who was arrested, or who might be compromised. Bruno gave orders and messages for the Youth Front, often inquiring about their mental and physical health before detailing which Fascist leaders to watch. Teresa found his care for his comrades endearing and rare among the partisan leaders with whom she had been in contact; many seemed focused only on action, not people.

But that day, Teresa grew impassioned about her role in the Resistance, barely keeping her voice down, despite the risk of conversations like these in public. Teresa demanded that she be seen as more than a courier, and that Bruno and the leaders of CLN represent the interests of the women as they made plans for the future of Italy.

Teresa had helped organize a local GDD chapter when their *giornalini* first made their way to Florence in mid-November and had been active in the organization's political education classes over the past weeks.

"You may see women as doing modest things," she told Bruno, "but we want change, too. We want to be a part of things; we want to be involved."

Bruno said he understood, and that the local gappisti could use someone with her fire and loyalty. The Florentine gappisti had heard of the recent successes of their Roman counterparts—how working in teams with women gave them cover as young couples, perhaps out for a stroll. They were also beginning to understand that they needed to allow women into their ranks, that their success would depend upon it.

Chicchi would soon be assigned to a squad.

CHAPTER 32

ANITA

REGGIO EMILIA
WINTER 1944

Anita continued her work as a staffetta, happy to help the many young men who seemed to be flocking to the mountains. Her family's bar was quieter now, and her brother and his friends had long left for the partisan camps. Whenever she wasn't working, Anita would willingly make deliveries in service of the Resistance.

Anita's neighbor Torelli came to her one day and said, "You do so much for the partisans and for us. But you need to think about what *your* future will be." He offered to have a member of the Resistance come and talk with Anita and some of the women with whom she had been working, to help them understand more about the political fight.

Anita agreed, and later reflected on her own lack of political understanding up to that moment. "To us, Communists and Socialists were just the same, what did we know about politics? We had never gotten involved in it. With Fascism, you could only read what they gave to you, and you didn't even have the right to make comments." Fascism, understood in part as an ideology in which the state dictates nearly every facet of life, had accomplished its goal: to bring up a generation of young adults—and in particular women—who didn't understand their own political agency or any alternatives to their political reality.

A representative brought pamphlets from the GDD, smuggled in with other clandestine papers that had news from other cities. This pamphlet explained who the GDD were and that they needed women to create their own local chapters to help spark political education and discussions and take up collections for the men hiding and organizing to fight in the mountains. The representative explained to them how this war was not just against the Germans but also a war for Italy's future. After the war, women would be able to vote and have the same rights as men; the women could—in fact they must!—think about what they wanted in their future. But, he emphasized, the women had to be organized. Within days Anita gathered a handful of friends to start the first chapter of the GDD in Reggio Emilia.

"At that point we understood that we could change our future," Anita later recalled. "We understood that we had to be more than partisans, that we had to acquire consciousness about our role in the Resistance."

CHAPTER 33

TO THE LAST MAN

The Nazi-Fascists understood that the men who ignored their calls to join the new Republic of Salò forces were forming an army of their own. While they might not be able to find all of the hiding bands, they knew that if they could keep the Resistance disjointed, it would remain weak and easy to subdue. To help achieve this, the Nazi-Fascists continued cracking down on clandestine presses—whose goal was to share news between regions around the country, inspire more actions, collaborate on efforts, and help the diverse groups feel less alone.

By the start of 1944, the Nazi-Fascists had also begun to understand the power of foreign radio. Radio London was believed by many in occupied Italy to be the best source of information about the war—and the Resistance. Their news reports, given on the half hour, often included coded messages—seemingly banal statements that had deeper implications for those who knew the code. Phrases like *The hen has laid the egg* might give the location or date of an airdrop, news about the movements of partisans, or a signal or location for an attack. The real meaning of these codes was known only by the few who had contact with an Allied agent, but even just the knowledge that what they were hearing was helping the cause was an inspiration to so many who were listening.

GERMAN COMMANDER KESSELRING understood the power of the Resistance. He testified after the war, "Rome had become an explosive city for us. . . . Security immediately behind the front line was a serious problem." So, as the new year neared, the Germans also made a concerted effort to root out the Resistance. They expanded their SS forces in the city from four hundred to two thousand, while the Fascists sent out one of their most ruthless men—the half-German, half-Italian Pietro Koch, along with his *Banda Koch*—the Koch gang—which would test the Vatican's resolve to stay neutral in the war. They ransacked Vatican properties to capture partisans, Jewish people, and men who had escaped earlier roundups, instilling fear in those who believed they were safe in monasteries and convents. The dozens they arrested would be sent to concentration camps, work camps, or prisons.

Pope Pius XII would have little to say about these bloody raids on church buildings, his secretary noting that he would "not want to be forced to utter formal words of disapproval." The German ambassador commended the Pope for striving for the "perfect balance" of placating the Germans and the Allies. The Pope was ostensibly trying to save what he could of the city's churches and art and support leniency—but not too vociferously—for those being terrorized under the occupation. Historians would later critique Pope Pius XII for erring on the side of riches over people, and failing to act boldly to stand up for basic Christian tenets of right and wrong.

———

ON JANUARY 12, 1944, the Allied forces attacked the Gustav Line, part of the larger Winter Line, which was the last main defensive hold between them and Rome. Hitler ordered his soldiers to defend it "to the last man" as he diverted more troops to Italy's front line. The Axis defense worked and the Allies failed to break through.

The next day a CLN leader had their own message to the Resistance, written in underground newspapers and passed around by staffette: "It is not possible to wait for the Allies. We must intensify our actions against the Nazi-Fascists, to weaken their organization now. . . . We must act now if we want the Anglo-Americans to find our government in office." The CLN, too, understood the necessity of unity and the power of the media. They wanted to show the Allied forces that the Resistance army represented the will of the Italian people and was capable of fighting for their own freedom—and governing themselves as well.

CHAPTER 34

TERESA

FLORENCE
JANUARY 1944

Finally, the Florentine gappisti began to act. Inspired by the underground news that made its way southward from their comrades in Rome, at the start of the year they began planting a series of bombs: at the main Fascist office, the train station, and the hotel that served as the command center for the German military. Teresa was among the few trusted staffette who helped transport materials and communication in the planning and execution of these actions, who traversed the city on bicycle and on foot, carrying fuses and pipes, hidden amid shopping or laundry, passed off to their contacts under the noses of the Nazi-Fascists.

The Florentine gappisti ended their January offensive with the burning of the prefecture and an explosion at the Teatro della Pergola when the Fascists were having a ceremony there. These actions had their desired effect. The Florentine Resistance, like their Roman counterparts, had demonstrated their ability to strike against the Nazi-Fascists, not wanting them to feel comfortable or safe in their city. And, like in Rome, the curfew was lowered in response—from eleven P.M. to eight P.M.—and the use of bicycles prohibited.

—————

THE FIRST MESSAGE was *L'Arno scorre a Firenze*—"The Arno flows through Florence." It was sent with the help of Gilda Larocca, who, with her boss, Enrico Bocci, were the coordinators of the first major Allied–Resistance line of communication, called Radio CORA.

Under her watch, in a quiet neighborhood across from a park, Gilda helped establish an information center, with detailed maps of the area to help track German movements, a cache of arms and munitions, a station for creating false papers and identification documents, and a list of ciphers and codes the Resistance used to communicate with the Allied forces. Housed in a building where a Fascist leader had lived before he'd recently escaped to the north, their base, Gilda hoped, wouldn't be suspected.

By the start of 1944, the Allies began to extend some trust to the Italian Resistance, realizing that their troops could accomplish much more by working together. They were already working toward the same ends in many respects: attacking the same German convoys, destroying Nazi communication hubs. The Allies had airdropped some resources over the previous fall—crates floating under parachutes filled with food, winter jackets, and munitions—and they had encouraged sabotage. But it was becoming obvious that the Resistance was already doing so much more and could provide intel from deep behind the front lines. The Allies had some success with a British spy and radio receiver located in Rome, transmitting messages to the Resistance there and precious information back to the Allies. Therefore, a recent drop near Florence had included a large radio receiver, which ended up in the hands of Enrico Bocci, the main connection between the Allies and the Resistance. Enrico enlisted a network of spies—mostly staffette like Teresa who were already moving around the city on other missions—to gather reports. Gilda Larocca, who ran the office, also helped to move the transmitter around the city. She and her team were always trying to stay one step ahead of the German radio detectors, who would ride around in a car with their own receiver, trying to find a strong broadcasting signal to track them down.

Gilda would hide the heavy transmitter in a shopping bag and cover the top with produce to make it look like groceries. She practiced walking with a casual gait to belie the weight of the bag, so as not to arouse suspicion as she carried it from one safe house to the next. Once, she was taking the trolley to the next transmission appointment, when the air raid sirens began to blare, causing the trolley to stop. She decided to continue on foot so she wouldn't be late. A Fascist walking in the same direction offered to carry the bag for her, but Gilda resisted. He wouldn't relent, so she agreed to each of them carrying one handle, trying to discreetly hold her side higher to keep up the ruse of the weight of the supposed groceries inside.

He finally asked her what was inside the bag.

"Women prefer to carry their most precious items with them—even while shopping," she replied. The Fascist accepted her explanation with a nod and continued on until their paths diverged.

And so began one of the most successful and essential spying and communication efforts of the war. This team noted train and vehicle transports, German soldier numbers and movements, and locations of possible German targets around the city. Their reporting was so detailed that they shared the insignia on the vehicles and the names of exact divisions, sending their size, resources, and movements. The precise and reliable information given to the Allies resulted in the decimation of entire German units in targeted air raids—in one case the eradication of a whole unit headed toward Rome as reinforcements in the defense against attacks on the Gustav Line.

And in the first few months of 1944, this consistent line of communication would also result in more resource drops to the partisans outside the city and through the north of Italy, with some of these new resources making their way back to Florence, disseminated to the gappisti and other partisans by Teresa and other staffette. The Allied leadership finally began to understand the benefits—perhaps necessity—of working with the Resistance, which had even more to gain from a German defeat.

CHAPTER 35

ANZIO

Early in the morning on January 22, the Allied forces finally landed at Anzio, a beachhead less than forty miles south of Rome. Despite their fears that they would lack enough resources for a successful landing, their arrival was a total surprise to the Germans, and they soon overran the small Nazi force defending the town, many of whom were still in their nightclothes.

General John P. Lucas quickly secured the beachhead, as his superiors had ordered, and began unloading troops and supplies, pleased with their luck. This news was greeted with excitement, particularly by those in and around Rome. Surely, many believed, the city would soon be liberated.

A British newspaper headline announced the landing and the troops' movement "several miles inland" the next day, further reporting that the beachhead was "rapidly increased in depth." But this was largely untrue. In reality, General Lucas kept his troops close to the shore, while the Germans began moving more than twenty thousand troops to this new front line. It would be a matter of time until the Allies were boxed in, with reinforcements able to arrive only by sea.

Meanwhile, another officer took a drive to gain reconnaissance, wanting to see what impediments lay between them and Rome. The small crew drove slowly, watching for hidden patrols, mines, or booby traps. After miles of uneventful driving, they thought they must have made a wrong turn, but then realized they had made it all the way to Rome's southern suburbs completely unopposed. Noting this wide-open road, they turned their vehicle around and drove back to the beach to report what they had seen.

But General Lucas would decline to move any farther inland, following his orders to the letter as he had trenches dug and established his troops on the Anzio shoreline.

It would be many long months before Allies would be that close to Rome again.

CHAPTER 36

CARLA

ROME
JANUARY 1944

The Allied forces have landed in Anzio—liberation must be near!
The Roman Resistance readied itself for what it hoped would be the final battle. Leadership sent Rosario and Carla to the working-class neighborhood of Centocelle on the outskirts of Rome, where there was a large band of partisans. With the Allies so close, the Americans had asked CLN to help rally locals for the final days of street fighting to help push out the Nazis while the Allies attacked. They hoped to preempt possible Nazi destruction and sabotage, like the trail of mines and rubble left as the Nazis retreated from Naples just a few months prior. Partisans came out of the shadows and were sent around the city and beyond, to the very suburb the Allied reconnaissance team had just chanced upon, uniting Romans with the same goal.

During these last weeks of January, while the Resistance believed the Allies were truly days away, their vigilance relaxed, and they met in larger numbers, sometimes openly in cafés. When Rosario gave an inspirational speech to more than a hundred of their new comrades, Carla stood by, a pistol in her pocket. She had no fear as she watched a handful of Nazi officers on the sidelines take in the large and raucous crowd, and then leave. It wasn't just the Resistance that was expecting the Allies—the Germans also seemed focused on the Allies' advance.

This is what victory feels like, Carla believed.

CHAPTER 37

HELLO, SUCKERS

H ello, Suckers," purred Axis Sally—the American female voice whose propaganda radio broadcasts the Nazis amplified over the Anzio battlefields, trying to sow doubt and strife among the Allied soldiers. The Italian state-controlled radio wanted their own "Axis Sally" to emulate the broadcasts by Mildred Gillars out of Berlin, and Italian American Rita Louisa Zucca, who had returned to Italy a few years before the war to reclaim family property, obliged.

Awaiting the next Nazi barrage, the American soldiers heard her trademark greeting, along with the popular song "Between the Devil and the Deep Blue Sea," reinforcing their precarious position on the beachhead. With a familiar accent, the role of Axis Sally was to destabilize the troops, questioning the fidelity of all the wives and girlfriends back home: *Do you think they will remain faithful,* she wondered aloud, *especially if you boys get all mutilated and do not return in one piece?* Zucca often ended her broadcasts for the soldiers on a disconcerting note. She would share a piece of sensitive intel Axis spies had gleaned, perhaps detailing the Allies' next move: *Well, we know where and when you're coming, and you will be wiped out.* And then she would sign off, *A sweet kiss from Sally!*

Rather than take that unfettered road to Rome, the Allies had hunkered down on the beach and given the Germans time to regroup. When the battle finally began in earnest, the Allied and Axis soldiers were evenly matched, with both sides relying on spy networks for information. The U.S. Office of Strategic Services, whose goal was to obtain intelligence and support spying and sabotage during the war, created a successful local spy network—from doctors and nurses at a hospital treating Germans, to children and farmers observing from the fields. This collaboration between the Italian people and the Allied forces helped transmit detailed intel—like exactly what resources the enemy had and where to bomb—to the Allies. This reliable network helped strengthen the Allied trust in the Italians, even as the Battle of Anzio hit a stalemate weeks later, with both sides battered.

The operation would later be considered one of the greatest Allied follies of the war. General Lucas spent days securing the beachhead rather than moving inland—indeed forgoing the opportunity to march straight to Rome on that unguarded road—or even move his troops farther into the Alban Hills, which would have given them a tactical advantage for future battles.

This Allied misstep would have repercussions for the Roman partisans as well. Once the Germans believed that they had retained control of Rome, they refocused themselves on destroying the Resistance, which they now believed was larger and more entrenched in the city than it was, due to their visibility over the previous few weeks. Helping to lead this charge was Erich Priebke, a horrific torturer in the Nazis' new interrogation center at Via Tasso—a small jail fashioned in a former police station where they sent their most prized prisoners. It was an old police headquarters, but the Nazis bricked over the windows and turned mop closets into pitch-black solitary confinement cells where desperate prisoners scratched messages and warnings into the walls. As January came to an end, the new wave of arrests began. Priebke's men began filling Via Tasso's cells and he got to work.

These developments impacted everyday Romans as well. Food and medicine were scarce, and even staples being sold on the black market, where many Italians went to obtain necessities like olive oil, had now skyrocketed in price. Nazis would break in and steal what they wanted from any home, store, or warehouse. The hunger and cold were causing discontent among the occupied Italians, increasingly willing to risk more for their own survival.

The gappisti, desperate after the wave of arrests, returned underground, rededicating themselves to doing everything they could to weaken the Nazis and make them feel fearful in Rome. They'd had a brief taste of freedom, and despite the new danger, they knew they couldn't allow fear to dictate their actions. It was clear now that the Allies weren't moving quickly enough for the gappisti. Their liberation would be up to them.

CHAPTER 38

BIANCA

PIEDMONT

WINTER 1944

On Tuesdays, Bianca went to the factories for her weekly appointments. There, she met with the women she was helping to organize. They would pass in the halls, perhaps give each other a look that indicated whether they were free to talk. If the woman she was supposed to connect with didn't meet her eye, or otherwise indicated it wasn't safe to chat, they had other ways to communicate—a message whispered to a coworker, a small note or token passed hand to hand.

More and more, women were meeting in small groups under the auspices of the GDD, and Bianca provided them with material to discuss or suggested actions that they could take part in. Women could still generally talk in low voices with little risk of suspicion. Fascist spies or German watchmen often thought they were just gossiping.

There were safe houses where they met in groups to discuss political ideas or hand out pamphlets or pass along intel from the factory floor. Word was quietly passed if a meeting place was no longer secure, and a new location would be established, shared through the same web of whispers and passed notes.

Bianca took the information she was given to her sector leaders—new worker issues or possible spies in the factories, potential areas of weakness the Resistance could exploit, tales of sabotage or retribution for perceived resistance. And back again the next week she shared directives from the Turin sector and GDD leaders. Evenings were often spent working on the flyers and pamphlets that would help direct these groups or share news or provide political education.

On Saturdays and Sundays, she went to the mountains—a difficult trip, first by train to the foothills and then uphill by bicycle—bringing supplies or weapons when she could, and information always. In addition to the clandestine publications she and others were starting to produce in fits and starts, she shared news on locations and movements of German and Fascist soldiers, larger war updates, or pending actions in the city. Bianca might be given orders to convey where the CLN leadership wanted the groups to attack, or, if they were lucky, perhaps word about a drop of supplies from the Allies. And then she would bring back what she was told or given, meet with her sector or provincial leaders, and make plans to do it all again in the coming week.

A single main road led from the foothills into each of the Alpine valleys, which passed through the heart of each village. Locals knew the paths up the ridges that connected the valleys and towns that could help them avoid the main road in places. But it was impossible, on some stretches, to hide. Bianca became adept at learning which of these towns were friendly, and where there were Nazi-Fascist outposts. She made the trek weekly, even as the temperature dipped colder than it had in years. Some days, she could walk miles toward the looming Alpine peaks and see no soldiers, but on others, she might encounter a new roadblock where none had been before, trusting that her stolen personalausweis would still work to keep her safe. The winter's only saving grace was the relative lack of snow, which meant that the hikes through the ridges were easier than they otherwise might have been.

THAT WINTER, ADA called Bianca and suggested, *"Andiamo a fare una gita"*—"Let's go on a trip." By then Bianca had learned that Ada's eighteen-year-old son, Paolo, had joined Alberto at La Gianna. Despite forged paperwork, Ada knew it was too dangerous for him to be coming and going between their home in Turin and the partisan bands with whom he had already been working—executing sabotage and helping to guide them around the valleys he knew well from his childhood spent at their country home in Meana, in neighboring Susa Valley.

Bianca was savvy enough to understand the subtext of Ada's message—the trip they were going on, which would be the first of many, was to bring supplies to their loved ones. The women filled bags with food—both nutritious snacks like cooked eggs, and also sweets—as well as clothes, newspapers, and messages.

The trip to this part of the mountains was long and arduous. Trains were canceled, sometimes leaving crowds waiting at the station, ready to storm the cars with their luggage in an attempt to get on. Or, at a bombed-out bridge the passengers might be forced to disembark one train, cross the crevasse on a makeshift footbridge, and board another on the other side. Many of the train cars headed north toward the Alps were repurposed carriages once used to transport animals, with no windows, only slits near the roof for ventilation. The trains would sometimes stop for hours on lonely stretches of the countryside, with no sense of when they might get moving again. It was during one of these moments, as the sun set, that Bianca asked Ada about her late husband, Piero, and Ada told her of the darkness that had descended upon her world in the aftermath of his death. She felt that same darkness now, Ada told Bianca, as she feared for the life of Paolo and the young men he was with in the mountains.

THESE TRIPS WOULD deepen the women's friendship, despite their age difference, and they began working together closely in the Resistance. Ada was connected to the upper-level partisan leadership and the local CLN government, and Bianca became one of their main organizers, sent to execute their orders. The trust gained on these trips paved the way for future collaborations—Bianca sometimes meeting Alberto at Ada's house in Meana—as well as for actions in the city. There would be many nights to come spent late by the fire, long after curfew, where the women envisioned a newspaper of their own, to speak directly to the women of the Resistance.

CHAPTER 39

FLORENCE UNDER OCCUPATION

For many people in Florence during that first winter of the occupation, life had some semblance of normalcy, especially for those who earned a salary from the government, or benefited from those who did. There were still theater, opera, and even boxing events, put on for the entertainment of well-off Florentines and the occupiers. Twenty-eight cinemas were open in the city and two literary magazines continued to publish. L'Accademia d'Italia was preparing to resume its activities the following month, with Fascist philosopher Giovanni Gentile serving as master of ceremonies on opening day.

Schools had reopened in late fall, and teachers were paid again if they affirmed their fealty to their Fascist leaders. Government employees—also expected to declare loyalty—were still paid, even as their productivity suffered amid a lack of leadership and resources and general ennui. People still went out to eat if they could afford to, and restaurants and hotels—many housing the occupiers—were generally paid for their services. Supply chains were greased if they treated these customers well.

But for others, this was a time of desperation. If members of the

Resistance had no other means of financial support, the Resistance would often give them a small salary, with money primarily supplied by donations, requisitioned from raids and arrests, or, more recently, from drops by the Allied forces. But this could not keep up with rampant inflation. February rations—the amount Florentines were allowed to purchase at set prices on the legal market—were scant: just 360 grams of beef, 100 grams of salami, 300 grams of dry and fresh cheese, 180 grams of oil, half a kilogram of sugar, 2 kilograms mixed between pasta and rice. Only children, the sick, and the elderly were allowed some milk and jam. And much of this was of poor quality. This, obviously, wasn't enough to live on, and most people had to resort to buying food on the black market, where prices were sky-high and fluctuating. By the end of 1943, the price of bread was five times more than it had been five years earlier and the price of pasta had tripled. A bottle of olive oil cost as much as a factory worker's monthly wages. For some Florentines, this made them more committed to the change the Resistance promised. For others, their despair pushed them to collaborate with the Nazi-Fascists, their tenuous loyalty bought with a few hundred lire or a few kilos of food.

CHAPTER 40

TERESA

ROME
FEBRUARY 1944

At the stroke of ten A.M., the Nazis sealed off the neighborhood and began pulling men from buses and trams near a fashionable shopping district close to the Tiber River. They were displeased with the numbers of Italians the call-ups for workers had produced. Led by Herbert Kappler, head of the Nazi secret services and police in occupied Rome, the Germans had begun surprise searches to find draft dodgers and kidnap able-bodied men. Someone walking down the street to work that morning might be on a train to Germany by the end of the day, disappeared to a new reality of forced labor that might include long hours in a factory or breaking stones in a quarry, their families unaware of where their husband or father had gone.

Often these captives were offered a chance to give up information about the Resistance in exchange for their freedom. Among those arrested that morning was a man who told the Nazis that he had seen suspicious behavior around the address of Gianfranco Mattei and Giorgio Labò's santabarbara. The pair had spent hours in that windowless room with weapons, munitions, and explosives lining the walls, working on developing two new types of bombs and improving the Rome unit's explosive-making efficacy and production. In the short time Gianfranco had been there, he and Giorgio scouted possible bombing locations by day, counting paces to use as estimated measurements, recording their findings once out of sight. Late into the night they worked making explosives like the ones that had caused such destruction at the cinema and the opera.

That evening the Nazis raided the bomb cache at Via Giulia 23, confiscating "enough explosives to blow up half of Rome," a German report noted. Gianfranco and Giorgio were arrested and sent to Via Tasso. It was February 1—Teresa's twenty-third birthday.

Word spread quickly about this arrest from the underground Resistance to the men's families. Within the first few days of Gianfranco's imprisonment, Teresa's grandmother contacted friends at the Vatican to plead for their help in his release. A cardinal and deputy of the Vatican secretary of state sent a recommendation for release to Colonel Kappler. The colonel tore it up on receipt, adding, "Lieutenant Priebke will have this talk by physical and chemical means with the terribly silent Communist."

WHEN TERESA HEARD of her brother's capture, she was bereft. The Via Tasso prison had already earned a reputation in its short existence for horrific torture, a place where inhuman screams and moans could be heard at all times of day. She felt the need to be with her parents and hoped being in Rome would allow her quicker access to news of his fate. So she volunteered to take a master copy of an issue of the underground Communist newspaper *L'Unità* to Rome for printing and dissemination, sewing the document into the seam of her dress.

Teresa didn't want to risk traveling by train under her real name or with forged paperwork. So she set off for the south on foot, memorizing a fake name and address, and practicing a cover story that was not so different from the truth: Her brother had been killed in the war and she wanted to be with her parents in Rome to mourn.

It wasn't long before she was offered a ride in a rickety box truck carrying silk. The trip, with roads in good condition, would normally take only a few hours, but with many highways impassable from bombing raids and sabotage, they were forced to drive more slowly on rough back roads, always under threat of Nazi checkpoints. Teresa kept her eyes on the road ahead, considering what she would do should she see German soldiers. What she didn't expect was guns from above. A few hours into her journey, near Perugia, aerial strafing knocked over the truck and killed the driver. Teresa was shaken but physically unharmed, and once she escaped the smoldering vehicle, she continued walking.

Soon after, an Axis forces truck pulled up alongside her. The young soldiers in the front seat had been sent to investigate the explosion and were headed southward to deliver their report. Her heart beat quickly as she waited for them to question and search her. But instead, they were friendly. Did she want a ride? Nightfall was approaching, so as she had practiced, Teresa played the role of a naïve young woman, telling them that she was trying to join her family in Rome. She knew better than to trust the ease with which they accepted her story, as they slid over to make room for her in the front seat, but she seemed to have no other option.

Not far up the road, they stopped at a Nazi checkpoint and Teresa's fears were realized. Finding a young woman with two junior officers, the soldiers there were suspicious. Why was she traveling by truck and not train? Why was an unmarried woman separated from her parents? Teresa kept to her story, and her hidden documents remained so even after they roughly searched her. Despite lack of evidence, they arrested her.

TELL US WHO you are going to meet. We know you're working with the Resistance! a Fascist officer demanded.

They had arrived at the nearby base after nightfall, just as the soldiers had finished dinner. Her presence became a spectacle, and many crowded into the room where she was being violently questioned.

Teresa repeated her answer, crying now. *Just my parents.*

The Fascist hit her so hard she fell off her chair. A Nazi kicked her prone body. She felt the sharp jab deep in her side from the butt of a rifle.

Where are they hiding? Tell us and the pain will stop. Another officer stomped on her face and her mouth filled with blood.

They accused her of vague crimes and demanded she give up names and information of local partisans, but Teresa maintained her innocence as the torture continued. For hours Nazi and Fascist officers continued their abuse, repeatedly raping and beating her. Teresa kept repeating her story, never considering offering information about her comrades in Florence or elsewhere. Weeping, battered, it was obvious to Teresa that this was sport to them. Somehow, throughout her night of terror, the newspaper was never found in the hem of her clothes.

When the officers grew tired, they dragged her to a locked room. *We'll shoot you in the morning,* one of them told Teresa as they left her collapsed in the corner, closing the door behind them. When she was finally alone, she tried to stand and found she could only hobble a few steps. Everything hurt; she was bleeding and missing teeth, and the soldiers' strikes to her side had ruptured one of her kidneys. Teresa began preparing herself for death.

TERESA FEARED MORE torture when someone came to her door later in the night. But instead, an Italian Fascist officer whispered into the dark room, *Ti alzi! Vai!—Get up! Go!*

She rose to her unsteady feet and limped out the door. Teresa was rightfully suspicious of this man—she had seen him in the back of the room while she was being tortured, though he had just stood silently, frowning. Could he truly be helping her? But she had nothing to lose, even if it was some kind of trap.

The guard left the door open and walked away while Teresa managed to climb over a high wall to freedom. She made her way through the brush on the other side, branches tearing at her ankles and ripping her dress. Stumbling through the night, Teresa found her way to a nearby convent, and collapsed in the doorway as daybreak neared. By a phenomenal stroke of luck, it was a friend of her mother's who found her. She would hide Teresa there, on the outskirts of Perugia, for more than a week until she was well enough to continue on to Rome.

"Perhaps I looked like his daughter," Teresa later said. "At great risk to himself, a Fascist soldier helped me flee." The two would meet again years later at his trial for war crimes and she would testify on his behalf, helping to greatly reduce his sentence. He told her that he became an anti-Fascist after that night, when he saw the brutal treatment of an unarmed young woman.

IT WOULD BE decades before Teresa publicly told the true nature of her torture—the repeated rapes that occurred along with the beating. She, and so many other female partisans, whispered among themselves that this was a regular weapon employed by the Nazis and Fascists—to expect sexual violence if arrested. It wouldn't be until Teresa's testimony in 2007 that the regularity of rape as torture would become part of the better-known Nazi atrocities during their occupation of Italy. While Teresa said that she didn't tell anyone at the time because she didn't want to add to her parents' anguish or detract attention from the tragic fate of her brother, the silence around sexual assault during the war was near universal for more than half a century. Part of this stems from the women's physical and emotional trauma, and the psychological pain of reliving the experience in the telling, especially when there is no opportunity for justice. But, perhaps, the greater reason for their silence was the accepted culture of female oppression—the feeling that women would be tainted, or were culpable or made weak by this act. This patriarchal culture is also what inspired so many women to risk everything for the promise of a different future.

"It was its own education," Teresa later said, "to have chosen the Resistance.... Because it is necessary to do all that is required for liberty and to have understood that fear is our nemesis."

CHAPTER 41

DESTRUCTION OF MONTE CASSINO

The Gustav Line was proving impenetrable. So the Allied forces debated a controversial move. On top of Monte Cassino, the linchpin of the Gustav Line, was a magnificent abbey of the same name. The Allies believed that Axis troops were using the abbey as a home base and weighed the decision to bomb it, despite its architectural, religious, and historical significance. Any tactical advantage, the generals decided, was worth the cost.

So on February 15, 1944, a fleet of big-bellied Allied planes reduced the Monte Cassino Abbey to rubble. Within minutes the cloisters were crumbled, the grand staircase leading to the basilica lay in ruins, and the statue of Saint Benedict was decapitated. In what would later be considered one of the most contentious bombing raids of the war, this Allied attack killed more than a hundred innocent people within the abbey, destroying an important center of religious scholarship and an architectural wonder, while the Germans camped nearby remained unscathed. The abbey had not been occupied by the enemy.

The Allied forces once again failed to breach the Gustav Line—

and the confidence of the Italian people in their supposed liberators was further shaken.

Meanwhile, less than a hundred miles west at Anzio, the Allied and Axis forces were evenly matched, resulting in major losses for both sides as the battle continued into its second month.

CHAPTER 42

BIANCA

TURIN
FEBRUARY 1944

Facing low draft rates and growing bands of partisans, on February 18, Mussolini ordered the death penalty for men who didn't report for duty. In some parts of occupied Italy, this worked to bolster numbers. In the mountainous region of the north, these recruits formed the Alpine Musketeers, a Fascist volunteer battalion that would be stationed in the Alps, working to root out the entrenched Resistance and draft dodgers there. Around two hundred and fifty Musketeers, with deep knowledge of the valleys, joined seasoned militiamen with an expressed goal to find and neutralize the partisans who seemed to have the run of the valleys as they stole arms and attacked communication hubs. Bianca's weekly visits into the valleys became all the more dangerous—and she feared for the safety of Alberto and his comrades.

THAT MONTH, BIANCA received a postcard signed by her friend Primo Levi and their two friends with whom he had been in the Fossoli concentration camp over the previous few months. Fossoli, situated in a rugged corner of Emilia-Romagna, had been a prisoner of war camp, but after the armistice was signed, the POWs were transported to Germany and the barracks had been rebuilt to house deportees. Originally under Italian control, its purpose was to hold Jewish people and political prisoners until the barracks were full, at which point they would be sent to Auschwitz.

Primo and their friends were on the second convoy to leave the camp and he had managed to write out a card that he had thrown from the transport with the hope that it would be found and posted.

"Dear Bianca, everyone traveling in the classic way—say hello to all—to you the torch . . . we love you." On the back, under the Italian war slogan *Vinceremo*—meaning "We will win"—Primo had written Bianca's address and "please send."

Primo Levi would send three more postcards to Bianca—his closest non-Jewish friend, for his family was in hiding at places unknown to him—all facilitated by a friend he met in Auschwitz. Lorenzo was a civilian worker who gave Primo rations and clothing, and he would post the notes from him when he could. The messages never said much more than "Primo is fine." Bianca would share these rays of hope with friends and family, not fully understanding the horrors of Auschwitz until after the war, when Primo and the few others who returned recounted them—personally and to the world at large. Instead, all that Bianca's and Primo's dear ones could conjure was stories of the concentration camps of the First World War. The tales of starvation and hard labor, sickness and exposure, seemed horrific enough to dampen their hopes of Primo's return. The truth, of course, was unfathomably worse.

CHAPTER 43

TERESA

ROME AND FLORENCE
FEBRUARY 1944

For more than a week, Teresa hid with her parents in Rome, awaiting word of Gianfranco's fate as she continued to recover from her injuries. Fellow partisans delivered frequent updates, letting them know that his body had not been found among those often dumped in piazzas around the city. This grim display was meant to serve as a warning for those who dared defy the Nazis.

And then one day a limping young man came with a message. He had been Gianfranco's cellmate in Via Tasso and was one of the few to ever make it out of this notoriously brutal prison alive.

He told them that Gianfranco was tortured for six days after his initial capture. Worse than the beatings and use of electric shock, Gianfranco especially feared the injections of various substances that induced great pain and a high fever that caused delirium. He had been afraid that in this altered state he would give up the names and locations of fellow partisans and his parents in hiding. So, he decided to take control away from his captors. During one walk to the torture room, he was able to whisper to Giorgio, who was held in another cell, to "throw all the blame on me." That night, he hanged himself with his belt. Before he died, he told his cellmate, "I know I'm dying but I'm happy because the cause is worth it."

The young partisan also passed along a final note that Gianfranco had written to his family, scrawled on the back of a bank check. It ended with the words, "be as strong and as tough as I was, too. I love you."

In the coming days, after mourning what she had been fearing for weeks, Teresa knew that she had to return to Florence.

DISEMBARKING FROM HER train, Teresa was surprised that Bruno Sanguinetti was there to meet her. When she saw his familiar face, she burst into tears.

"You have lost a brother," he told her as she wept into his shoulder, "but in me you will find another."

Between sobs Teresa told him of her fears for her parents' safety and implored him to help them return to Florence. Gianfranco's body had not been released, Kappler allegedly saying, "Let the father come and take it!"

Bruno assured her he would bring her family safely home.

Bruno and Teresa's younger brother Nino would soon drive to Rome to retrieve her parents, bringing them back on the dangerous roads. When they returned, Teresa told Bruno to put her to work. She was ready to avenge her brother's death.

CHAPTER 44

CARLA

ROME
MARCH 1944

Carla had returned with Rosario from the outskirts of Rome and found a city transformed. "Growing fear and despair, hunger and sickness were wasting people away," she described. Water was scarce, as were food and medicine. "Lice was everywhere in Rome," Carla continued, as was the nauseating smell of the medicine used to kill them. "We were all getting thinner and thinner, paler and paler."

But not everyone, Carla noted. "There were, however, those who still had their morning cappuccino and brioche, who spread butter on their bread when they took their afternoon tea. . . . You knew immediately who the people were who trafficked with the Fascists and the Germans. They were the only ones still driving cars; they were the well-dressed women in furs whom you saw on their way to the theater for an opera performed for the Nazi troops. The city had two categories of citizens, a minority who fraternized with the enemy, and the rest of the Romans, the vast majority, who suffered and died hoping for their liberation."

CARLA

———

THE STALLED ALLIED effort in Anzio—and the resulting reenergized Nazi-Fascist effort to destroy the partisans—left the underground army fractured and demoralized. Graffiti written on the walls in Trastevere even joked wryly, AMERICANS RESIST! WE WILL COME AND SAVE YOU! Those who remained active were hardened, known to greet one another with an upraised fist when they safely could. This new danger also meant that Carla could not return to Foro Traiano, but rather she set up her bed in the partisans' new santabarbara located in a coal storage room in the cellar of a middle-class apartment building on Via Marco Aurelio, a quiet street overlooking the Colosseum. This safe space was offered by the concierge, Duilio, who would also serve as a lookout and communication hub for the four partisans who would make this their home—and begin making bombs again. For safety, very few fellow partisans knew the address. Scavenged pieces of explosive devices were Carla's new roommates along with fellow partisans Caterina and Cesare; her bed, made upon a few planks of wood, would be shared with Rosario.

CHAPTER 45

BIANCA

TURIN

MARCH 1944

Turin workers!

Close ranks around your agitation committees, uncover, demonstrate unitedly against the attempted starvation of the Nazi-Fascists and their accomplices, the industrial magnates; demand full payment of all days off—including piecework and attendance allowance.

Shout about a stop to the persecutions, arrests, tortures, and shootings of patriots by the filthy Republican Guard. Demand the release of your arrested comrades.

Shout to the slavers who are deporting our young sons and vanguard workers to Germany.

Shout about a stop to the infamous Fascist laws that condemn to death young Italians who I know refuse to become fodder for Hitler's generals.

Shout out that enough is enough with the war production that provokes air bombing; enough with broken promises; enough with the lies, threats, violence, and starving maneuvers.

WORKERS! GARIBALDINI! Sabotage production; sabotage the electricity systems and communication routes. Stop the violence of the Nazis and the Fascist traitors! Answer blow by blow!

Death to the German invaders!

Death to the Fascist traitors!

Long live the general strike: Long live the guerrillas of freedom!

—The Committee of Agitation of the Piedmont and Lombardy and Liguria, Turin, March 1, 44

BIANCA AND HER Committee of Agitation had started organizing in February. They whispered the call for a mass strike weeks in advance and sent out instructions and encouraging manifestos on half sheets of paper. The day before, Bianca handed members of the agitation committees tiny pink slips to distribute. They read:

Workers, Technicians, Employees! Let's join the workers of Milan and Genoa. Let's go down fighting, comrades! Let's strike! Let's demonstrate: Against the starvers of our children. Against the oppressors of the Italian people. For bread and freedom. Tomorrow general strike.

A woman named Fiorina was among the Resistance members whom Bianca asked to help spread details about the impending strike to her fellow workers, distributing flyers surreptitiously, hand to hand. She recalled the fearful expressions when workers read what was expected of them.

"I saw the men's faces turn pale," she said, "while this did not happen on the women's." Perhaps, she noted, this was because of their fear of being deported, like so many of the men who had already been caught in worker roundups. But Fiorina also gives credit to the women organizing the strike: "I think that if it hadn't been the women who were so stubborn on that occasion perhaps it wouldn't have succeeded."

BIANCA AND HER staffette would often work on clandestine publications from Ada Gobetti's house at Via Fabro, 6. Ada had established a system with her trusted neighbors, who would leave a birdcage in a window if the building was safe from suspicion. If a neighbor had been visited by a German officer or if known Fascist sympathizers had been seen nearby taking particular interest in the building's comings and goings, the birdcage would disappear and Ada knew to stay clear. Other safe houses had similar systems to protect members of the Resistance, and those neighbors who helped keep watch were as integral to the cause as those who risked carrying newspapers or transporting guns.

Once the flyers were written, edited, and printed, staffette would disseminate them to workers around the city. The women hid the publications in stacks of laundry and would deliver them house to house as they dropped off the washing. They were delivered as gifts in bread pans or brought to other neighborhoods by making a secret handoff on the noisy Turin streetcars as two women stood next to each other like strangers, one placing a bag on the floor for the other to pick up and carry off at the next stop.

AS PLANNED, ON March 1, workers went on strike around occupied Italy. Some factories had been warned of the strike ahead of time and sent their workers on "holiday," a few claiming electrical issues. For those whose work did not close, the workers arrived on time, and then at the appointed hour—which varied by the orders of each factory's Committee of Agitation—they simply stopped working. "Stop the machines, close the registers. However, remain at your workplaces, compassionate and disciplined," one set of instructions read. They were to stand ready "for any demonstration that is deemed necessary, ready to repel any violence from whoever comes."

And so around the country, women and men did as they were instructed, bringing the country to a grinding halt. Women on factory floors stood silently, still, while factory bosses berated them to get back to work, eventually calling in the carabinieri for mass arrests. Others fought off beatings and violence from Nazi-Fascist soldiers brought in to threaten them. Some chanted and sang. In Turin and elsewhere, work stoppages closed down entire blocks of shops, and newspapers weren't published for three days as the printers joined the strike. Others paraded out together and down the street, their demands written on placards.

What they wanted was an adjustment in wages according to the increased cost of living, with a focus on the salaries of the lowest paid; more food rations; and the payment of past promised bonuses for their increased war production. They also demanded the end of violence against families of arrested patriots, the release of all political prisoners, and that the goods they manufactured not be used to support the war. One flyer declared: IF YOU DON'T GIVE US MORE BREAD, MORE PASTA, MORE FAT, MORE SALT: WE CAN'T WORK!

The orders were signed with a frequent chant: "Not a man, nor a machine, in Germany!" This referred to the end of roundups, as well as to the recent efforts of the Nazis to dismantle and steal factory machinery.

The workers did not stand alone. Around Turin, partisans

bombed a German command center the night before the strikes, and others sabotaged communication lines and train tracks, timed to create the most disruption to slow the Fascist retribution on the strikers and organizers. Some partisans came to factories on strike, to support the largely unarmed workers in case of violence, or to help prevent it.

Still, the response was swift. Some strikers faced violence, with workers—women and men—beaten and arrested. The Nazis demanded that one worker be deported for every twenty who went on strike. A new edict was passed making the organization of strikes a crime punishable by death. Over the next week of actions, workers were arrested en masse, taken to prisons, and loaded on trains bound for Fossoli.

CHAPTER 46

CARLA

ROME
MARCH 3, 1944

In the cool of the late-winter morning, Carla was outside a prison in a large group of mostly women, including the wives, mothers, and children of the seventh and most recent Nazi roundup of men who had been pulled off the streets and jailed ahead of their departure to Germany. They were taken from a neighborhood at the edge of Saint Peter's Square—in sight of the Vatican, where the Pope resided—resulting in another seven hundred men likely bound for forced labor. The family members were here to get information, donate food or clothing, and pass messages. A number of other women—Carla and fellow gappista Rosa included—had come to show solidarity in a protest organized by the women of GAP. While the worker strikes raged in cities across the north, here there were few large factories, so the Resistance focused on supporting local issues, like the persistent abduction of Roman men. Carla had come armed with her Beretta as well as anti-Fascist leaflets addressed to the WOMEN IN ROME.

When she was safe amid the crowded center of the throng of women, Carla tossed the leaflets into the air, many women around her stuffing them into their pockets or bags to read later. The Nazi and Fascist guardsmen saw this explosion of paper and tried to infiltrate the crowd to discover its source.

This effort was stalled when the crowd of women began chanting "Te-re-sa, Te-re-sa!" as they parted to allow a very pregnant woman to make her way toward the front to deliver a package to one of the many men at the barred windows. The crowd grew silent as Teresa Gullace, with one of her five young children following close behind, broke into a run through an opening in the police barricade, her son holding on to the hem of her dress. She threw her parcel of food toward the windows, her husband and his fellow prisoners leaning down to try to catch it, but it fell short. She grabbed the package to try again when a German officer on a motorcycle pulled up. Carla was near the front of the crowd, watching the scene from a few yards away.

The women around her started shouting again, this time at the officer, demanding he leave Teresa alone. The crowd surged toward the barricade, leaning on Carla, and she had trouble catching her breath as she watched the interaction play out in front of her, her hand clasped around the gun in her pocket.

Carla watched the German grab Teresa, but the words they exchanged were lost in the cries of the crowd. Teresa freed herself and the officer grabbed her again, nearly lifting her off the ground. Teresa's little boy bent to pick up the package, and Carla heard an explosion. The Nazi had drawn his gun and shot the woman dead.

The crowd began to wail and Carla, incensed and with no thoughts as to the repercussions, pulled her gun from her pocket and pointed it at the German. She was grabbed by Fascist guardsmen who tried to disarm her, while women from the crowd attempted to pull her free. Rosa squeezed close to Carla and whispered, "Give me the gun!" As the women pulled Carla in one direction and the guards in another, she was able to release the weapon into Rosa's waiting hand as she was tossed about in a roiling ocean of furious, grieving women.

Carla was finally pulled from the crowd by the guards and forced to walk toward where Teresa's murder had taken place, past the small wailing child, who still clutched the clothes of his dead mother. One guard kicked Carla to make her walk faster.

"Let's kill her here," that guard said to the other.

"No," he responded, "at the barracks."

CHAPTER 47

TERESA

FLORENCE
MARCH 3, 1944

Teresa showed up as if prepared for a picnic, perhaps with flyers hidden in a basket, not unlike she had done when she was a teen. She was meeting the workers of the Taddei glass factory in Empoli—a small medieval town seventeen miles west of Florence—at a rendezvous in a park among the rich wooded areas that surrounded the town. The picnic was a ruse to cover the planning of the strike, with small groups of genially chatting women arriving together, carrying satchels, supposedly holding food to share. Once the workers arrived in the hidden clearing in the trees, Teresa shared orders from the central GDD as well as news from the agitation committees in the north. Then they finalized their plan and prepared to act.

The group of about a hundred workers, mostly women, descended on the center of Empoli. Like the workers across the country in the days prior, they marched and chanted, waving placards they had pulled from their bags with slogans shared among the strikers: PEACE, BREAD, LIBERTY! and NOT A MAN, NOR A MACHINE IN GERMANY!

The whispering started when they seemed to be making little impact: "Let's go to the mayor's office!"

The group marched down the main street and crowded at the office door. Their demands were straightforward: They hadn't been given their rations in months. In fact, they'd watched the Germans carting away their food.

"We just want bread and a little meat," one woman pleaded.

Then the Germans pulled up in a big truck, a machine gun pointed at the protesters, and ordered the group to disperse or they would fire. The workers wouldn't be intimidated and stood their ground. Finally, armed partisans from the hills beyond arrived and defused the situation. While they did not immediately have their demands met, the workers understood their collective power. That day, at least, there wouldn't be a massacre.

CHAPTER 48

CARLA

ROME
MARCH 3, 1944

Carla took inventory of the room the guards had locked her in. It appeared to be a break room, with a beaten concrete floor and no windows, furnished with benches and a table. There was no obvious route of escape. Carla racked her brain to come up with a believable story that might keep her out of Via Tasso, where she imagined her next stop might be. Shoving her hands in her pockets, she first found an unspent ammunition cartridge, which she was able to hide in the ashes of an unlit wooden stove. When she returned her dirty hands to her pockets to clean them on the lining, she felt something else. It was a membership card for the Honor and Combat Fascist society, with the name Marisa Musu inscribed on it—fellow gappista Rosa's real name. Rosa must have dropped it into her pocket when she grabbed the gun amid the chaos of the crowd. Carla was thankful for this gift and crafted her cover story.

When the Fascist officer came in a few minutes later, she was ready. He looked at her with surprise—a reaction that Carla took to mean that he had not expected someone so well dressed, as the roundup had taken place in a working-class neighborhood.

"They tell me that I have to question you because you were armed and tried to shoot someone," he said to Carla.

"Do I look like a person who could shoot someone?" she responded calmly. "In the confusion the soldiers were so furious that, instead of taking a subversive who was next to me, they dragged me here without hearing reason."

The officer looked dubious. "Why are you here?"

"I'm a member of the Honor and Combat group. We came to keep the women calm, to convince them to go back home, that the Party would do what it could to help."

The officer was tall, slim, and handsome, and he appeared to take notes with as much precision as he took with his uniform. He also seemed to believe Carla.

"Do you have any documents?" he asked her.

"They stole my bag with all my money and documents," she told him, now acting impatient.

"I can't release you without identification," the officer responded.

"My mother will be so upset if she hears that a woman has died here—" Carla stopped short and interrupted herself, pretending to find the card in her pocket. She handed it to him with satisfaction. A smile formed as he read it.

"Good, good, I can let you go," he responded. "I'll keep the card."

Both of them were relieved at the resolution, and Carla understood that she had to continue to play her part.

"If you allow me, I can give you the card back in person, wherever you'd like," he said.

Carla smiled and met his eyes. "Let's meet in Piazza Colonna, where the party headquarters are. Around five?"

They were interrupted by a great noise from the hall. Officers were bringing the husband of Teresa to identify her body. The officer let them pass and then led Carla to the outside gate, offering her his hand.

"See you later," he said. And she walked out the door.

The cheers of the remaining women greeted her release, but she forced herself to walk past them, lest her cover be blown. Ignoring the calls from the crowd, she continued toward Piazza Vittorio Emanuele II, where the gappisti were to rendezvous, willing herself not to look back.

CHAPTER 49

NAZIS STRIKE BACK

After the factory strikes during the first days of March, momentum grew around occupied Italy. A few days later, the women of the GDD—women like Lidia Valeriani, from a small town in Emilia-Romagna near where Anita grew up—helped to organize mass demonstrations in the countryside, too, among farmers in support of the factory workers.

Lidia's father had seen her off, telling her, "Lidia, you're doing the right thing because it's important, but you must remember that your life is going to change after this."

But she wasn't thinking about how different her life might be after the strike at noon. Rather, Lidia and her friend were finding neighbors milking their cows or feeding the pigs and reminding them: "Remember, there's a strike later! After you take the milk to the dairy, join in!"

They'd already handed out their flyers and had numerous planning meetings. Lidia wouldn't get the news for more than a day, but while she was rallying farmers and a few local factory workers, the mass factory strikes in Turin and Milan were already in full swing a few hundred miles northwest.

The group Lidia would join met in the town square and chanted. They wanted a stop to the war, the crowd yelled. They demanded that the Nazis and Fascists stop stealing their food.

A bus came up on the narrow town road, pausing as it waited for the crowd to disperse so it could pass. Lidia and a few others climbed aboard and told the passengers, "There's a strike. You can't pass!" Among them were a handful of Italian soldiers. The women demanded they get off the bus, and the soldiers did so without a fight.

The bus turned around and the soldiers gave up their weapons and started walking back the way they had come. Lidia felt powerful and proud of the work she and her comrades were doing.

IT WAS GROWING late and there was an early curfew. Lidia and her comrades knew they had to return home before they felt the wrath of the Nazis.

But it was too late. Close to home, Lidia saw the sky fill with smoke and then a German van coming from the home of a neighbor who had been at the strike. The Nazis had set the house on fire. They would later find out that rumors of arrests and violence squelched turnout in some towns, so that the Nazi-Fascists could focus their retribution on other towns where the strikes had gone well.

When Lidia returned home, she found her mother caring for her youngest siblings, bags packed nearby with valuables for easier evacuation in case their house was set on fire as well. Along with numerous neighbors, her sisters had been arrested—her father would soon be arrested as well—many of them sent to concentration camps as punishment for their involvement in the strikes.

That night, Lidia and her family who remained at home could

see the orange glow from the neighboring town of Scampate, which the Nazis had set ablaze.

"These battles had to be done, they were part of what we were fighting for," Lidia would later say. "We had to fight in order to get rid of all this."

ANNA ANSELMO WAS among the first to line up at the appointed hour of the strikes at a Fiat factory in Turin, to march to the manager's office and demand pay raises. The striking workers were mostly women, with some men joining, including an older laborer who declared, "I'm old now and have nothing to lose!"

While the group stood chanting, the Fascist officers, who claimed they were there to keep order, began beating and whipping strikers at random. Finally, Anna and other strikers realized the strength they had in numbers and marched together to the relative safety of their workshop. The factory had been recently bombed, and there were piles of debris. The women threw tiles at the Fascist officers and created a rubble barrier to stop them from entering the workshop. One woman, in a green beret, who rarely spoke but who allegedly had escaped occupied France, where her husband was imprisoned for political reasons, bloodied her fingers prying tiles off the wall. And then, when the officers retreated, the women locked the doors to their workshop and returned to work, unsure of what the fallout might be. Some women had already been taken prisoner. The older man had been beaten to death.

Later a German soldier came and spoke with the foreman. He pointed at the woman in the green beret and a few others in the room. The foreman opened his book with information about his workers and wrote for a long time.

The next day the woman with the green beret and a handful of others did not show up to work. They had been arrested in the night, their addresses given up by the foreman. Most of them would end up on a train to the Mauthausen concentration camp.

THE WORLD TOOK notice of Italy's massive mobilization of worker power. On March 4, *The New York Times* published an account of the six million general workers striking or locked out since March 1, citing their protest against the "sweeps for conscripting 'voluntary' workers for the Reich." This report also included updates of the German response from around Italy: In Milan, the Nazis turned their machine guns on a "parade of workers," killing at least twenty people. Martial law was declared, and gatherings of more than three people in public spaces were now illegal. Despite the large number of women striking, the article referred to the workers only as "men." The threatened Nazi response, the *Times* reported, would be the deportation of one million people to work in forced labor in Germany.

TWENTY THOUSAND WORKERS from factories around Tuscany had also joined the movement. While the workers marched and picketed, like in the north, the local resistance supported them during that week of strikes. In and around Florence, they sabotaged tram lines and set fire to local Fascist offices where worker cards were being gathered to collect the names of workers to be deported in retribution for the work stoppages. In one factory there was a thirty-six-hour sit-in, as workers occupied the factory, refusing to work. Elsewhere, a gappisto dressed as a Fascist infiltrated an office and set off a bomb, destroying all their paperwork with names and contact information.

These efforts might have saved some strikers from being targeted by name, but the Germans retaliated in other ways. In the days during and after the strikes, a heavy military presence in Tuscany checked documents of everyone they came across, near the cinema or along the cobbled streets or in piazzas. Newspaper propaganda said they were targeting "the lazy and idle" but it seemed to be indiscriminate. Primarily targeting men, they arrested anyone whose paperwork seemed out of order—or for no particular reason at all. More were arrested at factories once striking workers returned to work, because Nazi leadership considered the initial number of workers arrested too meager.

In one Florentine piazza, men young and old were surrounded by German and Italian Fascist soldiers and rounded up at gunpoint, while women and children cried and screamed as their loved ones were torn from their arms. These men would be sent, with only the clothes on their backs, to one of the nine empty trains waiting at Santa Maria Novella, which would soon be filled with both strikers and the merely unlucky, swept up in the arrest. On March 8, those trains left Florence with around six hundred men and women bound for Mauthausen after stopping in Verona and Fossoli. Ultimately tens of thousands of workers from around occupied Italy would be deported in retaliation for the strikes. Few would return home.

IT HAD BEEN exactly a year since Turin's worker strikes of 1943, which had shown Bianca and others that resistance was even a possibility. But the strikes of 1944—which were much broader in scope and much more dangerous considering the increasingly vindictive Germans in control—would be the largest worker strikes of Nazi-occupied areas during the war. And they would be a turning point for the Piedmont Resistance, as well as partisans in Milan and other areas with many participating strikers—and in the Nazi-Fascist fight against them. Seeing so many people—a majority of them women—of the supposedly passive working class taking a stand, the Nazi-Fascists would become more brutal. Likewise, this would be the moment that many workers—women and men—would feel they had joined the Resistance in the fight for their future and the future of their country.

CHAPTER 50

CARLA

ROME
EARLY MARCH 1944

On March 4, Carla left their hideout early, in the dark, stepping over the sleeping bodies of her comrades. Her mission that day was to bomb a fuel depot outside the Celio prison not far away.

She had hoped to place the bomb before anyone had begun their workday, but when she arrived, German soldiers were already in the process of filling and loading barrels onto a truck. She waited in the shadows of the trees lining the sidewalk above the depot as the sun started to rise. Then, as children and their parents began walking to school, she tried not to attract attention.

It was hours before the truck was finally full of heavy barrels, and Carla watched a soldier move toward the driver's seat. She knew this was her moment to act. Carla pulled the bomb from her pocket and lit the fuse, hearing the sizzle after a few anxious attempts, and then ran a few steps toward the truck. She paused and looked around. No one had noticed her. Cocking her arm, she threw the ignited bomb toward the back of the truck, where it landed among some barrels, and then she walked quickly around the corner.

Moments later she heard an enormous explosion, followed by a series of smaller explosions as the filled barrels caught fire and were blown into the air, one after another. Carla didn't allow herself to turn around until she entered the gate into their hideout, where Rosario was waiting for her, and then they watched in awe as a high column of smoke rose into the air.

It was still early but the others had already left. Carla and Rosario were expected in Piazza Vittorio Emanuele II, where they would get the news from the night before, including any reports of their comrades who had been executed. There they would learn that fellow gappisti, including Giorgio Labò, had been shot, their bodies dumped with signs of horrific torture. The bomb Carla had set off that morning, which ignited twenty-five hundred gallons of gasoline and echoed for miles, was the first since Giorgio's and Gianfranco's arrests.

Witness reports immediately after this conspicuous attack noted a blond woman in the vicinity, and the Nazis were now on the lookout.

CARLA'S COMMANDER INFORMED her that she had an appointment with a young female Resistance member who expressed interest in joining the gappisti. "She cares a lot," he had told Carla. "Talk to her and you'll see."

She made her way to their meeting place near the dramatic travertine double archway of Porta Maggiore at one of the city's eastern gates. Carla soon spotted the petite young woman, who was wearing long gloves and an immaculate dress and stockings. Since she had left Foro Traiano, Carla's accommodations had been much less comfortable. While she could look presentable with her well-made trench coat, and perhaps a visit to the hairdresser, who was a supporter—offering services to the Resistance and intel about his

Fascist customers—she felt immediately ashamed of her wrinkled clothes and ankle socks stuffed into her too-big men's shoes. Carla approached the young woman and, after sharing a greeting, the young woman asked what the gappisti did. Carla leaned in close to keep her words more private, and caught a whiff of the woman's sweet perfume.

"Look, you sleep in cellars," Carla told her. "You eat whenever you can and whatever little bit that you can. I haven't changed my shirt for two weeks. Forget hot water. You must always be on the move, avoid the same places. You must never meet any of your relatives, not even your mother; it's as if you are dead. They hunt you for twenty-four hours a day; you have to know how to use weapons; you go out at night after curfew to attack Germans and Fascists." Carla stepped back to watch her companion's reaction.

"You are crazy!" the young woman murmured, horrified. Then she turned and walked briskly away.

A FEW DAYS later, further emboldened, Rosario and others opened fire and threw bombs on a parade of Fascists who were marching along Via Tomacelli singing, "To arms, we are the Fascists, the terror of the Communists." Three Fascists were killed and several others injured in one of the gappisti's most audacious actions yet, the first in which they revealed themselves in broad daylight. The gappisti would escape easily, having honed their ability to plan successful attacks and melt into the crowd. Rome's Nazi commanders subsequently banned outdoor or public rallies or marches by the Fascist Party.

CHAPTER 51

SURGICAL STRIKES

Before dawn on March 11, U.S. airmen were meeting to receive the day's orders. One airman remembers the shock of seeing the map of their mission: "Florence! We're to bomb Florence!"

But after the surprise of the destination—a city filled with priceless architecture and art—the airman and his colleagues were next stunned by their exact targets. The seventy-eight B-26 Marauders were to drop 145 tons of explosives on the marshaling yards at the Santa Maria Novella train station, located in the middle of Florence. While they had already been hitting targets outside the city center, this was the first mission to focus on the compact ancient heart of the city.

The commander giving the briefing that early morning tried to make eye contact with as many of the young pilots as he could. "We've got to be very careful."

In addition to maps with the exact targets the men were to hit, they also had custom maps with numbered white triangles indicating historic landmarks that were not to be damaged in any way.

One pilot looked at the map and commented, "Sure got a lot of things we can't hit."

Once the Americans joined the war, the Allied airpower was unmatched by that of the Axis powers and was, over the course of the war, an element that tipped the scales in the Allies' favor. They had long been bombing factories and railways at cities across occupied territories, becoming better at hitting their targets as the war went on. But they were also criticized for the many civilian targets they hit mistakenly, with vast destruction and life lost, all considered collateral damage—in addition to other bombing mistakes, such as the destruction of the Monte Cassino Abbey.

In the first months of 1944, the Germans had been entrenched in the Gustav Line south of Rome and mired in the prolonged battle near Anzio just north of that. German reinforcements and supplies were coming from farther north, through major railway hubs like in Florence. Taking out the supply lines, the Allies decided, was essential to their success in these battles.

But precision bombing had still not been invented. To determine when to drop a bomb, there was an airman whose job it was to do a precise calculation—taking into account wind and air speeds and the aircraft's altitude, all in a matter of seconds. Clearly, this mission carried great risk—and not just to irreplaceable monuments and art. Many people lived in the city's center. To miss this narrow target would cost lives as well.

The exact targeted area was about 2,000 feet long and just 400 feet wide. The airplanes traveled at an approximate ground speed of 327 feet per second, giving them a very small window to drop their payload accurately. Some of Florence's greatest treasures, including the Duomo and the Uffizi, were a fraction of a mile from the train station—and the city's oldest basilica, which shared its name with the station, was just 426 feet away from their primary target.

With these instructions—and warnings—echoing in their ears, the bombers took off for Florence, due to arrive at ten-thirty A.M.

That morning the air raid sirens had screamed their warning across Florence. Residents made their way to nearby bomb shelters if they could. Like in most cities, there were not enough to provide everyone safety. But perhaps few were worried. Florence had little in the way of industry, and the city had made it years into the war without major damage.

And then the bombs began to drop. The ground shook with each wave of explosives, with a brief pause before the next round arrived. Those belowground wondered: Would Brunelleschi's spectacular dome still stand? Which of the ancient churches had rung their bells for the last time? Much artwork had been carefully stowed away, but many outdoor statues remained, a number of them covered in heavy cloth or wooden boxes offering scant protection.

When the sirens stopped and the people emerged, the air still heavy with dust, they found the train station and rail yards destroyed—but nothing else. Miraculously, every bomb, without exception, had hit its mark that morning. Many historians consider this the most precise bombing mission of the war.

FLORENCE WASN'T THE only city facing the terror of bombing, although it was unique in the precision with which the bombs hit their targets. The Allied air force also had Rome in its sights. Rome had been targeted more than forty times since those first explosives fell on San Lorenzo just eight months prior. While the "surgical strikes" largely missed the city's historical, artistic, and religious treasures, in addition to military and infrastructure targets, churches and residences had still been affected, and thousands of Romans had been injured or killed. For the first three weeks of March 1944, Allied forces dropped bombs almost every day, doing what they could to avoid the treasures of the Eternal City.

Despite the Germans' insistence that Rome was an open city, it was clear they were using the city's resources to support themselves in battle, and this usage had increased threefold since the Anzio landings. A *New York Times* correspondent described the "perpetually clogged" streets during curfew, with "unending waves of tanks, motorized artillery and trucks loaded with munitions which filter through the maze of streets." The Allies considered it fair game to target transportation, utilities, communication hubs, and other Nazi assets, and rebuffed the Pope's plea to cease targeting Rome. The Allied leaders suggested that the Pope use his influence to tell the Germans to stop using Rome as a safe harbor for their war efforts. Instead, the Pope looked the other way when the Nazis built command posts "practically under the shadow of the Vatican" and the Nazi-Fascists requisitioned food and other necessities, causing a crisis. This was only compounded by the increased Nazi-Fascist police presence around the city, intended to punish any illegal behavior. But the many edicts meant that a typical Roman broke the law multiple times a day just to move around the city or procure food to survive. Everyone felt threatened, and this German quest for control was tipping toward chaos.

AROUND OCCUPIED ITALY, feelings toward the would-be Allied liberators were mixed. On the one hand, the Nazi-Fascist terror was indiscriminate and unending. But many had seen the state propaganda showing Germans carefully transporting the treasures from Monte Cassino Abbey to the safety of the Vatican vaults. These images were at odds with the destruction the Allied bombing had caused, decimating this architectural treasure. Many others were personally affected by the seemingly never-ending bombing raids. One gappista questioned why the Allied landing at Anzio had gone so slowly in a place where "there were no mountains, no large rivers, where there's nothing but flatlands," asserting that the delay was strategic to keep military "casualties down, and . . . clear out the partisans."

While historians know now that the slow advance at Anzio was not purposeful, the feeling in Rome and elsewhere that spring was that the Allied forces cared little for the Italian people.

CHAPTER 52

CARLA

ROME
MARCH 1944

Nearly every day that winter, at the same hour, a platoon of German soldiers had marched through the streets of Rome, from Piazza del Popolo and down Via del Babuino, deep voices in song. "Jump, my girl, jump!" the lyrics went in German, translated once for Carla by her comrade. They described a victorious return home from war. Local residents heard the guttural chanting coming from blocks away, the city still quiet as the midday respite was nearing its end. Once the soldiers grew closer, they could also hear the crisp click of the boots on the centuries-old cobblestones. If a Roman dared look out the window, they would see a symmetrical formation of a hundred yards of Nazi soldiers, rifles on their shoulders, marching in perfect synchronicity.

Members of the Roman Resistance saw them, too. Intel had reached them that this was a new unit being trained to root out partisan bands. Since the end of February, gappisto Giovanni remembered seeing the "rotten green" of their uniforms, which reminded him of the Nazi who had taken his parents. Their presence taunted the gappisti as they began to concoct a plan.

Thus, an action came together. The soldiers of Eleventh Company traveled to shooting practice at daybreak and then back in the early afternoon, always in perfect lockstep. At first Giovanni watched with great annoyance, and then deep ire, which turned finally to curiosity. This parade occurred like clockwork, passing beneath the apartment where he was hiding, and then up a narrow residential street called Via Rasella, this turn made to avoid a tunnel that was being used for unhoused Romans.

Giovanni brought this intel to his fellow gappisti in mid-March and the group considered this an ideal target for their most audacious plan yet. They decided to attack on March 23—the date of the founding of the Fascist Party.

For the past two decades the Fascists had held great parades and rallies on March 23, with banners and music. But this year the Germans declared there would be no pomp, which would be an "unnecessary provocation." Perhaps, too, they were thinking back to the action on Via Tomacelli, and the persistence of the gappisti. They knew that the city was on edge after weeks of Allied bombings. Hunger was turning residents desperate and the Germans sensed that it would take little for this anger to boil over. They instructed the Fascist Party that any celebration had to happen indoors.

Once the plan for the bombing was in place, Carla, Rosario, and Cesare and Caterina—who had married that month—started to work on the explosive device. Carla and her network of staffette put out the request for needed elements and then met with contacts from other GAP zones or Resistance groups, or with their contacts at Romana Gas, who would provide heavy piping and even perform complicated welding on request, to help build the biggest bomb they had ever constructed for an action unlike any other.

IN MID-MARCH, CARLA and a GAP leader, whose nome di battaglia was Spartaco, were standing at the base of Via Rasella, where the narrow residential street headed uphill from Via del Traforo. Carla had initially been asked to accompany Spartaco as cover, but he had grown to value her opinion. And so they walked arm in arm and pretended to whisper lovingly in lowered voices as they discussed details. Their intel from Giovanni was that the column passed this way at midday when the area was empty and any businesses—greatly diminished anyway because of the war shortages—were closed. This was key, as the gappisti wanted to minimize the possibility of civilian casualties.

They walked together up the quiet street, their footsteps echoing off the walls of the buildings constructed tight against the trim sidewalk, not even wide enough for two people to pass. These buildings created a narrow corridor two-thirds of the way up the road, to where Via Rasella meets Via del Boccaccio.

The pair walked past this small intersection where the column would turn—there stood an apartment building with a small courtyard in front—and then up the hill. They noticed the heavy shadows from the buildings, mostly residential, with just a few quiet businesses on the ground level.

"Do you agree with Cola that Guglielmo should be trusted with the bomb?" Spartaco asked Carla as they neared the top of the rise, referring to fellow gappisti.

"No," she quickly responded. "The action against the guardhouse in Piazza Vittorio failed because of his indecision." Carla then went on to tell Spartaco about the time Guglielmo had ordered her to take his revolver perilously close to curfew, saying that as a man he was more likely to be stopped. He had left her stranded, far from home, with contraband that could have gotten her killed.

"He just shrugged when I protested," Carla said, "and then he turned around and left me there alone."

"Who do you think can replace him?" Spartaco asked her.

"Paolo," she replied, referring to Rosario by his battle name. "He is decisive and reliable. All of our actions together have been successful."

Spartaco seemed pleased with this suggestion and said, "Let's get to work, then, and wish each other good luck."

CHAPTER 53

BIANCA

PIEDMONT
MARCH 1944

In the Alpine valley the weather was bright and sunny, with clear blue skies encouraging the first violets to push their purple buds through the cold ground—a harbinger of spring. Bianca was making one of her frequent visits to La Gianna; the voyage would be long thanks to delayed trains and roadblocks, but that was mitigated by the ease she felt when she arrived at the towns near the camp. It was in this small, partisan-controlled area where she felt most free.

That day she again met an acquaintance from Turin, the historian and scholar of Judaism Emanuele Artom, whom she had known through friends at the university, and who had been named the group's political commissar. This position was one of great importance in the partisan bands; the commissar was charged with political education at the base, informing members of the reasons they were fighting, keeping morale and motivation high. Bianca had come with news and supplies as usual, and as she left, the thin young man asked if she might bring up books the next time she came.

"As a political commissar I would like to do some education among these young partisans," he told her. He seemed excited to take on this role that played to his strengths, knowing he wasn't as physically robust as others but had much information to share. Emanuele continued, "I think when it comes to rebuilding the country, they know nothing about parties, about trade unions, about democracy. We run the risk of things going back to the way they were."

Bianca quickly agreed, despite the heft and space the books would take up in her baggage for the next arduous trip. She understood the importance of political education and began setting aside books as soon as she returned home.

CHAPTER 54

TERESA

FLORENCE
MARCH 1944

On March 22, five young men were led into a crowded piazza in the Campo di Marte neighborhood on the west side of Florence. Their families and neighbors had come to hear the sentencing of this group, who had been caught in a recent roundup and were being tried for draft dodging. Within minutes, trucks of Fascist soldiers armed with machine guns and rifles arrived. They spread out around the square, throwing insults at the crowd, who jeered their presence. There were other Italian Fascist soldiers there, too, known to be less enthusiastic about their post, according to accounts, and required to be present as a warning against deserting.

Once the prisoners arrived in the center of the square, their guilty verdict was announced, reached quickly by a sham court. The young men would face the death penalty.

"Today," the Fascist thug Mario Carità said, "otherwise I will take care of it."

The families cried out in anger and disbelief, while the neighbors yelled at the Fascist soldiers. Above the din the crowd could still hear the young men's anguished cries of "Mama!" as they were tied to their chairs.

A group of soldiers, chosen from among the less ardent Fascists, were ordered to act as the firing squad against their peers. They slowly assembled as directed while fellow soldiers quieted the crowd at gunpoint. In the silence all could hear the murmuring and blessings of the priest, sent to give the young men their last rites. His hand waved over the heads of the weeping men in the shape of the cross, causing a wail to erupt from the crowd.

And then the commander counted down.

"Fire!"

After a brief volley of bullets, only two of the five young men had been hit, their chairs falling backward, one still alive and crying out in pain. Most of the firing squad had declined to fire.

Sharp orders could be heard from the Fascist officer in charge, and then the resisting soldiers were forced to walk up to the victims and fire an entire magazine into their heads, some of them now weeping as well. The crowd cried out in horror and anger as the soldiers fulfilled their orders, in fear of their own death if they refused. Some members of the crowd fainted.

Next, five coffins were brought to the scene of the massacre. The firing squad was ordered to move the bodies. But one victim was found to still be alive. Carità stepped in, seemingly disgusted.

"Cowards!" he yelled. "Why don't you kill them?" He decided to finish the job himself.

The entire city would soon hear reports of what happened in Campo di Marte. Of course, Teresa and other staffette shared the news through their network, but with so many Florentines present by design, word spread quickly without their help. The Fascists wanted this massacre to strike fear in those who dared defy their

orders. But, for many, it had quite the opposite effect. It galvanized the Resistance to keep up the fight, to free themselves from
the tyranny of the Nazi-Fascists. This barbarity also prompted
Bruno to call for an assassination of his own. And he would need
Teresa's help.

BRUNO'S REQUEST OF Teresa was seemingly simple. He asked her to
identify her former philosophy professor, Giovanni Gentile, who
was widely considered the architect of the Fascist ideology in Italy.
It was Gentile who had justified the unequal and gendered Fascist
education reform and had written multiple manifestos defining,
and in defense of, Fascism. Bruno considered him, through his decades of Fascist ideation, responsible for countless deaths. Despite
his known political views, Teresa had a friendly relationship with
the professor, and he was known to quietly help protect Jewish colleagues and, for the most part, keep explicit politics out of the classroom. But Bruno made a compelling argument that Gentile had
provided Mussolini with the philosophical justification for more
than twenty years of repressive policies that had harmed so many
and directly resulted in the war they were currently fighting. His
death would send a message, Bruno believed.

Teresa agreed to help him. The plan was to wait outside the Palazzo Serristori, where Gentile had recently moved the Italian
Academy of the Republic of Salò from its previous headquarters in
Rome. The grand three-story palazzo stood across the street from
the Arno River. Teresa and her fellow gappisti leaned against the
wall at the river's bank, waiting for Gentile to exit. The plan was
simply for Teresa to point him out to her companions. But Gentile
noticed his former student and greeted her from a distance with a

wave. Teresa was suddenly embarrassed at being seen, and broke away from the men she was with, as if the physical distance could undo the significance of that simple greeting. Now her fellow partisans could identify the stout professor, with his white hair, neatly trimmed facial hair, and round glasses. There would be no mistaking him when they decided to act.

CHAPTER 55

CARLA

ROME
MARCH 22-23, 1944

On the evening of March 22, Carla tried to get some sleep in the basement at Via Marco Aurelio, where Duilio kept watch. The guns of the continued battle at Anzio could be heard in the distance, as they had been for months. She could feel that her days in this hideout were numbered. The air reeked of burning fuses from their bomb construction, as the team had strived to discover the correct fuse length to allow enough time for escape. This was only compounded by the smell of used coal coke, which seeped through the walls from its dumping ground just outside their room. They had been working and sleeping on the cold, dirty concrete floor, with only a low table as furniture. Carla's bedding, which failed to keep her warm, smelled of mildew.

Carla tried to quiet her mind, knowing she needed her rest. But she couldn't stop thinking of the fate of all the lives that would intersect the next day. "These men were educated," she thought, "accustomed to murder; the dedication toward 'race selection' was for them a rehabilitation of society." This wasn't a belief, she decided, that inspired pity.

She remembered the larger reasons for her actions. Despite the deadly power of the bomb, Carla and her fellow gappisti—just a few ragazzi with guns in their pockets and homemade explosives—were not on equal footing with the 156 well-armed men they were targeting. "We were outside of every law, of every right, even that of piety," Carla considered. "We were 'bandits' and not patriots fighting for the freedom of the invaded homeland; we were young people whom no law protected and who anyone could have killed or handed over to the enemy to collect the ransom."

And she thought back to her friends who had been killed in action, or those who had been tortured at Via Tasso. To the many Jewish people who had been killed or detained, and even the woman she and Rosario had tried to help after the Nazis raided her shop months earlier. She recalled the bombing of San Lorenzo, and the voices of the children from the orphanage imprisoned by the collapse, which had haunted her since. "For all those who had suffered and died unjustly, who were unjustly persecuted, I have to fight for them," she thought, and she finally drifted off into a fitful sleep.

THE NEXT MORNING, March 23, Rosario donned a street sweeper's uniform and began pushing his wooden cart, laden with nearly forty pounds of explosives under a shallow pile of garbage. Even refuse was becoming increasingly hard to find in a city desperately hungry and poor. He started across the city center and toward Via Rasella. The group hadn't considered how unwieldy the heavy cart would be, particularly on cobblestones and hills, and Rosario struggled to control his heavy load.

En route he was regarded suspiciously by other street sweepers, who knew he was not meant to be there. But Rosario managed to convince them that his cart was full of black market goods, and continued on his way. He reached Via Rasella with plenty of time to set up before the soldiers would pass at midday, as they had consistently for more than a month. He took out his broom and lit a cigarette while he waited.

CARLA, TOO, HAD left the basement with time to spare that day, carrying a bulging bag with a tuft of greenery sprouting out of the top, making her package look like grocery shopping. She had a gun in her pocket and Rosario's trench coat over her other arm, to provide his cover after he planted the cart and walked away. Her first task was to deliver the bag, which actually held bombs, to another comrade, who would use them for a secondary attack planned for the Germans retreating from Rosario's attack. Carla's bombs were initially going to be used in a different action, hidden in a baby carriage that Carla would push, pretending to be a mother. The plan had been for her to ignite the bombs in the midst of a Fascist demonstration. But this action had been canceled when the Germans forbade public demonstrations. Now she was charged with delivering them to the waiting contact and then walking toward Via del Traforo, at the base of Via Rasella, and awaiting the signal.

THAT SAME AFTERNOON, the Nazi soldiers of Eleventh Company were returning from their daily rifle drill. But it was their last drill, and they left later than their normal time, and in a slightly different formation than usual. Today the noncommissioned officers marched in the front rather than the center, and all their rifles were loaded, unlike their many marches in the past weeks. Something must have felt ominous to the Germans; perhaps they were nervous about what that day's anniversary might bring.

But the gappisti knew none of this.

241

CARLA ARRIVED AT the intersection in plenty of time and tried to make herself disappear into the background. The area was deserted, except for two easily recognizable plainclothes Fascist police officers, still in charge of day-to-day safety and order in the city, and another GAP comrade who gave her a surreptitious wink as they passed each other. Her role was to wait until she saw her comrade's signal that it was time to walk to the top of Via Rasella, where she would rendezvous with Rosario after he lit the bomb.

Carla walked to the newspaper stand, which was closed for midday, and began reading the front page posted under glass. She was surprised to read that Mount Vesuvius, barely one hundred fifty miles south of Rome, had erupted, burying Allied warplanes under ash while they waited for reinforcements from as far away as New Zealand. She couldn't believe that her life had been so focused on her immediate actions in Rome that everything else, even something so extraordinary, escaped her attention. She read the entire article while watching the street behind her reflected in the glass. She had been waiting too long, she knew.

The two plainclothes officers approached her, suspicious of her movements and the fact that she was wearing a trench coat, with another over her arm, on such a warm spring day.

"Excuse me, *signorina*," one said. "Are you waiting for someone?"

Carla willed herself to release her pistol, which she had been clutching in her pocket, as she turned to the two men with a forced smile.

ROSARIO WAS AWAITING his signal at his station at Via Rasella as well. He had been there much longer than expected. Rosario would later reflect that this action wasn't as challenging as others in some regards, "but it was very, very tough from the point of view of mental endurance, because it lasted so long, it lasted so long." While he waited, he nervously smoked, using up most of his matches, not considering that he might not have enough to light the fuse.

"I'm just reading about the eruption outside of Naples. Can you believe it?" Carla said to the officers. When they didn't respond she continued, "I'm here waiting for my boyfriend who's at the officers' club in Palazzo Barberini."

She felt calm and put together. The indoor Fascist event at the officers' club was not widely known, and she was pleased that this intel from her sources helped alleviate the policemen's misgivings. Carla was making every effort to play the part on this important day. She had even had her hair styled and dyed dark brown to better blend in among her mostly dark-haired comrades after hearing that there was talk of a suspicious "blond Englishwoman" working with the Resistance.

"But why are you carrying that raincoat on such a beautiful day?" the other asked, seemingly more friendly.

"Oh, this? I cleaned it for my boyfriend and I'm returning it to him."

Behind the policemen's backs she saw her comrade Pasquale pass by. She thought he was giving her the signal to move, but she couldn't be sure.

"Excuse me, gentlemen." She turned her attention back to the officers. "What time is it?"

"Two forty-seven," one answered.

"I'm late! I must be going," she replied and hurried off.

As she walked by Pasquale, his back to her, he whispered

something that she didn't hear, but the officers were watching her rush away, so she couldn't stop.

Carla walked up Via Rasella, where she could see Rosario sweeping clumsily. He noticed her, too, and put his broom back in his cart. Her appearance was the sign for him to light his pipe.

The hill's ascent seemed steeper than when Carla had walked it with Spartaco days before. She had expected to see Guglielmo, who was providing cover, and Cola, who would remove his hat to give Rosario the signal to ignite the fuse and walk away. But neither was anywhere to be seen.

On the way up the hill, she stopped at the small garden near Palazzo Barberini where some children were playing with a ball. Her breath caught at the image of them witnessing the carnage that was about to occur.

In her most stern voice she scolded, "You can't play ball in the garden. Go home and do homework!" The boys ran off.

Carla kept walking to the gate of the palazzo and leaned against it, waiting for her comrades, praying this action would move forward, wondering at what point Rosario might join her in retreat. The Germans had always been on time.

After minutes ticked by, the undercover officers approached her again. Someone had said that she looked suspicious, they explained, did she meet up with her boyfriend yet?

"He came out and said he would be a little late," she said with an annoyed air. Carla was trying to think of how to get rid of them without compromising the mission. Just then luck shined upon her, and Carla saw a friend of her mother's walking across the street. She ran to her and embraced her, grateful for an excuse to leave the officers.

"What have you done to your hair?" the older woman asked, hugging her back, adding, "I didn't recognize you, you're so thin."

"What are you doing out here today?" Carla said in a whisper. "There's a rumor of roundups in the center—you must go home!" The woman's face turned fearful, and she hurried off. Moments later, she saw Guglielmo, and Rosario moved from her view and into position.

Then Carla heard the boots clicking in unison. She turned to look downhill and saw the column of soldiers in the square. They had been marching through the streets quietly that day, the Germans feeling as uneasy as the partisans. But as they reached the turn toward Via Rasella the lieutenant marching with them commanded, "A song!" And they began singing "Hupf, Mein Mädel."

THE STREET HAD been quiet when Rosario first arrived, but as the three-o'clock hour was turning toward four, the neighborhood began to come alive again. Midday lunch and rest time were almost over. Children were starting to come outside and play. Shops were opening up. A group of men came back to work on the street. The action would have to be called off if the soldiers did not arrive by four, or else Rosario would have no chance of getting the bomb back to the santabarbara by the five-o'clock curfew.

And then Rosario saw Cola walk into position and take off his cap—the Nazi formation was on its way.

Rosario told a group of children to run away, grabbing two and throwing them into a shop, slamming the door shut.

To the men unloading a truck he whispered a warning, "Go, get out of here, because in a minute here, with the Germans, it will be havoc." They didn't question his advice and ran off.

Rosario used one of his last matches to light the fuse and then he, too, walked briskly away.

CARLA HAD JUST reached her position at the top of Via Rasella when Rosario appeared, and she slipped the trench coat over his street cleaner's uniform. She looked up. The undercover officers had been watching from across the street and were now walking toward them. Carla took her pistol out of her pocket and turned to face the oncoming threat as a bus passed in the street between them.

DOWN THE HILL on Via del Traforo, other gappisti were stationed to attack German soldiers as they retreated from the bombing, and they, too, noticed the Romans emerging from their midday respite. A group of children—the same ones Carla had shooed out of the garden—had moved their play nearby. Concerned for them, Pasquale kicked their ball farther away. He heard them cursing him when they turned to run after it. It was then that the bomb ignited. Among the insults of the children came the roar of the explosion.

CARLA AND ROSARIO had turned toward the bus, pistols in hand, ready to confront the officers after it had passed, when the explosion happened. A violent gust of air blew up the hill, causing the bus to skid sideways onto the sidewalk, its momentum carrying it forward and past them as it continued on its way.

The policemen were no longer focused on the couple—they ran downhill toward the blast while Carla and Rosario ran in the opposite direction. After a moment the gunfire began, and they dodged shots coming from down the hill as they made their retreat, shooting into the clouds of dust as they ran.

———

THE SPOT AT which Rosario had placed the bomb was in the middle of a narrow street, with multistory row houses rising from the narrow sidewalk. At sidewalk level were a few businesses—a shoe shop, a bar—and above were apartments. The vacuum force of the bomb "created a ceiling of glass [from] all the windowpanes," which were sucked upward and then "suddenly—as if it had been suspended in mid-air—crashed down upon the German column," as Pasquale would later describe it. Shards of glass rained upon the parade of soldiers, in some cases setting off the grenades the soldiers wore around their waists. A giant crater opened in the street where the bomb was placed, bursting a water main so that a bloody river ran down the hill.

The Germans who were still standing began returning fire in all directions, not knowing where the gunfire was coming from. Many believed that residents or partisans were shooting at them from the apartments or rooftops above.

When the dust settled, the scene was gruesome. Nazi soldiers were decapitated or bleeding profusely from severed limbs. Gappisti at the bottom of the hill engaged the retreating Nazis until they ran out of ammunition, but amid the chaos the Germans couldn't focus on a clear adversary. The platoon's commander ran around screaming: "Run, you pigs!" But as a surviving soldier remembered, "We were in pieces, many already dead, and he kept calling us pigs. . . . And where on earth were we supposed to run?"

THE GERMANS FOCUSED on the residents of Via Rasella as the source of the attack. Some continued shooting upward all afternoon, others ransacking the local businesses. Word had traveled quickly to Nazi command that dozens of their newly arrived soldiers were dead, many more injured. They were bent on making someone pay. Nazi officers searched the apartments along Via Rasella, separating the men from the women and children. They tore crying babies from their fathers' arms and put teenage boys under arrest. *Who is responsible?* they wanted to know. The residents, of course, knew nothing. At least two civilians had also been killed in the bombing or resulting gunfire, with dozens more injured.

The city's top German leadership arrived, some coming from their weekly alcohol-infused luncheon. One demanded that the entire block be blown up and had even called for the German army's explosives experts. Another sought to calm him, promising a full investigation. Meanwhile, two hundred local residents were lined up on the street, fully expecting to die.

But by then the gappisti were far from the neighborhood. None of their comrades had been injured or caught—and the Nazi casualties were greater than they had anticipated. With thirty-three dead and sixty wounded, Eleventh Company had ceased to be.

CHAPTER 56

REPRISAL

Within hours of the attack on March 23, top German officers in Rome would be on a call with Adolf Hitler, who demanded a reaction to "make the world tremble." His first command was to destroy an entire Roman neighborhood including the people living there, murdering thirty or even fifty Italians for every German killed. There had not yet been an explicit reprisal in Rome for the actions of the various Resistance organizations, although there had been plenty of acts of general terror in supposed retribution for partisan actions around occupied Italy. Here the Germans preferred to keep the partisan successes quiet to hide their weaknesses from the general populace. But there was no ignoring this action. The explosion had been heard across the city; it had interrupted a Fascist celebration just as a war hero was reciting "Salute to Il Duce."

Local Nazi leadership decided that despite Hitler's demands, those to be killed would come from their prisoners who had already been sentenced to death. They decided upon the more "reasonable" number of ten Italians for every German killed and ordered their subordinates to come up with a list of the three hundred and thirty people who would die. The Vatican would be informed of this reprisal ratio by midmorning of the next day. The official response would be a concern that "a full-scale war could explode in all the streets of Rome," but little else would be done to stop these murders.

CHAPTER 57

BIANCA

TURIN
MARCH 23, 1944

Bianca, Ada, and a few other women of the GDD were meeting in a semi-bombed-out apartment, in hopes the decrepit surroundings would be a safe place to speak freely. On the agenda was the writing and printing of propaganda with a goal to convince Italian teachers not to pledge loyalty to the Republic of Salò. By the end of the meeting, the women had written a letter and copied it with the help of a handheld mimeograph machine often used for smaller printing runs. Then they addressed the envelopes to teachers around Turin, most of whom were women, using the letterhead of various publishing houses to sneak past the censors. More were stuffed into a suitcase to be hand delivered. Even in the chill of the exposed apartment, the women felt satisfied with their hours of work.

It was then that a staffetta arrived to tell them the terrifying news that Nazi-Fascists had led a surprise attack on the partisans up and down the Alpine valleys. The men of La Gianna partisan camp—including Alberto and Paolo—were nowhere to be found.

CHAPTER 58

CARLA

ROME
MARCH 24, 1944

Carla awoke early on March 24, eyes red, curled on the couch of supporters of the Resistance, who had offered up their home as a safe place for some of those involved in the action. The previous night Cesare and Caterina had gone to bed early, having a plush double bed with clean sheets all to themselves, one of their first moments of privacy since they had married. Rosario had spent hours playing chess with one of the owner's sons. Despite having had her most comfortable accommodations in more than a month, Carla had a hard time falling asleep. She kept going back over the events of the day and dreading the certain and cruel Nazi response.

Soon after curfew lifted that morning, the four gappisti returned to their basement santabarbara to eliminate every shred of evidence. The fuses, the filings, their few personal effects were all scrubbed from the room. The only thing remaining was an extra bomb from a canceled action, which they hid among the old ashes of an unused furnace. Their discussions returned to what they would do next; how they could continue to help push the Nazis from Rome.

Nothing had been broadcast on the radio—despite the entire

city having heard the explosion. And there would be no reports in the newspaper that day, either.

THAT MORNING THE Nazis' roundup of prisoners began as surreptitiously as possible. The story of the roundup lives on from the testimony of the few who witnessed it: from inside the prison with detainees looking through peepholes, or from those who broke the wicket that the German officers shut tight on their small cell window when the terror began. Outside, a daughter keeping vigil for her father at the Regina Coeli prison watched the trucks leave; a field hand saw the same trucks arrive at the caves on the outskirts of Rome not long after.

In the prison, the officers claimed they were taking the men to work detail. But as one man was being carried out on a stretcher, those who remained knew this was not true.

"Murderers!" one prisoner yelled, and the rest joined the refrain. The charge of "Murderers!" echoed in the hallway as the Nazis led or carried out dozens of prisoners, men they were sentencing to death without even the pretense of a trial.

To reach the number Hitler ordered, the Germans took those who had already been sentenced to death for partisan activity and also some who had been arrested but not yet tried, as well as detained Jewish people and many unlucky others. Witnesses in one prison claimed that there was chaos and that prisoners were chosen at random. The group included elderly men and teen boys, prisoners who had just been brought in and others who were finishing the paperwork for their release. There were still not enough to satisfy Hitler's demands, and so the Nazis also took the men and boys from the apartments along Via Rasella whom they were holding overnight under suspicion of complicity with the bombing.

Once they had their victims, Colonel Kappler later testified, they next had to find a "natural death chamber." The Nazis settled on the abandoned caves on the Ardeatine Way that had once served as catacombs, on the outskirts of Rome, a mere three miles from the city center. He would not allow any final religious rites or comforts, as prisoners are usually allowed, and also demanded that all officers take part in the slaughter.

The ancient catacombs were built into a low hillside, just beyond the walls. Here, the densely settled city quickly turned to fields and farmland. The trucks began arriving in the late afternoon, and the murders would continue until well after dark. Prisoners, with hands tied behind their backs and feet bound so they could only take short steps, were ordered into the caves in groups of five and told to kneel—eventually upon the corpses of the previous victims. A Nazi soldier would then shoot them in the head, leave the bodies in a pile, and return to get the next group of five. Priebke, the infamous torturer at Via Tasso, held the list and crossed off the men's names, one by one, as they were pulled off the truck and led into the cave. There were five men, grabbed in haste from Regina Coeli prison, whose names were not on the list.

Kappler asked, "What should I do with these five men who saw everything?" They would be killed as well, bringing the total to three hundred and thirty-five murders.

And then by eight in the evening, after the last prisoner was murdered, German engineers mined the entrances to the cave to seal the bodies behind the rubble.

AT ELEVEN-THIRTY A.M. on March 25, the state press agency issued its first and only statement:

On the afternoon of March 23, 1944, criminal elements carried
out an attack by throwing a bomb at a column of German police
officers in transit on Via Rasella. Following this ambush, 33
officers were killed and many injured. This cowardly ambush
was carried out by Communists from Badoglio. . . . The German
command is determined to stamp out the activities of these
wicked bandits. . . . The German command has ordered that,
therefore, for every German killed, ten of Badoglio Communists
will be shot. The order has been carried out.

In the days that followed, nothing more would be said on the
radio or in the newspapers about who was killed or how or where.
No one would know the fate of the missing men for weeks, even as
the cobbled-together reports from the few witnesses made their
way around the city.

WHAT HAPPENED IN the days following has been misremem-
bered and misreported, and no doubt tainted by the pain of losing Romans from all corners of the city to senseless Nazi violence.
But what is true is that there was no call for the perpetrators to
turn themselves in, in exchange for the lives of the murdered soldiers.

It is also true that the gappisti had no reason to believe that
their action would result in murders of this scale, as there had not
yet been an explicit person-for-person retribution from any of the
previous bombings or assassinations. The Nazis had been system-
atically torturing and killing anyone suspected of anti-Fascist behavior. And thus, the gappisti decided early on that they had to act
with a mindset of war; they could not consider the possible Nazi-

Fascist acts of retribution or their work would be stopped before they even began.

Yet there remains anger at the perpetrators of the Via Rasella attacks for starting the series of events that resulted in these deaths, even though the massacre was at the hands of Rome's oppressor. And even today, there are those who believe that the gappisti had to know they were provoking the Nazis when they planned such an extreme and brazen action.

THE GERMANS DIDN'T begin sending death notices until the second week of April, and never published the names of those killed in the paper, as was customary. The reason, most logically, was to prevent the families from organizing and to quell any protests. But their omission was also, surely, an attempt to cover up evidence of this obvious war crime. There would not be a neighborhood in Rome untouched by the deaths at the Ardeatine caves.

Consequently, the Germans could no longer deny the power of the Resistance. Kesselring finally acknowledged the danger the partisans were to his occupying forces. He issued instructions to his troops around occupied Italy. The Resistance was more than a nuisance, he admitted, writing: "It must be hammered into every man that every civilian may be either an agent or a saboteur, who uses the trusting nature of the German soldier to do him harm." He stressed that "every civilian of either sex" might be a "fanatical assassin."

CHAPTER 59

BIANCA

PIEDMONT
LATE MARCH 1944

The serene, almost festive rhythms of life in the mountains had come to an abrupt end. The sides of the ridges, teeming with new spring growth, now had an aura of death. Scorched areas of the mountainside could be seen from the valleys below, still smoking. Partisan vehicles, sabotaged so they couldn't be requisitioned by the Nazi-Fascists, had been sent careening into the river. The few bridges that led to camps like La Gianna were destroyed by the partisans themselves to halt the enemy's advance. But while that might have stopped the trucks and tanks, individual soldiers still waded across the river and planes flew low overhead, raining bullets on any sign of life.

Days went by with little information. Ada had taken the train into the mountains, trying to get more news, learning only that the partisans had managed to shoot down a German airplane during the battle. But what had happened after that was unknown. The camps were still vacant, the locals reported. Ada returned home to Turin late at night, having to endure the last dark hours on the train with only her tortured thoughts of the uncertain fate of her son.

Ada and Bianca kept in constant contact in the coming days,

promising to share whatever news they received, both women anxious, sleeping poorly. And then, on Wednesday, March 29—nearly a week after receiving the first news of the attacks—Ada received a note in Paolo's messy handwriting. He was safe in Meana with Alberto and two other friends. Ada contacted Bianca and they left together for the foothills.

THE STORIES PAOLO and Alberto told the women were harrowing. Days after Bianca had last been to La Gianna, the partisans had received word that the Germans were advancing and made quick plans to transport weapons and supplies into secret caves in the mountains, and sabotage what they couldn't save. But the Nazis advanced faster than anticipated and the men had to make a run for it. They had been together in a larger group, including political commissar Emanuele Artom, who they feared—correctly—had been captured. Paolo, Alberto, and a small band of partisans found themselves together on the mountain, wandering for days, unsure what direction might be safe from the encroaching Nazi army.

They ran out of food, and at one point heard the sound of a low-flying plane spitting bullets into the forest. The young men threw themselves against the trunk of a tree, Paolo later telling his mother he could feel Alberto's heart beating fast like his own while they waited for the strafing to end.

A few days later, they realized they had entered an area that was not affected by the roundups. The group split into two, with Alberto, Paolo, and two others headed to Meana, where they knew they had a safe place to rest. On the way, supportive locals gave them food and offered them cigarettes; another offered his barn for the men to sleep in. Eventually, they arrived at their destination and sent word.

And so Bianca and Ada could breathe deeply again, with the knowledge that their loved ones were safe, at least for the moment. Both felt the sentiment that Ada wrote about in her diary that night, after listening to her son's deep breathing as he slept soundly for the first time in many days: "This miracle nearness . . . seemed to me a privilege for which sooner or later I would have to atone."

CHAPTER 60

TERESA

FLORENCE
APRIL 1944

Bruno decided that the time to act was now. The Florentine Resistance would assassinate Giovanni Gentile, the "mastermind" of Fascism and Teresa's former professor, to send a message to their oppressors and occupiers. Within days the plans were made: The same gappisti who had watched Teresa identify Gentile on the street, along with others there as cover, positioned themselves at each of the avenues converging onto the entrance to Villa Montalto, the estate of a wealthy antiquarian bookseller on the outskirts of Florence where Gentile was staying.

At midday on April 15, two gappisti, their guns concealed, approached Gentile's car window as he was headed back to the villa for lunch. When he rolled it down to speak with them, the gunmen shared a look to confirm it was the professor, and then they both let out a volley of shots through the open window. They, and the three other gappisti who had been monitoring traffic, made their escape on bicycles.

This assassination, considered political rather than a direct act of war against an armed combatant, was among the few actions by the Resistance that would be debated among the ranks of the CLN for decades. Some believe that Bruno ordered this as retribution for the death of Gianfranco Mattei—who was his close friend as well as Teresa's brother. Others, including Teresa, justified this as an act of war. "We were at war and the law was also war," she would say at an inquiry decades later.

AFTER THAT ASSASSINATION, Teresa began to work more with the Florentine gappisti. They had tasks only an intrepid young woman could do.

One of Teresa's first actions was to plant a bomb near the Arno Hotel where a German commander was known to pass on his daily commute. Like their comrades in Rome, the Florentine gappisti used spies to study a target's every move, to plan an action that would minimize risk to passersby and have the best chance of success. But most important, they needed the right person to place the bomb without suspicion.

To play the part, Teresa put on makeup and her most fashionable dress—she had taken to wearing pants and would later say this was the only time she ever wore lipstick—to blend in among the women running errands around the city.

Teresa walked with purpose along the narrow streets of her city, her sack heavy with the bomb. Close to the hotel perhaps she willed herself to smile to soften her gaze as she pretended to mail a letter. Teresa turned to leave and walked toward a garbage can as if to throw out scraps. There she lit the fuse and gently placed the bomb inside. Less than a minute later the bomb detonated, mortally wounding a Fascist police chief.

THOUGH TERESA KNEW that violence was necessary, she never wanted to carry or shoot a gun. But that didn't stop her from embracing the power that could come from wielding one. Teresa would arm herself with a black fountain pen and hold it like a pistol. Using her weapon, she demanded hams from farmers to feed her fellow soldiers and intimidated Fascists during a gappisti action to requisition Salò government money from a train, to help finance the partisans. With her fellow armed comrades, she carried her weapon confidently despite not having the means to defend herself. The quest for justice was the most important thing.

CHAPTER 61

CARLA

ROME

APRIL 1944

Rome was starving. By the start of April the daily bread ration had been reduced to a hundred grams—about the weight of a deck of playing cards. At the Tosti ovens in the southeast of Rome, desperate mothers lined up early, waiting hours for their food distribution. As the day went on, the line grew longer and more agitated. A woman started yelling at the soldiers who were there to monitor them, calling them "bullies" and mocking the measly rations. One responded by pulling her out of line. The women grabbed her and succeeded in pulling her back. It was then that they realized the power in their numbers and rushed to the front of the bakery, breaking down the door, grabbing the bread and flour.

The baker cowered in the back while the women found the bags of white flour—presumably to be used to bake bread for the German and Fascist elite, since the average citizen hadn't seen white bread in months. They stole that, too.

In another neighborhood, women heard whispered intel from the Resistance of the specific time that a truck arrived at Borgo Pio—a main street in a neighborhood near the Vatican—to collect bread for the troops. Women surrounded that truck, too, overpowering the soldiers in charge. They opened the back and swarmed the bread like ants, making sure everything was evenly distributed. When a soldier finally wrestled himself free and shot into the air, the women dispersed.

And then on April 7, a group of women from neighborhoods near the Ponte dell'Industria heard there was a bakery that made white bread. They arrived in a large group, and the baker, perhaps out of charity or out of fear for his own safety, agreed to let the women take small amounts of the flour. But someone called the Germans, who arrived and surrounded the women, guns drawn. Some dropped their loot and fled along the river; others threw their hands in the air and started praying.

The Nazis rounded up ten women and led them to the middle of the bridge, made them turn away from their captors, and then shot them all dead, like "animals at a slaughterhouse," a witness would later describe. The bodies were left lying on the bridge all day, among the abandoned loaves and blood-soaked flour.

The Allied forces knew about the hunger—even if they did not know the details of these women's actions or their murder. But to help feed the Romans would aid the Germans and Fascists as well, for any supplies going into Italy risked interception. They knew that a hungry populace would make the city increasingly dangerous for the occupiers. "Rome must starve till freed," Churchill said.

THE GAPPISTO NAMED Guglielmo was also trying to feed his family. Father to three young kids and from a working-class neighborhood, he dabbled in petty theft, though few of his comrades knew that. In mid-April, the carabinieri caught Guglielmo in the act, and as soon as he was brought back to the station, he asked the police commissioner if he could offer up information on the Via Rasella bombing in an attempt at freedom.

The Fascist police quickly took him up on his offer. Thus, a deal was struck. Guglielmo would receive a million lire for each arrest made in relation to the bombing. He gave them what info he had— luckily because of the use of battle names, his knowledge kept families safe—and then agreed to resume his appointments for the next day. Their plan was for the Banda Koch, the mercenary thugs who aided the local police, to lie in wait to facilitate the arrests after Guglielmo identified members of the Resistance. The Koch gang would be allowed to have their way with the prisoners before turning them over to the Nazis for questioning.

Guglielmo's first appointment was at the frequent GAP meeting point near the Colosseum. In the shadow of the ancient amphitheater, two central GAP leaders, Spartaco—a mastermind of the Via Rasella attacks—and Cola, passed along the next directives to another member, named Raoul, who was to take a message to Duilio, the concierge at their former santabarbara. Guglielmo, sensing his opportunity to earn more money, tagged along to this former top secret hideout. Once the pair left, the Koch thugs arrested Spartaco and Cola, shoving them into a car. Raoul and Duilio were likewise arrested at the santabarbara.

Spartaco and Cola were brought to the Banda Koch's new headquarters, recently relocated to a palazzo not far from the Spanish Steps. This was surely just a first stop before Via Tasso. The Banda Koch dragged them into a room on the first floor, shoving them roughly, kicking them once they were on the floor. The mercenaries were congratulating themselves on such high-profile arrests, and Cola saw an opportunity with their good mood to rid himself of some papers.

"May I use the bathroom?" he asked. The thugs threw him into a supply room with a toilet, mocking him, perhaps, about this final comfort before the torture began. Cola scanned the dark room, looking for someplace to destroy the incriminating evidence. The only light came from a narrow, high window. His thoughts turned to escape. Cola—especially tall and thin—hoisted himself up and through the small opening, dropping into the garden beyond. He was alone. The garden wall had been destroyed—"given to the homeland" as was the euphemism—and he easily bolted to the street beyond.

Once outside the compound, he resisted the urge to run among the Romans going about their day, knowing it would only arouse suspicion, especially because he was noticeable in any crowd thanks to his stature. He knew he only had a few minutes before the Koch gang realized he had escaped and came looking for him. Cola walked away from the city center. He passed walled palazzos and tall apartment buildings, moving quickly past churches and schools. The city wall was visible now and he kept his brisk pace until he turned to a less traveled street near the closest city gate. Running now, he crossed Corso d'Italia and slipped onto Via Tevere, beyond the city center. Here, he was safe.

Over the next two days, Cola warned the entire organization about the Koch gang's hunt and Guglielmo's betrayal. Guglielmo could no longer lead the Fascists to unsuspecting Resistance members, but he knew their habits and meeting spots and took to riding around in cars with Banda Koch, trying to spot his former comrades on the street. Everyone went into hiding to wait out the danger.

Carla and Rosario knew they were now the hunted—and with Duilio arrested, even their secret cellar hideout was compromised. For Rosario's role in the Via Rasella bombing, the Nazis raised the bounty for his arrest or murder to 1.8 million lire.

CARLA

———

CARLA, ROSARIO, AND two other gappisti were soon installed in a new safe house in a wealthy neighborhood on the outskirts of Rome, aided as always by the large web of allies who might never have held a gun or placed a bomb, but were willing to offer what they could to support the Resistance. The four knew they had to stay hidden as much as possible, their risk of being recognized now too great. The house had nothing—no cooking gas, no oil, not even a crumb of food. They were instructed to stay as quiet as possible, lest neighbors grow suspicious.

It had been a few days since they had arrived and one of the gappisti had gone out in search of food. He returned with a few eggs and a small sack of flour. Carla offered to make pasta—even though their only option would be to eat it raw.

She emptied the bag on the counter and began to make a well in which to crack the eggs when she realized the flour was filled with mealworms.

"Even better!" Rosario joked. "It adds protein."

Carla kneaded the dough and then rolled it thinly while the others watched with anticipation. She was starting to cut the fettuccine when they heard a knock at the door. It was late. The four stood in place, unmoving and silent. Finally, a voice said, in perfect Italian, "It's me, Elgio! I stayed out past curfew and need to come in!"

Carla took off her shoes and tiptoed to the door. She could sense a number of people on the other side through the creaking of the floorboards and the rustling of clothes.

In a Venetian accent that Carla had often imitated as a child, she claimed she was the housekeeper. "I'm alone," she continued. "The lady of the house is not in Rome."

Another voice responded, "Open up, lady, it's the doorman. The police are here."

"I'm coming, I'm coming," she responded in her fake accent, indicating with a wave of her hand that her three comrades should make a quick escape. "Just let me put on my dressing gown."

She took a bomb that she had cleared out of Duilio's basement after his arrest—the Fascists had luckily missed its hiding place in the boiler when they searched their former hideout—and triggered it, placing it carefully at the base of the door. She hoped it would explode when the police forced their way in.

Then she followed the others to the bathroom window, where they had slid down the drainpipe to safety. As soon as she touched the ground, she heard the bomb exploding, followed by bursts of machine-gun fire—she had escaped just in time. Rosario had waited for Carla, the last to evacuate; the other two had already disappeared. It was only when she was running across the street to escape illumination from headlights on the road just outside the building that Carla realized that she wasn't wearing any shoes.

She heard yelling from the windows above—she and Rosario had been spotted. The two had no choice but to keep going.

CARLA WAS UNFAMILIAR with the Quartiere Coppedè, where they were, but Rosario knew it well. They ran from the shadow of one grand oak tree to the next, which shaded the sidewalks of the well-heeled neighborhood during the hot summer months. That spring night, they were providing another kind of protection. A car turned a corner coming toward them, zigzagging to shine its lights on one side of the street and then the other, and the two threw themselves to the ground behind a tree. The lights passed over them but didn't stop. They hadn't been spotted.

They stayed there for many minutes before getting up and heading down a side street. Rosario said he had a friend in the neighborhood who would help them. They just had to get there undetected.

Suddenly a night patrol appeared, demanding to know why they were out past curfew. They clutched at each other like lovers, Carla explaining that her mother didn't approve of their relationship.

"She even hid my shoes to keep me from leaving!" Carla exclaimed. The patrol believed their story and told them to go home. To go along with the ruse, the couple walked in different directions, Carla hopping a fence into a garden outside a nearby villa. She knew Rosario always had his hand in his pocket, clutching his revolver, and she was glad that he did not feel the need to use it.

THE PAIR WOULD spend the night at Rosario's friends' elegant villa nearby, where they were welcomed without question. They gave Carla a new pair of pink satin slippers—the only shoes Rosario's friend had in her size—and the two left early the next day to seek help from the Resistance leadership. The decision was for the two of them to separate. Rosario was sent to hide in the infectious disease ward at the hospital, where he had hidden in the days after September 8, and where the Resistance continued to have contacts. Carla would be sent to another safe house.

When they were leaving each other there was a sense that something had changed between them. They still did not know each other's real names, but they now seemed linked together in a way they were both only starting to feel. "We understood that we might never see each other again," Carla later remembered. "And suddenly this separation revealed a richness of emotions that united us, that had grown without our knowledge." Sharing a long look into each other's eyes, they parted without saying goodbye.

_____

CARLA'S NEXT SAFE house had many books and no food. She was led there by a young woman who gave her a backpack with clean clothes and a small amount of money. She was told that someone would check on her daily and bring necessities and news, but she was not to leave the apartment and should make as little noise as possible. Carla began to read, starting with _The Communist Manifesto_ by Karl Marx, a book she had heard about but could never find because it had been banned. She read it in one sitting. She would read many more books over the next few days, trying to keep her mind off her hunger when no one came with supplies. Her favorite was a collection of poetry by Rilke, signed by its Italian translator.

ON THE SIXTH day, Carla broke a rule. She went outside to a nearby bakery and bought hard biscuits made from acorn flour for herself and her new roommate, who had joined her a few days before. Her roommate had come with just enough food for one meal, which she ate quickly. Carla had been too afraid to ask her to share.

FINALLY, CARLA'S CONTACT returned. There had been a communication mix-up—she was sorry no one had come with food or updates. But now she had news. She was sending Carla to get Rosario and they would both join a partisan band east of Rome in the Prenestini Mountains. She gave Carla two hundred lire and a bag of salt for the partisans. That night, Carla feasted on biscuits and anchovies.

CHAPTER 62

CAPTURING MONTE CASSINO

At 11 o'clock about a thousand big guns from Cassino to the sea fired at approximately the same moment," recalled American general Mark Clark about the evening hour on May 11 when his soldiers assaulted the Gustav Line for the fourth—and final—time. The moon was full and bright, illuminating the Allied soldiers who army-crawled into position. The blasts from the guns split olive trees in half and shook the ground.

The Allies had tried to break through the German line at Monte Cassino three times already. The first was days before the landing at Anzio, which they had hoped would result in Nazi troops being diverted to defend the rocky mountain stronghold, allowing for those on the shore to have a relatively easy passage toward Rome. But the mountain's excellent vantage point had allowed the Germans to anticipate the Allied attack. The steep, rocky terrain leading to the top was difficult to traverse, even when not under fire and carrying a heavy pack and a weapon. The second attempt had resulted in the controversial bombing in mid-February of the beautiful Monte Cassino Abbey. A third effort to overtake Monte Cassino a month later had also been unsuccessful.

It was necessary to breach this stronghold of the Nazis' Gustav Line, about seventy-five miles southeast of Rome, if the Allies hoped to move toward the Eternal City and push northward in Italy. Every inch the Allied forces had gained in central Italy had been difficult. They had vastly underestimated the difficulties presented by the mountainous terrain and the challenging winter and early spring weather. And the Germans, with their excellent planning, had dug in well using forced labor and their own Organization Todt construction team. As the Allied forces advanced, they would be surprised at the relative comfort of the Germans' bunkers, sometimes with sleeping quarters and the ability to cook hot meals, not to mention their tactical advantages.

By this fourth attempt, the Americans, British, French, and Polish armies decided to work together to attack on four fronts, building bridges as they went to facilitate the movement of supplies to continue the assault. As a war correspondent reported the next morning, "The first blow for the freeing of Europe had fallen in the night."

The Allied forces advanced quickly once they'd broken the line, and the Germans reluctantly retreated from Monte Cassino. By May 18, the Polish forces had hoisted their flag above the ruins of the abbey and the Germans had been pushed back to their next defensive line. Finally, the Allies could turn their sights on Rome.

But this victory came at a great cost. Among those who helped breach the challenging terrain were Moroccan Goumiers, who were skilled in mountain warfare. Their efforts were essential to beating the Germans, but they terrorized the Italian population. In the aftermath of battle, survivors whispered stories of the Goumiers raping hundreds of civilian women and pillaging the houses of those who had already lost so much. But these atrocities would not be widely reported—within Italy or in official war histories—for many years.

CHAPTER 63

TERESA

FLORENCE

MAY 1944

In the first weeks of May, any sense of normal life was coming to an end in Florence—even for the Fascist sympathizers. A bombing had destroyed the stage of the Teatro Comunale and it closed down, as did a number of other forms of entertainment. And then literary magazines stopped production.

Also in May, rations were cut once again. Florentines now could only purchase 250 grams of sugar per month, 120 grams of meat per week, 1,750 grams of mixed grains per month—and no oil. The hunger that had taken over Rome was now in Florence.

AND THEN TERESA received the news that Bruno had been arrested. Foolishly, he would later admit, he responded to a request to meet someone claiming to be a partisan who needed help. It was a ruse—he was captured and taken directly to Villa Triste.

But little was known of Bruno's true involvement in the Resistance. Teresa had succeeded in keeping his secrets—only she and very few others knew that he was the mastermind of the assassination of Giovanni Gentile, or the one giving orders to the Youth Front. And Bruno's family had Fascist connections, which made his claims of innocence more plausible.

Perhaps we can strike a deal? Bruno offered. Despite his being targeted for arrest, initial questioning—which had not yet included violence—seemed to indicate that his captors didn't have much evidence against him. The atmosphere around Florence was starting to feel desperate for the occupiers as well. Now that the Allied forces had captured Monte Cassino, besides Rome there were few major impediments between the front line and Florence. Bruno could sense some of the officers were planning their retreat farther north and saw an opening for negotiation to help them in exchange for his freedom.

The Nazi-Fascists allowed Bruno's wife to visit to help sort out the details. Bruno asked her to contact his father, to see if he might be willing to offer money or food in exchange for Bruno's release. And he asked her to contact Teresa as well.

Teresa agreed to meet, perhaps at one of her and Bruno's usual spots, such as the benches outside the Santo Spirito baths. Bruno's wife's health seemed frail, her nerves shaky. She was trying to help negotiate his freedom, she told Teresa, but the Fascists kept wanting more. Bruno wanted Teresa to know he was doing okay, and to keep working. And there was another cryptic message for her, too, that Bruno's wife repeated but did not understand. The two women bade each other farewell, both anxious about the fate of their beloved Bruno.

The next evening, under cover of darkness, Teresa snuck into Bruno's empty house—his family was staying elsewhere for safety. His communication to her was a request to find sensitive documents that he had hidden and destroy them. They included reports of actions that would surely earn Bruno a death sentence, and names and locations of Resistance members around Tuscany, whose lives would also be compromised should they be found. Once she was in a safe place, Teresa made a small fire and watched them burn.

CHAPTER 64

ANITA

REGGIO EMILIA
SPRING 1944

Anita parked her bicycle outside the pharmacy and walked to the hotel behind it. The hotel was tucked among the warren of buildings in the center of town, just off the main square where the local markets were held. Inside the dark lobby she saw her contact—one of the Ferrari brothers. They greeted each other briefly and he handed her a package—it might include messages, maps, or bomb-making fuses. Perhaps that day it was small enough to fit between her breasts. Sometimes he gave her revolvers as well—those she strapped around her waist in the bathroom before she left.

The Ferrari brothers were butchers, and there were three of them. Two were connected with a detachment in the mountains, and one was with the Fascists. Anita had asked the partisan brothers soon after she met them what they would do with the third when the war was over.

"Come on," one of them had replied. "He's with the Fascists because we sent him! They were glad to take him. Now he sends out weapons for us." Sometime later Anita would be sent to meet the Fascist brother as well, who also gave her packages to deliver.

After the meeting, Anita set out for the Apennine foothills, riding her bicycle on roads she had been traveling for months, often with some kind of contraband strapped to her body or hidden among her items. As she took the main road that led out of the city, the trees growing denser and the road starting to slope uphill, she felt her pulse quicken. Up ahead was a checkpoint, she knew. Soldiers had built a barricade with scraps of wood and metal across half the road at a place where the small town's old stone buildings rose just beyond. There was barely enough room for a car to pass. She slowed at the calls by the Nazi officers to *halt*.

Anita had dressed for this mission as she often did. The weather was growing warmer, so gone were the bulky layers. She had worn her tightest skirt and a shirt that showed off her body. She stopped and smiled at the German soldiers. They smiled back. Still far enough away that they might not notice a bulge in her clothes, she stuck a leg out provocatively as she steadied her ride. The soldiers watched intently as she pretended to lower her skirt, flashing the young men a lascivious look. As she recalled, "They, stupid little fools, whistled and I passed."

CHAPTER 65

CARLA

ROME AND THE HILLS NEAR PALESTRINA
MAY 1944

Carla and Rosario left the outskirts of Rome at five A.M. They had finally reunited the day before, spending the night at a safe house where they had feasted on egg pasta—the first warm meal Carla had eaten in weeks. By the time the sun was rising in the sky they were already out of the city, walking along an abandoned train track that had been bombed during the Anzio battles. They had a backpack and one bicycle between them, which they walked down the center of the track. It was safer to travel this way, they were told, because the roads were more visible and highly patrolled from the air by the Allies, who had already done them much damage.

It was a beautiful spring morning—sunny and warm—but there were scenes of destruction all around. The road, when visible from the track between the trees, was pocked with bomb craters, often with the targets in the ditch alongside: singed military trucks and cars, some with rotting corpses still inside. The tracks themselves were destroyed in places as well, and difficult to traverse. As the pair walked, they could hear the Allied airplanes in the distance, swooping down and attacking any possible German targets.

Around noon, they heard the same sound of the incoming fighter planes that seemed impossibly close, as if the two of them were the target. The sound was deafening as the aircraft opened fire just over their heads. Carla and Rosario ran toward the only cover they could find and dove onto the tracks under the shadow of a small tree as the machine gun bullets sprayed around them. The tree was sliced in two, the branches bearing spring buds falling around them. The two clung to each other as the planes turned around to make another pass.

Carla remembers lying still amid the branches while the airplanes returned, so close to them that the leaves and dust swirled in the breeze they created. But the planes held their fire and disappeared in a bank of cirrus clouds. Carla and Rosario lay there for minutes, overcome by fear. And then they began to kiss. "It came as such a surprise," she later wrote. "We had both been so frightened and then we were both embracing, thinking that this journey might separate us forever."

BY THE END of the day Carla and Rosario had met up with the partisan band as ordered; Rosario was to take charge of organizing them for the final push toward liberation. Together, they moved into a cave in the hills near the small city of Palestrina. Like in Rome, they planned actions against Nazi and Fascist targets, and struggled to get food and stay hidden from the enemy. But much was different as well.

One of Carla's first actions was to position herself at a crossroads and wait for the inevitable group of Nazi soldiers to pass by, asking for directions to Rome. For days there had been a steady stream of what was left of small battalions from the south and east being called to the front line after losing the battle of Monte Cassino. Many took the secondary roads, knowing the danger of the air strafes on the main thoroughfares. Carla's job was to direct them the wrong way, toward where her partisan band was waiting.

The first group of about ten soldiers arrived soon after she took up her post. As directed, she sent them toward her comrades and then she scurried up the hill that flanked the road and then down the other side, her gun drawn to help with the attack. They shot three soldiers immediately, and the rest dropped their weapons and raised their arms in surrender. The soldier Carla disarmed of grenades and bullets was surprised at her presence, now with a gun, just minutes after their initial meeting.

Later that night, the dead were buried, and their cave was full of prisoners—from whom they always removed their dog tags. It was a safeguard against them escaping, for without the tags, the Germans would consider them deserters and shoot them. As Carla stared into the darkness during her shift as night watch, she reflected on the different kind of war that was happening here, beyond the city. She did not have the constant fear of wondering who was lurking around the corner, but rather she knew she would have the courage to face her enemy full in the face when the time for battle came. In Rome they would often set a bomb that killed or maimed without ever having to see its target. She felt a serenity, almost, in being able to face her adversary, even in having to deal with the bodies afterward.

OVER THE FOLLOWING weeks, their days were filled with caring for the prisoners, connecting with the other partisan bands, and taking part in various actions in the area. Sometimes they were alerted by local contacts that Germans were nearby, and planned an ambush that might provide weapons, medicine, or food. Other times they encountered Germans on the road. They were proud of the

ACHTUNG BANDITEN signs posted along the road, warning German troops that the area was dangerous—rife with partisans. But when they met Carla, a seemingly unassuming young woman, she disarmed them with her smile, before doing it with a gun.

One day a local sentry came to their cave, asking for help. A group of Germans had taken over a nearby farmhouse. As Carla and a few partisan comrades headed up the hill to the house, a German popped up from the wheat. She trained her gun on him, ready to take him prisoner, when she saw his eyes widen, focusing on something behind her. A moment later a shot was fired, and a heavy body fell next to her. A fellow partisan had shot another German who had emerged from the wheat behind her and was about to kill her. She shot the soldier she had at gunpoint, noticing his surprised expression when he realized that she was going to kill him. The decision had happened quickly—she didn't feel safe taking a prisoner, not knowing who else was also hiding around her.

Later that night, she lay awake in the cave, the distant Allied shelling now constant. She couldn't help but conjure the look on the soldier's face as she reckoned with the ease with which she killed someone. Who had the war turned her into, she wondered, and who would she be afterward should she make it out alive?

BY THE END of May the Allied bombs were getting louder as the front line neared. Standing outside their cave, Carla gazed down from the hills over the flat plains to the south, thinking that "it looked as if there was a giant plow, working the earth, but the only thing it was sowing was destruction."

Houses and roads and farmland were destroyed. Some partisans still met with Rosario and Carla, determined to do all they could to hasten the German retreat. But their numbers had dwindled. The villages around her had already suffered from previous bombings, and now many partisans returned home to help save their houses and families from this new—and hopefully last—wave of terror. Others couldn't stand the thought of falling days before freedom.

During a meeting in the field beyond the cave that they had called home for nearly a month, a mortar exploded near them, raining down ash and embers. The trees under which Carla had caught respite from the midday sun were now on fire. Metal slivers singed her skin. They could no longer meet in the open or spend any more time than necessary outside with the burning shards falling like rain from Allied bombings.

CHAPTER 66

CROSSROADS

On the misty morning of May 23, the Allied forces' big guns would finally break through at Anzio—more than four months after they first landed on Italian shores. Over the next two days both the British- and American-led forces had decisive victories south and east of Rome, advancing quickly. British general Harold Alexander had ordered his counterpart American general Mark Clark to take a right turn before Rome, toward the town of Valmontone. Capturing this strategic location would cut off Highway 6 and trap Germany's retreating soldiers, landing another serious blow to the Nazis.

On May 25, General Clark neared the crossroads with his troops, where he saw the right fork toward Valmontone and the left fork toward Rome. As his soldiers marched forward, quicker and with fewer casualties than expected, Clark had a choice, the ramifications of which could change the war. The goal had long been Rome—for psychological reasons, if not strategic—for the soldiers had fought a long and difficult winter with the Eternal City in sight. Only a weakened line of defense stood in their way, and if Clark were to turn left at the crossroads, he could claim the liberation of Rome.

But the German army could be surrounded, likely stopped from moving northward, if he turned his soldiers right instead. In a decision later described by eminent historian Carlo D'Este "as militarily stupid as it was insubordinate," General Clark sent most of his army left. He won the prize of liberating Rome but lost the opportunity to shorten the war.

CHAPTER 67

CARLA

ROME
JUNE 1944

The code words were *La neve è caduta sui monti*—"The snow has fallen on the mountains." If the Resistance—which now included anyone who was willing to defend Rome from the Nazi-Fascists in addition to the bands that had been established for months—heard this phrase broadcast on Radio London, it was their signal to emerge, ready to fight.

The code word *elefante* would be the sign that the Allies had entered Rome itself. This was shared among the resisters in the city and the hills beyond, with many ready to join the last push to rid Rome of their terrorist occupiers.

The CLN Military Council had struck an agreement with the Allied Command to allow the partisans to usher the Allied soldiers into Rome, with Rosario leading them from the hills toward the city, distributing weapons to citizen soldiers along the way. But they didn't know what to expect during this first German retreat from a major Italian city since Naples the previous autumn.

ON JUNE 3, the Allied soldiers' descent upon Rome was a day away. Italian Fascist diehards were burning papers and securing their valuables, planning their post-occupation penance in a newly free Rome. Some—like the Banda Koch—were packing up to move northward with their German allies. Yet many Nazi leaders seemed inured to their coming reckoning. That night, top German officials even took in a performance at the opera.

LIKE IN THE days before that first deadly strike on San Lorenzo eleven months before, Allied bombers dropped leaflets over the city. They littered the streets like winter flurries, and their message was reinforced by the broadcast on Allied Radio: "Rome is yours! Your job is to save the city, ours is to destroy the enemy." The Eternal City was ready for war on its ancient streets.

BUT THE ARMED insurrection would not be necessary. Under the light of the full moon, Romans who could not sleep from the noise or elation at imminent liberation might have been able to see the line of German trucks and tanks retreating back over the Tiber River. Dirty, exhausted, humiliated soldiers stared straight ahead, averting their eyes from the residents who watched with excitement as their occupiers left the city without a fight.

THE NEXT MORNING, on June 4, Carla and Rosario were now officials, wearing the red, green, and white armband of the Roman partisans, authorized by the provisional government of Rome. For the first time since the occupation began, they did not need to hide their true intentions in public, although they could not yet let down their guard entirely. Rosario was stationed at one of the city gates, monitoring the retreat amid isolated reports of looting, sabotage, and sniping. This continued throughout the next day as the partisans first assigned to lead Romans into battle were now charged with keeping the peace.

By six P.M., the streets were nearly empty, despite the June sun still shining brightly. The Roman partisans had been directed by CLN to cease combat with the enemy, to aid a peaceful retreat. A few hours earlier, the last German stragglers had trudged out of the city.

And then a single military vehicle drove through the gate and stopped. Rosario approached warily. The soldiers were wearing helmets covered in camouflage and their uniforms were coated in dust, obscuring any identifying markings. Romans crowded in doorways, staring at the men, who looked exhausted. One of them said something in a language that might have been English, "but the way they said 'yes' sounded like 'yeah'—a little too close for comfort to a German 'ja,'" Rosario later recalled. He watched as one of the soldiers took out a pack of cigarettes, tapping it upside down to release one. The camel on the pack was clear. These were Americans. The crowds began to rush from the dark of their apartments and into the streets, their voices rising in cheers.

THE NEXT DAY Carla was sent to the new offices for the anti-Fascist newspaper *L'Unità,* to help produce the first issue printed openly in more than twenty years. This time she wasn't playing the piano as the editors met secretly in the other room; she was guarding the door with a gun in hand, keeping away Fascist looters.

Carla spent more than a full day standing watch at the newspaper offices, then helping to organize the shifts of guards. It was there she ran into friends from before the war and from the start of the occupation, some bearing the marks of torture or injuries outwardly, everyone sharing a knowing look of all that they been through together—of what they had lost and what they had sacrificed. Rosario arrived later that afternoon as well, and they rejoiced at those who survived, and mourned those who had not. They learned that Spartaco and Duilio had both resisted horrendous torture and lived. GAP leader Luciano Lusana had been arrested and murdered at Via Tasso. Carla desperately wanted to see her family, but to leave this group would also mark the end of something that had changed her in ways she couldn't quite yet understand. Still, she knew it was time to go.

Carla walked toward Foro Traiano, her first time returning home in months. There had been no way to contact her family, and she knew they had no idea if she was still alive. Her friends at the newspaper office had said she looked different—one good friend from school apologized when he hugged her, thinking that he had accidently grabbed a stranger.

Walking now without fear through the streets she knew so well felt surreal after the intensity of the last eleven months. Around her there was celebration, the Nazi swastika replaced everywhere by the same beloved tricolor displayed on her armband.

As she approached her building, Carla saw her mother and brother emerge from their open door and pause, their eyes staring into space as if wondering which direction they would go. Carla wanted to see if her family would recognize her, and so walked by them a short distance and stopped, as if willing them to feel her presence. She turned and walked toward them again. Finally, her brother called out, *Carla!*

Her mother turned to her, and they ran toward each other, embracing, the physical contact of their bodies convincing them both that this reunion was not a dream. Her mother sobbed into her shoulder, before pulling away briefly, to look at her.

"You're all skin and bones, my little daughter," she said. This gave her brother the opportunity to squeeze his way between them, and the three stood on the sidewalk, clutching one another for a long time.

While Carla would be able to take a bath and sleep in a comfortable bed that night in newly liberated Rome, she knew that so many of her comrades farther north were continuing the fight. The Germans still had many miles to go before they left Italy.

PART 3

LIBERATION

CHAPTER 68

TERESA

FLORENCE
JUNE 1944

Teresa and another young Resistance fighter surveyed the task they had been charged with, hidden among the rolling hills and majestic cypresses of the Tuscan countryside. They were inside a railway underpass on the outskirts of Florence, where the Germans had stashed fourteen carts of explosives. From each end of the long train, daylight—and freedom—seemed perilously far away.

The carts were deep enough within the tunnel that they would have to be both careful and quick. Each would ignite a bomb on their side of the tunnel and then run out to safety in time to beat the ensuing vacuum of air and propulsion of heat and shrapnel. The space inside the tunnel would concentrate this power outward down the track, like a huge version of the Nazis' flamethrowers.

Teresa didn't know her partner well. He was from a local Resistance band and had been tasked with helping her because of his knowledge of the area. The pair separated from each other and headed to each end of the long train, perhaps testing their voices along the way to make certain they could hear each other when they lit their fuses simultaneously. Timing was essential.

Okay, ready, one called to the other. *Tre, due, uno.*

WORD OF ROME'S liberation had just reached Florence. Less than two hundred miles separated the two cities, and between them was little in the way of German defenses. For weeks now, anticipating their retreat, Germany's construction arm had been building a new line of fortifications. The Gothic Line stretched across the country north of Florence, along the southern edge of the Apennines, spanning most of the width of Italy save for a river-crossed corridor between Bologna and the Adriatic coast in the east. Using mostly forced labor to construct more than two thousand bunkers, observation posts, and machine-gun nests, the Nazis prepared to hold off the advancing Allied forces.

After the liberation of Rome, spirits across occupied Italy had been high, even as the Nazis became more desperate to annihilate the partisans they believed had helped the Allies push them into retreat. The Allied forces had now fully realized the benefits of working with the partisans and had shown it by air-dropping more resources—from food to arms to money—that made their way to the partisans beyond the occupied cities, with staffette bringing them to the Resistance groups in Florence as well. These drops were largely coordinated by Radio CORA and the growing number of radio operators around the north who offered detailed information on the movements of the retreating Nazis in return.

TERESA AND HER partner lit their fuses and began running down the tracks in opposite directions. Maybe Teresa heard her companion's yelp of pain and surprise as he tripped, but hadn't fully understood what that might mean as she focused on her own escape while sprinting toward safety outside the tunnel.

Teresa took cover as the detonation of the pair's bombs triggered one cart after another. During the long moments of the chain of explosions, she waited for her companion to come around to meet her as they had planned. As her breathing slowed, she was filled with a new sense of dread. She put together the sound of him hitting the tracks, his cry, his absence now. He hadn't made it out alive.

TERESA KNEW SHE was being pursued by the Germans. Perhaps they had received a tip that a young woman, seemingly in a hurry, had made her way into one of the protected courtyards of the University of Florence. How many petite and dark-haired female students were also wearing men's pants and knew the university well? She knew that she needed an alibi. Teresa ran through the halls of the palazzo that held offices and classrooms, looking for her professor Eugenio Garin, her leather soles echoing against the stone floors.

At the start of the occupation, she had been close to defending her thesis for her master's degree in philosophy. It was a goal some of her friends had made fun of her for. *What's the use?* they asked her. *What job could a woman have with such a degree?* Women weren't even allowed to teach the subject in school. But her persistence was also a symbol of hope—that things would soon be different after the war, when women might have the freedom to pursue what paths they wanted.

Finding Professor Garin in a meeting with colleagues, Teresa explained her predicament, gasping for breath. Her professor was a friend of the Mattei family, and a known Resistance ally.

"Professor," she implored, "the Germans are chasing me. Please say I'm here to discuss my thesis."

He agreed.

The professors instructed Teresa to explain her thesis, and then various members of the group asked her questions to defend her work. As Teresa spoke, German officers arrived. They were looking for a young woman who fit this student's description, they said.

"You must be mistaken," Professor Garin told them calmly. "The girl has been here the whole time."

And thus, not only did Teresa escape with her life. That day, she also earned her master's degree.

CHAPTER 69

BIANCA

PIEDMONT
SUMMER 1944

One warm day, as Bianca had many times before, she collected packages and messages from her comrades in the city and rode into the Alpine valleys to deliver them to her contacts, who often came down from their camps to meet her partway. Bianca was prepared for the danger—partisan bands held Alpine areas that Nazi-Fascists sought to infiltrate. From where the train dropped her off in the foothills, to where she was going dozens of miles into the valley by bicycle, she would be passing through territory that was being fought over, heading toward an area that had just seen warfare.

Despite the losses from the battles earlier that spring, the partisans had regrouped and taken back a growing number of towns in the mountains, like the one where Bianca's fiancé, Alberto, was stationed. As new Fascist Alpine groups became active, so did the partisans become better organized. Alberto's group had merged with other smaller bands in May. Over the next few months they took part in attacking local Nazi-Fascist garrisons, stealing arms and explosive devices, interrupting road transport, and sabotaging power lines. But these actions created the need for more resources.

With the improved weather after the spring thaw in the mountains, and then the emotional boost from Rome's liberation, Bianca had been traveling beyond Turin more and more often. She came with supplies for Alberto and his group—but she was also among those connecting the strengthening CLN leadership with the partisans. The Resistance around the Piedmont region was among the best organized in occupied Italy. They were learning from the stories of resistance and liberation in Rome and elsewhere.

But so had the enemy.

The Germans had streamed northward in their retreat, and there were now more of them in the small towns and cities of the north—angry at their losses and seeking to regain territory, willing to fight for one town at a time.

Bianca's ride into the valley took her past homes and shops built up close to the mountain roads in the towns, with miles of rugged forest between them. Despite the warm day cooled by a light breeze—the kind of weather mountain folk wait all year for—Bianca saw no one. The townspeople were hiding from the fighting, windows barred, creating a sense of a place abandoned, suspended in time. The signs of life outdoors—drying clothes or a garden nearly ready to harvest, a necessity in those times of great hunger—only increased the impression that the people had disappeared into thin air.

There was an eerie silence during Bianca's ride into the valleys, but it would occasionally be torn apart by the crackling of weapons. These areas that she had come to know well in the previous months now felt cold and unreal as she pedaled her bicycle at full attention, trying to decide which paths would be safest to avoid an unseen enemy. The dense trees of the valleys, which had long been her respite, now seemed to hide potential danger around every bend.

It was dusk when she finished her meetings. In the past she might have found a secluded place to sleep outside, curled in the nook of a tree's roots perhaps, rising at dawn to ride home once the overnight curfew had lifted and the sun could light her way. She had spent many nights under the stars, sometimes with others, sometimes alone. But Bianca had been warned of roundups nearby, had felt the heavy presence of the enemy, so she was not eager to test her luck. She would have to find a better shelter in which to spend the night.

Her memory struck upon the holiday years earlier that she spent with her family at Albergo dei Tre Re in the nearby town of Fenestrelle. She remembered the long, two-story guesthouse on one of the narrow cobblestone streets, tucked up under the base of a ridge, with a restaurant and bar on the first floor. She had heard the owners were friendly to partisans. Fenestrelle was one of the larger towns in the valley; the quaint downtown had many small hotels for those who had, in peaceful times, sought to escape the cramped city for hiking and fresh air. Looking up from its narrow main streets during the day, Alpine ridges were visible, snow dusting the peaks any time of year.

Bianca arrived at the guesthouse door after dark, feeling exposed as she stood in the doorway on the empty street. She could hear vehicles in the distance, driving down the main road between towns. It could only be soldiers out this late.

At her knock the door cracked, and wide eyes met Bianca's before it opened and a woman ushered her inside. Bianca explained her situation to the proprietors—a married couple named Lina and Mario—and she was welcomed. Bianca was not the only partisan they were housing that evening, she was told. Lina led Bianca into the darkened dining room, where in summers past there would have been groups of people still eating and drinking at this time of night. Today the chairs were tucked in tight, the wineglasses washed and hanging near the bar. Lina pulled out a chair and offered Bianca a bowl of soup, which she quickly ate.

Give me just a moment and I'll have your room ready, Lina told her and turned to go, when a sound made her stop. The same trucks Bianca had heard on the main road were now audible again and getting louder, their wheels noisy on the cobblestones, the engines reverberating against the close-built homes and hotels along the narrow lane not built for such vehicles.

Moments later there were three hard knocks on the door.

Open up, a deep male voice commanded from the other side. *My officers and I need rooms.* Lina moved quickly behind the bar and grabbed an apron, handing it to Bianca.

Get them drinks and distract them, Lina whispered to her, *so I can get the boys out.*

Bianca surveyed the bar and began lining up glasses while Lina took her time answering the door.

Welcome, gentlemen, Lina effused, as if they were friendly hikers up for a weekend jaunt instead of a large group of Fascist officers whose troops were camping nearby.

You're in luck! My summer help arrived today and can serve you all drinks while I get your rooms ready.

Nearsighted and resistant to wearing glasses, Bianca pulled bottles from the shelf and squinted at the labels, attempting to fill orders, not wanting anyone's glass to remain empty for long. The officers were jovial, happy with the flowing drink and the promise of a comfortable bed.

And then a familiar-looking Italian Fascist soldier recognized

Bianca as a fellow student from her university days just a few years prior. This now seemed like another time.

"Weren't you a fencer at the university?" he asked Bianca. Perhaps his eyes narrowed, and Bianca felt his thoughts clicking into place. Her seemingly incongruous presence, her ineptitude at serving, her advanced degree and family in the city.

"You're a partisan's girlfriend!" he deduced.

Perhaps she laughed it off and insisted she was there to work, refilling his glass to the brim. He might have continued to watch her with suspicion, but he did not push the matter any further.

Upstairs, Lina roused the sleeping partisans and secreted them to a space hidden beneath the hotel, allowing them to escape into the night. When she reemerged in the bar, Lina announced that the officers' rooms were ready. They would sleep in the still-warm beds the partisans had just vacated.

Bianca muddled through the breakfast service the next morning as well to keep up the ruse, and then helped make up the beds and clean the rooms while the officers were still watching. As soon as they lost interest and left for actions in the mountains, she grabbed her bicycle and thanked her host.

Cycling through the narrow valley, Bianca felt relief for the first time in days. With the wind blowing through the trees, if she closed her eyes for just a moment on a straightaway, she might pretend she was riding with Alberto and Primo and the others during those long and lazy summer days before the war. The road was mostly downhill, and she barely had to pedal as she whipped down the pass, making good time toward home.

And then she was pulled out of her reverie by the frightful rhythm of machine-gun fire. She was being shot at, her colorful jacket and speed making her a target. Was it Fascists who were shooting, or partisans? With bullets flying, it didn't matter their provenance.

Bianca threw herself to the ground and hid behind a low wall with her bicycle, waiting for the gunfire to cease. She would stay there a long while in the silence, too, as time elongated, questioning when it might be safe to get up again and resume her trek home.

CHAPTER 70

RADIO CORA

The Radio CORA operators had been busy for the past five months, coordinating the spying network and broadcasting the information to the Allies, changing locations often, sometimes twice daily. The team had various safe houses, all on the top floors of buildings throughout the city. Eventually, through airdrops, each space would have its own transmitter and transformer, so the bulky equipment, which filled heavy suitcases, would not have to be moved from location to location as it was in the beginning—a difficult task that had fallen to many staffette in Florence and around occupied Italy. At the scheduled time, the transmission team would open a window and drape a few yards of the antennae outside, hoping it wouldn't be noticed. A typical transmission began with a partisan trained in Morse code trying to establish a connection with their Allied counterpart. The call signal was the date of the month followed by the first letter of the day of the week. They would transmit for three minutes before listening for a response for another three minutes, repeating this about three times before being allowed to give up trying. If a connection was made, the message usually took only a few minutes to transmit, and the response was quick as well.

The intel they shared was often the deciding factor in close battles, giving precise locations for Allied air strikes, or details about troop movements, in addition to having a direct line to request specific supplies from the Allies and plan future airdrops. And the Germans knew this, dedicating more and more resources to their own radio detection teams. Those twenty minutes or so were an anxious time for the partisans, as ears strained for trucks driving by on the streets below, the sound of an engine slowing. Discovery often meant death for radio operators, preceded by torture.

The Radio CORA team, led by Enrico Bocci and Gilda Larocca, had been extremely careful. They never broadcast from their home office, where codes and maps and other sensitive information was stored, and always worked with armed guards. But by the beginning of June, they had become less vigilant. On June 6— just days after Rome was liberated—the Allies had stormed Normandy, France, in an apparent surprise to the occupying Germans. When the partisans of Radio CORA received the news, they rejoiced. Their own liberation felt tantalizingly near. Like in Rome after the Allied landing at Anzio, their excitement slipped into carelessness.

The next evening, on June 7, they were broadcasting from their home office without guards, when they were surprised by the Germans, who finally found the spying network that had cost them so dearly. They heard the sound of heavy boots stomping up the stairs just moments before a pistol shot open the locked door. One partisan had time to grab a gun and kill three of the advancing Nazis, but he would suffer a fatal wound when they fired back. The others were captured and taken to Villa Triste.

———

THE NEWS THAT partisans from Radio CORA had arrived made its way around the prisoners at Villa Triste, who whispered messages as they passed one another in the hallways. Bruno worried about what their arrest might mean for the Resistance, or what was found in the search of their home base. But this fear was quickly replaced by the terror induced by the classic Neapolitan melodies a Fascist monk, who was an associate of the Carità gang, began to play on the piano. When these songs began, perhaps the playful "Funiculì, Funiculà," about the funicular built on the slope of Mount Vesuvius in the late 1800s, the inmates knew what was coming. The incongruous songs couldn't mask the sound of the inhuman screams, which echoed down the corridors and across the courtyard, from the horrific torture their compatriots were enduring.

The members of Radio CORA were subjected to five days and nights of torture, during which none of the members broke. Then some were led to their execution. One member yelled to the cells above as he was dragged away, "Goodbye, boys! Courage!"

Gilda Larocca would be sent to Fossoli concentration camp, from which she was able to escape before being sent northward.

A FEW DAYS after the arrest of those working for Radio CORA, Bruno was released. His true role in the Resistance was never discovered. Bruno's freedom had been bought with a large shipment of canned goods and a bag of ransom money, paid as a bribe to one of his jailers. The leader of the Banda Carità intended to take his spoils and escape the imminent liberation of Florence, along with the other Nazi and Fascist leaders.

"I fooled that pig," Bruno later said with a laugh. Most of the tins he gave him were damaged and spoiled.

The day after he was released, Bruno was back working with Teresa and the Youth Front, wanting to capitalize on the desperation of the occupiers that he had witnessed at Villa Triste. But Bruno and the Resistance knew that their job wouldn't be easy—they had to start planning the final insurrection.

CHAPTER 71

ANITA

EMILIA-ROMAGNA
SUMMER 1944

They hoped for a cloudless night because that would increase the chance of success, even though it also brought more dangers. The plan was for an Allied aircraft to fly low over the intended drop zone, a place whose coordinates had been communicated via code from Radio London or from another transmitter still active after Radio CORA fell. The large cargo plane opened its bay doors. Partisans on the ground might be shining colored lights into the sky or they could have set up small fires to help direct the aircraft.

As the wooden boxes floated down by parachute toward a friendly farmer's field or a clearing in a wooded area—if the moon was bright enough to illuminate them and they had been released at the right moment and they weren't under fire—this might even be beautiful. And once they touched down, the partisans swarmed like ants at a picnic, prying off the tops of the crates and ferrying the items back into the woods. The partisans could only hope that they wouldn't be spotted by the Germans, who were watching from their new fortifications high upon the Apennine ridges. Sometimes the drops contained food and guns and clothing to supply the growing partisan army—other times the offerings were much smaller, frustratingly padded with sandbags. Why not send more supplies to fill out the additional weight? Even old uniforms would be welcome, as many of the partisans had just one outfit—and cold weather would soon be upon them.

One time that summer, a drop contained a large radio transmitter that made its way to a nearby factory. Then another staffetta brought it to Anita, who was tasked with transporting it in whatever way she could manage to the partisan bands outside Reggio Emilia.

THERE WAS NO easy flirting with this heavy luggage on her bicycle, no chance of pretending it was laundry or potatoes. So she and her friend Maria Montanari, who was now working with the Resistance as well under the nome di battaglia Mimmi, made a plan to transport the machine, riding part of the way by train.

It had only been a few weeks since the horrible news of the Florentine radio operators who had been found by the Nazis was shared by staffette across occupied Italy. Anita and her fellow staffette understood the risks of carrying and operating this cumbersome equipment. Still, this was work that had to be done. The Allies had not yet reached Florence—and Reggio Emilia lay on the other side of the newly fortified Gothic Line. While the German line held, the Resistance and the Allies would be relying on information that could only be shared using these radios.

As planned, Anita boarded the train and sat in a specific car by the window. Maria arrived with the transmitter and placed it in the baggage hold at the end of Anita's compartment and then got off the train, perhaps preparing for a shift at a local Nazi-Fascist hospital where she stole medicine and collected intel for the Resistance. They knew if train cars were searched, as they often were, the officers might inspect every package and each traveler's papers. Their hope was that this package wouldn't seem to belong to anyone in the car. Perhaps Anita looked out the window at the verdant summer greenery, feeling the breezes from the open windows cool slightly as the train chugged toward higher elevation.

As soon as it pulled to a stop at the San Polo d'Enza station, about a dozen miles into their journey, Fascist officers boarded the train. Anita sat, terrified, as they searched each passenger's luggage and under seats and in overhead compartments. But somehow, they missed the transmitter, covered as it was by newspapers. Anita felt herself relax again as the train resumed its journey toward the mountains.

At her stop in Ciano, just a few miles farther down the line, Anita got off with her package and bicycle, a clumsy affair made easier by the relative quiet on the platform. Anita parked her bicycle and hid the package nearby. The partisans had forged routes around the area, through forested areas and up into the mountains. Following ancient shepherding paths or subtly marked ways between newly camped bands in the foothills and valleys of the Apennines, these connected them to the cities and towns beyond. Anita was becoming adept at navigating these paths, and she found one that followed the Enza River uphill, toward the camp where she was meant to deliver the heavy transmitter.

Briars tore at her dress and arms until she emerged into the clearing, where the soldier on guard raised his rifle at the rustling. Anita announced herself and he lowered his gun, greeting her with a smile. Known to be funny and fiery, Anita was well-liked. She told the partisans of her mission but that there was no way she could ride her bicycle with the transmitter undetected, let alone carry it up the hill. She knew what was possible for a woman alone, in contested territory.

"Go pick up the damned radio yourselves!" she ordered the partisans, to their surprise. They would do as she said.

"I had no chance of getting through the roadblocks, and so I solved the problem that way," she later reflected with a laugh.

CHAPTER 72

TERESA

FLORENCE

JULY 1944

At the end of June, the Resistance circulated a manifesto calling for Florentines to defend their homes from Nazi-Fascist sabotage during the coming fight for liberation:

> Tuscan citizens, the war of liberation is approaching our provinces . . . each of you has the task of defending with all of your means and all of your strength your country, your home, your job, your family, your life. Everyone has a duty to be at their fighting station. Everyone must deserve freedom. Everyone must work for the insurrection and future of their homeland.

At the end of the document, the CTLN, the Tuscan arm of the national CLN government, claimed all government powers.

The Resistance leadership had a larger goal than merely surviving until liberation by the Allied forces, which was certainly coming, although the timetable was unknown. They learned this much during the nine long months it took for the Allies to reach Rome from Salerno. The Resistance wanted to prove to themselves—and to the Americans and the British, who clearly had an agenda for

Italy post war—that they fought for their own freedom, and that they were worthy and able to defend and rule their own country.

THE CITY OF Florence, with its winding streets, bifurcated by the Arno River, was not as advantageous for the Nazis to use as a storage or transportation hub as Rome had been. There were neighborhoods, especially in the city center and around the Oltrarno across the river, with winding, shadowy streets, only wide enough for the smallest German trucks. Aside from the destruction of the main train station and some infrastructure damage on the outskirts of the city, the buildings of Florence remained largely untouched by Allied bombs or German sabotage.

But that did not stop the Nazis from using central Florence to their advantage. There were wider main thoroughfares that led from some of the city's grander piazzas out of the city, and the Germans used these as they had in Rome: parking trucks in accessible piazzas unlikely to be bombed, patrolling the streets with machine guns drawn to enforce increasingly strict edicts, and requisitioning apartments around the city for their own use.

Meanwhile, the Youth Front and local gappisti planned frequent actions to wreak havoc on Nazi-Fascist communication and transport. Small acts of sabotage—like blowing up transformers or bridges—might be fixed in a day or so, but were still worth the effort since these disruptions would effectively cut direct lines between the city and elsewhere, halting actions and redirecting resources. But actions that affected the Germans usually affected the general population as well. They had no telephone communication and food was becoming scarce. And as the Allies moved northward, they were working to cut off supply channels to the Germans on all sides, which further affected the daily lives of Italians in occupied areas as well.

ON A HOT evening in early July, Nazi-Fascist officers converged on a nondescript building near the city center. With some soldiers standing out front under the massive closed windows and others stationed in the gardens behind, there would be no escape for those inside. One of them walked to the door and knocked sharply. *Come out!* They had the building surrounded.

The young men inside, including Teresa's younger brother Nino, did not want to surrender so easily. But, with a quick glance outside, they also knew there was no way past the enemy. This was the core of the Youth Front's team of saboteurs, and thanks to a tip from a neighborhood spy, they were about to be arrested and sent to Le Murate prison to await their own sham trial.

Teresa waited with Bruno and other local Resistance leadership for any scrap of information they could get about the arrests. Bruno had negotiated his own release, Teresa knew. Could Nino do the same? But Bruno's family had money and Fascist connections, and the Matteis were known anti-Fascist instigators. The Nazi-Fascists seemed not only desperate to keep their grip on Florence but also realistic about their imminent retreat.

Surprisingly, the Germans came back with a proposition. They would release the Youth Front prisoners in exchange for the immediate end of the group's sabotage and propaganda efforts.

"Please," Teresa begged Bruno in one of their meetings, perhaps sharing a table at a café, "give me a few days." To passersby, they might have seemed like lovers having an argument. Teresa no longer looked like the young girl she was barely a year before, when she'd first met Bruno. Gone were the collared dresses and neat barrettes holding her hair off her face. Her hair was wild, and her arms were brown from the long bike rides into the country. She was not afraid to speak her mind, even to this leader of the Resistance. She knew about the order for the Youth Front to destroy a communications transformer station the next day. Teresa wanted to plan Nino's escape but was afraid of immediate retribution for the strike.

She also knew that no matter Bruno's affection for her or her family, his belief had always been to never pause the larger goals of the Resistance for the benefit of individuals, no matter how beloved.

"It is not possible to change the order," Bruno said. "War is war."

THE NEXT DAY, as planned, other members of the Youth Front who were dressed as technicians evaded German detection and blew up a communications hub. Telephone lines between Kesselring, now head of the entire Mediterranean front, and his various commands around the country were silenced for a day and a half.

ON JULY 8, the Germans lowered the curfew yet again and began heavily patrolling during the evening hours. Anyone caught out after hours would be shot on sight. Meanwhile, the Fascist heavies, including Mario Carità, began their escape. The Nazi army also received their plans for retreat: Soldiers were told to destroy pasta factories, grain mills, and telephone exchanges when they moved northward in the coming weeks. Nothing would be safe in their trail of destruction.

TERESA WAS RELIEVED that there were no reports of immediate assassinations after the Youth Front strike, but then the Resistance received word that Nino and his Youth Front comrades had been sentenced to death. They only had a few days before the action would be carried out. Teresa contacted her oldest brother, Camillo, who was a well-known doctor in Florence. Together, using information from Teresa's fellow Resistance members, they made a plan.

On the eve of Nino's planned execution, Camillo snuck into Le Murate prison with other medical personnel who regularly treated prisoners. Teresa had told him where to find Nino's cell and Camillo made his way along the damp and dark hallways, the small windows letting in only slivers of moonlight, hoping no one would question the actions of a man with a red cross armband performing a medical check.

He found his little brother, perhaps raising his finger to his lips at Nino's surprise. *This won't be pleasant,* he might have told him, *but it's better than death.* Camillo gave him an injection that induced a high fever within minutes. The brothers waited together while the concoction went into effect. According to prison policy, Nino was sent to the infirmary.

The next day Teresa received word from a breathless staffetta—*The plan worked!* Nino's sentence had been delayed.

CHAPTER 73

A DESPERATE FLORENCE AWAITS

By July 22, Allied soldiers were advancing to Empoli, less than thirty miles from Florence. The Germans knew that a full retreat was imminent but did not want to leave without their consolation prizes.

Nazi officers sent their soldiers to institutions around the city, ransacking museums and universities and laboratories, apartments and hospitals and barns. More than five hundred paintings and a hundred and twenty sculptures would disappear in the looting, as well as ambulances, hearses, even the lenses out of microscopes. They stole as much food, household furniture, and livestock as they could manage, selling lame or slow animals to butchers along the way as the task of moving them became too burdensome. The city had no electricity—which meant that there was almost no running water because there was no power for the pumps.

Florence was hot and desperate. There were long lines at the few running water fountains, and no one had enough food. Few people were out at midday—hiding from not only the Nazi-Fascists but also the sun, for fear of passing out from heat or dehydration. By the last week of July, most of the Germans had left Florence, except for some top officers and around a thousand paratroopers ordered to garrison the city and keep the incoming Allied troops occupied while the rest of the Nazis retreated.

The most ardent Fascist leadership had escaped northward by that time—something most of the working-class Fascists did not have the resources to do. Before they left, Fascist leaders frothed up the remaining loyalists and recruited as many as two hundred to hide among the rooftops and stairwells of the city to act as snipers, in a final act of blind loyalty to a barbarous party. Camouflaging themselves in civilian clothes, these men were tasked with killing innocent Florentines indiscriminately, targeting not just possible partisans, but the women and children waiting in water and food lines.

Meanwhile the Resistance leadership spread the word across the city and into the surrounding countryside: Get ready for the final battle. More than twenty-five hundred partisan fighters were called back to Florence to prepare for the insurrection, with a similar number of fighters readying themselves from the city center. While they might have had the advantage in numbers against the remaining Nazi-Fascists, many of them were poorly armed, with barely enough firepower for a half hour of fighting. But the partisans had already faced nearly a year of fear and terror at the hands of the Nazi-Fascists and were not willing to passively wait for the Allied forces while their city was stolen or destroyed in their retreat. They had no playbook for insurrection—the Naples uprising was spontaneous and the transfer of power in Rome was peaceful. As they made their plans for battle, the partisans knew that Florence would surely be different.

The local Resistance leaders were preparing to call for the uprising in the last days of July. By then the Allied forces were just a few miles outside the city, and their arrival close at hand. More than half of the factories had ceased to operate after workers disassembled the machines and hid the parts to stop the Nazis from stealing them. Workers received a final distribution of food rations and some went into hiding as well, to resist the German efforts to round them up and deport them to work in Germany. Through a coordinated effort facilitated primarily by women, weapons were transported from beyond the city to the center in broad daylight, using handcarts, bicycles, and baby carriages to get through Nazi-Fascist roadblocks.

But on the afternoon of July 29, the Germans posted an announcement. Thousands of Florentines who lived along the Arno were given less than a day to move all of their possessions out of their homes. Where they would go was not the Germans' problem. For the next frantic hours before curfew, carts ferried clothes, kitchen items, and mattresses, children sometimes precariously perched atop, as people made agonizing decisions about what to take and where to go. No one would tell them the reason they had to suddenly leave. Amid this chaos, the uprising would have to wait.

CHAPTER 74

BIANCA

PIEDMONT
JULY 1944

Bianca's current print shop was in an old apartment on Via Santa Teresa, near Piazza Solferino, a large square surrounded by apartment buildings, ensuring plenty of foot traffic. The apartment's residents had fled the city, and so there Bianca and her team typed articles during the day, the Olivetti clicking and clacking, an unmistakable sound that could be heard in the hallway if one walked by quietly.

At night they printed, as was their practice, hoping the low humming and thumping of the mimeograph machine might not be noticed by the sleeping residents.

Early one morning, Bianca and her team were in the midst of production when the door opened and a woman looked in, studying their faces in confusion before closing the door and leaving. The comrades' fear of being found out was real. Seemingly every day there was news of members of the Resistance who had been arrested or killed, some for infractions of Nazi law much less egregious than this.

Bianca and her comrades silenced their printer, hid the most damning evidence of their actions, and debated what to do. Would the stranger call the carabinieri? Should they leave their precious printing press behind and make their escape? Before they could decide, the door opened again: It was the concierge who had given them access and the other woman, who they discovered was the landlady. The concierge made excuses for them—they were just young women working on a photography project, she said. But it was no use. Their presence could endanger the building, the landlady said. They would have to find a new location for their work.

After finishing their printing—a manifesto for local women to join the Resistance—Bianca and the women took their parcels of flyers out as early as the curfew would allow, hidden in satchels and amid laundry. Then they returned and moved the printing press as well.

Their call to arms read:

Women of Italy,

The struggle of the Italian people has entered an insurrectional phase and needs all the forces of the people, men and women. We women no long have to merely collect money, food, or clothing for the "Freedom Volunteers," but we must actively participate in their lives and their battles.

We have to be fighters, we have to be on the front line. The Groups for the Defense of Women and for the Assistance to Freedom Fighters have taken the initiative to organize groups of "Volunteers for Liberty" who are women who must join the detachments, the brigades, the partisan divisions, and make themselves available as . . . fighters, nurses, cyclists, couriers, informants, and for everything that women may be necessary and useful for in the battle for liberation.

. . .

And the time has come to give everything to save our homeland. Our life, our bread. There must be no hesitation. Let us demonstrate that we, too, know how to fight, that we, too, are capable of any sacrifice.

Women's Defense Groups

SOON AFTER, ON July 25, the first issue of Bianca's *Il Proletario*—"The Proletarian"—the official newspaper of the central sector of the Turin Resistance—was published. It was an undertaking more challenging than the pamphlets she'd written in the past, for the goal of the newspaper was to share news of actions and arrests, brought in from staffette, as well as from front lines beyond Italy from other illicit international sources. Bianca and her team also wanted to provide political education about the power of collective worker action. This newspaper had to speak to those who were already members of the Resistance and work to bring others into the fold. There was much to report.

CHAPTER 75

ANITA

REGGIO EMILIA
AUGUST 1944

Another mission for Anita. She was to go to Ceresola and pick up a revolver to bring back to Reggio Emilia for a local gappisto to use in an armed action in the city. Guns were so scarce that staffette were often critical in helping to transport them where they were most needed—an hours long, dangerous commute for the sake of one assassination attempt or raid, and then the staffette might bring the weapons elsewhere for another action.

Anita and her cousin Sandra went together on a trip they had made many times—taking the train a few stops outside Reggio Emilia and then walking to the small town beyond. Summers in that region were hot and humid, and the pair sought the shade of the trees when they could as they walked along the country roads, side by side. Perhaps as they had before, Sandra stood lookout while Anita checked for the gun in the usual hiding place, just off the main road, in the hollow of a tree. It was empty.

Anita was unconcerned—these things happened, she knew. And it was a lovely day for a walk. She and Sandra headed back to Reggio Emilia.

As they walked back to the train, the two women were stopped by someone who claimed to be a partisan. He looked the part—dirty olive drab pants and work shirt. He asked their names, which they gave—first and last—and then he wrote them down on a piece of paper and put them in his pocket.

What are you doing up here? the man asked them.

We're getting eggs, Anita answered, giving him their cover story.

I know your brother, he told her, sizing her up. *Are you armed?*

No! she answered truthfully. Did she trust him? She desperately wanted news of her brother who was in a partisan band nearby but she didn't want to compromise her safety or his.

Were you transporting weapons? he asked. The young women denied this. One could never be too careful, plus, they had nothing on them.

Take this gun, he told them, brandishing it in broad daylight and giving them directions for the drop-off.

Anita took it and hid it among her things without saying a word and, before she could think twice, whispered, *Tell my brother I am well.*

ANOTHER MISSION A few days later was a typical one. At one of her meetings in Reggio Emilia she was given a note. It was folded up very small, written in code in tiny handwriting. She was to take this to the mountains when she went next.

THE NEXT MORNING, when the Fascist officers came to Via Dalmazia, her mother happened to be home. This was unusual, as she had been sent away from the city because of her nerves. By the summer of 1944 she had taken to fainting at the sound of bombers overhead, conjuring images of the many casualties from the Reggiane factory bombing, now well more than a year earlier. When they heard the sharp knock, it was Anita who opened the door.

Are you Anita Malavasi? an officer asked. She nodded.

You need to come with us, he commanded.

Behind Anita, her mother began to cry softly. *Why are they here? What happened?* she asked in a shaking voice.

Okay, Anita said to the officers, *but may I get dressed first?* The officer nodded and Anita closed the door.

Inside she ran from room to room, looking for a window she could escape out of. But the Fascists had her home surrounded. She put the note she received the previous day into her mouth and chewed, willing herself to swallow the pulpy paper. She knew she—and most likely her room—would be searched. She hoped her mother's surprise and fearful emoting might save the house from being ransacked.

While she changed, she whispered to her mother, *Look, there is ammunition and medicine in my room. Go find them and hide them in the cellar.* Her mother, to Anita's surprise, hurried to do as she was told. Anita slowly strode to the door to speak with the officers to give her mother time.

I'm sorry, sir, I am just so surprised to see you, she said with honey dripping from her voice. *I can't imagine how I can be of help.*

AT THE POLICE station, Anita found herself with Sandra, locked in a windowless interrogation room as the Fascists began their questioning. "Who sent you? What were your orders?" the officers demanded. "What were you doing in Ceresola?"

"I was only going to get eggs!" Anita insisted. The officers tried yelling and intimidation, but Anita and Sandra kept to their cover story. The women hadn't yet been physically harmed, which Anita took to mean that perhaps the Fascists' evidence against them wasn't solid. She was trying to figure out why they had been brought in, in hopes of finding a clever way to freedom.

"We have a witness," one officer finally claimed. "Bring him in!"

Perhaps Anita and her cousin exchanged a glance, fearful of who might have been arrested. When the door opened again, in strode the man who had asked their names a week earlier. He was dressed nicely, without evidence of any torture. Was he a partisan as he had claimed, but had sold out his comrades to escape torture? Or was he working with the Fascist police to root out the Resistance? In many ways it didn't matter.

"I just lost the light of reason!" Anita later said, calling the man names and questioning his logic.

"You're a scoundrel!" she accused him, finally admitting to carrying the gun the man had given her. "How could I say no to you? You had a gun, and I only had a basket in my hands!"

Her emphatic self-defense disarmed the interrogator. The officers were at an impasse. Had they caught two partisans, or had their man set up innocent women? Perhaps they conferred privately before agreeing to release Anita and Sandra.

The women were told to sign the minutes from the interrogation and then were allowed to leave but instructed to return the next morning for further questioning. Anita knew not to let her guard down—sometimes they allowed people to go home so they could follow them. Whom did those they released, unnerved and terrified and briefly elated at their luck, go to once they were free? Anita had been hearing the stories of more and more staffette being caught, and had known she needed to take more care even as she was asked to do increasingly difficult jobs. It was finally dawning on the Nazis and Fascists how many women were active participants in the Resistance.

Anita asked if she could go to the house of her aunt, who she said was the secretary for a local Fascist organization, and the Fascist officers agreed. Once she was released, she and her cousin did as they had said—hoping that the officers surely following her didn't know that her aunt was actually a partisan who lived in the Fascist secretary's house. Once behind closed doors, she asked her aunt what to do.

"Are you joking? Tomorrow, they'll torture you," Anita was told. "Don't think that they won't come to get you. After what happened, you must run away."

The only stop Anita would make before she left was home, to gather what supplies she could and say goodbye to her parents. She would not even contact her longtime fiancé, whom she had never told about her anti-Fascist work, knowing he would have disapproved. They had spent little time together recently because of his factory job and the difficulties of travel during evening hours. Privately, Anita had welcomed this respite from what felt like the inevitable trajectory of marriage and motherhood after the war.

At home, Anita told her father what happened and that she had to escape to the hills. His first reaction was shock. "You have children, and you think you know them, but you don't know what they do," he said, and began packing a bag for her with her brother's clothes and a blanket, and whatever food scraps they could spare. His eyes were wet as he moved around the house finding supplies for his eldest daughter. Anita later said that her father was not a particularly brave man, but he was a good person who believed in justice. Sending her to the mountains as prepared as he could was perhaps one of the bravest acts of his life.

Her father handed her the sack and embraced her. "I never

thought you would be entangled in this reality because you are a woman, but you have to go," he told her. "You made the right choice. I have a lot of respect for you. If you can, fight and defend yourself. Just remember that your father thinks a lot of you." Releasing her, he walked Anita to door. And then she set off under darkness to join the partisans.

CHAPTER 76

FALLING BRIDGES

FLORENCE
AUGUST 1944

When August dawned, there were thousands of refugees from the Oltrarno living in the Palazzo Pitti. Inside the luxurious castle guarding the Boboli Gardens, families created beds using their blankets and clothes in the grand ballroom and vast halls, making themselves at home in the palazzo where generations of royalty—and even Hitler, during his last ostentatious visit to Florence—had once slept.

ON AUGUST 2, a new German edict: Florentines were to stay inside, lock their doors, bar their windows—and never come out, upon threat of being shot on sight.

And then, sometime after ten P.M. on the evening of August 3, the city was shaken by the first of the explosions.

OVER THE FIRST days of August, the Germans were focused on destroying the main bridges that spanned the Arno, connecting the north and south sides of Florence. To the north were the Duomo, the Palazzo Medici Riccardi, and the Uffizi—some of the city's most precious architectural and artistic treasures. To the south were the Palazzo Pitti, once the Grand Ducal residence, and its accompanying Boboli Gardens, as well as the popular Piazza Santo Spirito. Here, too, was the new secret headquarters of the Resistance fighters who were coming down from the hills beyond, readying themselves for the insurrection.

The bridges, hundreds of years old and built with huge boulders, were found to be challenging to destroy. The initial rounds of dynamite—placed by German soldiers who then became targets for partisan snipers—couldn't complete the job, so land mines were brought in. First the Ponte alle Grazie was destroyed, then the Ponte Santa Trinita. Dust filled the stagnant summer air as these ancient structures, over which generations of Florentines had traveled, were turned to rubble. Finally, only the Ponte Vecchio was still standing as the remaining link between the two sides of the city.

Before they retreated, the Germans had to decide what to do with the Ponte Vecchio, arguably one of the most recognizable sites in Florence, lined with multistory buildings and providing only a narrow roadway for pedestrians, carts, and small vehicles. After watching the other bridges fall, Cardinal Della Costa, the same church official who had mourned Hitler's visit in 1938, could guess the Nazis' next target and decided to work quickly. He contacted Gerhard Wolf, the German consul and a known Italian sympathizer, to make the case to save the Ponte Vecchio: The bridge was too narrow for tanks, he rightly argued, and, judging by the effort it took to destroy the other bridges, the buildings that lined the Ponte Vecchio would prove even more of a challenge. Plus, what would be left would be such a huge pile of debris that it could serve as its own pathway. *Be the hero—save this piece of Florentine history!* the cardinal implored.

The Nazis were convinced—but the solution they came up with was painful. Their demolition team set about mining the now-empty apartments on either side of the bridge to create a rubble barrier to make crossing the Arno nearly impossible.

Later that night, from their makeshift beds in the grand ballroom or along the wide halls of the Palazzo Pitti, the refugees heard a series of deafening booms, dust from the crushed rock seeping through cracks in the closed shutters. Their fears would be confirmed the following morning—the Germans had blown up the massive buildings spanning a city block on either side of the Ponte Vecchio. To further dissuade anyone from using the last remaining passage to the north side of Florence, they mined the two-story-high debris pile as well. Only then did the German soldiers retreat to the north of the city.

The Resistance was now in control of the Oltrarno. Their first order of business: Find a way across to the other side of the city, where most of the CTLN leadership and many other Resistance members resided. The answer was the Vasari Corridor, the same passageway at the top of the Ponte Vecchio that Hitler and Mussolini had traversed six years earlier, waving to cheering crowds below. The Vasari Corridor had been closed since the beginning of the war, and while the corridor was seemingly intact, the question was how to reach it.

THE SAME DAY—August 4—the first advance Allied officers reached the south side of Florence, although the main army was still many days away. But the Oltrarno was far from a safe haven. While the Germans had abandoned it, they'd left behind dozens of Fascist snipers on this side of the river as well. The Germans also placed men high upon the hills, and they began firing large mortars toward both sides of the city at random times and targets, terrorizing residents and unleashing more damage and death. One landed in the baptistry of the Duomo and caused some of the only damage of the war to Florence's architectural treasures, which otherwise remained intact. One of the most significant casualties from the mortars was the young partisan leader Aligi Barducci, who was struck by a mortar that landed in Santo Spirito during the planning of the insurrection. In the coming days, the partisans would rename a division of soldiers in his honor.

The Oltrarno became the logical base for the Resistance to coordinate with the incoming Allies. The Allied forces said they would make plans to establish temporary bridges upstream and downstream from the city, and continue to pressure the Germans from beyond the city center. But these efforts still seemed days from starting. Most of Florence—including many members of the Resistance army and their leaders—were on the occupied side of the river, alone. Residents were still ordered to stay inside, essentially imprisoned in their homes. The Resistance understood they needed to fight for their city now.

CHAPTER 77

ANITA

EMILIA-ROMAGNA
AUGUST 1944

Anita and Sandra knew where the partisans were and they knew how to get to them. But because of the curfew, they were rarely out at night. Gone was the relative safety they had enjoyed walking through the streets as women. They were now *bandite*—and could be shot on sight. Once they reached the deserted roads beyond Reggio Emilia, where they would have plenty of time to hide if they heard or saw the lights of an oncoming vehicle, the women could breathe a little easier. And so they walked toward the Apennine Mountains, the only sounds the crunch of their shoes on gravel and the rustling of the wind in the trees.

"FROM THIS MOMENT you're not men or women anymore, you're partisans. You'll do what others do, share things with us and sleep in the same rooms," the commander told Anita and Sandra when they had reached the camp. They were among the first women to seek shelter there, and though they had been known collaborators for months now, their presence was still met with skepticism by some.

That first night, Anita slept between a partisan from her hometown and a deserting carabiniere from Sardinia, who had refused to follow the Germans' orders. Side by side, sharing the too-few woolen blankets that would protect against the chill of the mountain air, they whispered all night long. The novelty was astounding to Anita. Coming from a traditional farming family, she had never even been alone with her fiancé after dark. And now she was sleeping shoulder to shoulder with men.

The next day, her education as a soldier began. First, she had to learn to use a weapon, assemble and disassemble it, clean it, fire it. She practiced this for hours until she was proficient. And then she was assigned guard duty.

On her first night shift, Anita was partnered with a partisan named Saetta. As they sat in the cool of the evening, she found herself jumping at every noise.

"*O dio!* What's that noise? It's the Germans!" she whispered, raising her gun to an unseen enemy in the dark of the forest.

"It's just the wind in the leaves," Saetta assured her.

Well before her shift was up, Saetta sent Anita to bed. "Just go to bed, I'll do it myself. Otherwise, you'll get us all killed!"

ANITA'S PARTISAN BAND lived in an abandoned stable at that time, sleeping on a few inches of straw. When there was food, it was shared, with everyone equally charged with cooking, cleaning, and guard duty. She was assigned to a battalion, and when her group went out, she had the role typical of the few women among them: relay.

A woman, even in the mountains, aroused much less suspicion than a man when walking alone. While a number of female partisans had been arrested, it was still difficult for many men to conceive that a woman could be a soldier, and so they could travel with relative ease. A relay, sometimes also called advance guard or *battistrada*—outrider, would be the one who went out alone, in search of enemy encampments, spies, or intelligence.

"We acted as explorers for a bit," Anita described, and then they returned to their battalion and let the others know whether it was safe to go out. When her battalion had an action planned, she scouted out ahead and then came back to guide them. The safety of dozens depended on her, and she walked with a gun ready to use, not strapped beneath her clothes, inaccessible.

CHAPTER 78

TERESA

FLORENCE
AUGUST 1944

Teresa darted into an empty piazza, hoping to draw fire. Her comrades were in the shadows, ready with guns, looking for the location of the sniper. Shots rang out as she ran to the cover of one of Florence's narrow streets, slicing between the palazzos on the far side of the square. Fellow partisans swarmed the building from where the gunfire had originated and broke down the door. A long minute later, sounds of a brief firefight echoed across the piazza, and then silence. One more threat had been eliminated, but many still remained. This dead body, like the others, would have to be buried in a garden or stripped bare and thrown into the Arno if they were close enough to its banks. Despite these attempts at disposal, the stench of death hung over the hot city, the air still heavy with the dust from the destruction of the buildings and bridges.

ON AUGUST 6, in still-occupied Florence, the Germans had allowed women and children to finally leave their houses for a few hours in search of food and water. Nurses and doctors with appropriate papers and red cross armbands were also permitted. Staffette posing as nurses used this opportunity to connect the Resistance once again, transporting messages among the partisans, hiding—impatient, hungry—in basements and behind closed windows in stuffy rooms. Among them was Teresa's brother Nino, who had been unceremoniously freed with fellow Youth Front members as most of the Germans retreated. Other imprisoned partisans were not so lucky—their bodies would be found heaped in rushed mass executions in the city or beyond.

Still the remaining German patrols continued to terrorize the families waiting in line for necessities, using any pretext to search houses, ransacking them and stealing what valuables might be left. Snipers continued to shoot and kill indiscriminately from rooftops. Often the bodies of the murdered had to be left in the street for fear of further attack.

IT WAS ESSENTIAL, the partisan command on the Oltrarno knew, to establish contact with the city center. So, evading the mines on each side of the Ponte Vecchio, a Resistance member was able to run a telephone wire through the Vasari Corridor, finally making this crucial connection. If that brave partisan had been foolish enough to open the same window at the bridge's apex and look outward as those architects of war had six years before, the view would have been very different. The bridges in either direction were piles of rubble—reduced to dust and crumbled stone in a few moments' time after serving centuries of Florentines. Most of the apartment buildings that once lined each side of the Arno had also been destroyed to block access to the river in case anyone was foolish enough to use the debris as stepping stones to cross it. What they would not see was the presence of any Allied forces, who seemed in no hurry to fully liberate the city center that the Nazi-Fascist leadership themselves had already largely abandoned.

THE GERMANS WERE retreating from the center of the city, although they did not plan to go far. In their wake they left leaflets scattered in the streets:

We'll be back! Soon England will not tolerate the effects of the new German weapons. . . . In a short time we will launch the offensive and it will be in that moment that the Italians faithful to their homeland will be compensated. In that moment the traitors will have the response they deserve. Observe them and remember their names and their betrayal. . . . God will punish traitors and reward the faithful and steadfast.

It was clear that the Nazis would not retreat in the orderly, peaceful way they had left Rome. To bolster the population, one of the local clandestine newspapers printed an issue that members of the Resistance also plastered on walls around the city. "Let's attack our killers! With no bread, gas, electricity, water, or medicines; between the explosion of mines, the rumble of mortars, the hissing of bullets—what more could frighten us?"

The staffette, Teresa among them, helped to spread the word: The battle would start on August 11, at the sound of the bell.

ON AUGUST 11 at six forty-five A.M., the "people's bell," known as the Martinella—the bell that medieval fighters would ring as a call to battle—began its alarm in the Palazzo Vecchio, from its iconic tower, which rose more than three hundred feet above the city. The partisans emerged with weapons drawn, ready to fight the rearguard of Germans and defend their city from further sabotage.

The battle was meticulously organized despite the challenges of the urban landscape, using intel received from staffette of where the Nazi-Fascists remained. Partisan bands were assigned to areas of the city that had not been cleared of snipers or patrols, and were tasked with pushing out the enemy, building by building. Teresa was first assigned near the Giardino della Gherardesca—a private garden once owned by the Medici family with flowering bushes, towering trees, and a bathhouse. As the partisans fought the occupiers, shooting through windows and in the narrow streets, Teresa dragged the dead bodies into the garden and buried them, until finally they pushed the Nazi-Fascists beyond the ring road that encircled inner Florence.

As they moved on, Teresa then became the advance guard for a band named after her fallen brother, Gianfranco, leading them through the streets. She would race from her soldiers to the top commanders, zigzagging between doorways to receive orders of where to move. Then she would run back and lead her team through the city. When they neared their target, a shot would be fired and the fighting would begin. Without a gun, she attended to the injured, gave orders, relayed information, and acted as lookout.

Through these scattered battles around Florence, there were many staffette who led groups of soldiers and shared messages and intel about German locations and firepower to and from the Resistance commanders and among the formations, crouching behind piles of rubble as they waited for a pause in the shooting to move forward once again. Some had guns to attack the enemy and defend themselves, while others wore red cross armbands, hoping they wouldn't be targeted while they tended the injured.

In some cases, there were heavy losses as formations found themselves cornered in an area still held by remaining Germans. One formation faced heavy attacks early in the fighting as they sought to save a railway viaduct from German sabotage. They suffered the loss of two leaders, but emerged victorious. There were similar stories from around the city that staffette shared with the central command. Those leaders, Bruno among them, would confer with their comrades on the Oltrarno side by telephone. Together they made battle plans and sent the staffette out again to deliver the orders. Groups were sent to occupy factories to keep them intact, or clear Germans from various neighborhoods as they continued their retreat.

Because of the manner in which the Germans retreated, however, some bands of partisans were cut off from one another as they pushed toward the infrastructure on the outskirts of the city that they were charged with protecting. These bands were only connected to one another through the staffette, who helped them regroup after heavy losses or when sections of the city were cleared. With the fighting continuing for days without pause, it was hard to find a safe place to eat or rest. At one moment in a quiet alley, Teresa saw a dog gnawing on a piece of moldy bread. Teresa grabbed it from the animal, fighting for any sustenance, no matter how compromised.

As the formations changed, Teresa was sent to deliver the most sensitive messages between the central command and the leaders in the midst of battle, relaying information about the locations of remaining German strongholds and where to attack next. In one meeting, she was handed a stack of documents and ordered to bring them to the leaders on the Oltrarno side of the city.

Teresa faced the pile of mined rubble at the base of the Vasari Corridor, hoping to follow the supposedly safe route traversed by just a few people before her as she climbed the rocks to reach the empty hallway. Across the river she ran, the sound of gunfire and grenades echoing around her. Then, in the relative quiet of the south side of the city, she passed on her information and received the next order, running back across and down the dangerous route, then diving back into the fray.

TERESA WOULD ONLY later learn the fate of her brother Nino and his partisan band. After the first days of fighting, he was able to sleep for a few hours on the roof of a nunnery, clutching his rifle, until he was awoken at dawn to news that his formation's leader—who was also his good friend—had been shot. Nino went to him and was by his side when he died, then took his place as leader.

During the ensuing battle Nino had emerged from a doorway to shoot at a target in an upper window of a building and was shot in the back. Staggering forward, he fell down and passed out from the pain. The Germans took him for dead and the fighting moved on. When Nino awoke hours later, he was alone. He was able to get himself up and find medical attention in a second miracle of survival.

THE BATTLE CONTINUED in earnest for five days, as the Germans were slowly pushed farther and farther beyond the city. When the partisans cleared a zone, some members stood guard on street corners, and others tended to the wounded and worked to get the city back in order. Finally, on August 15, the Allied forces announced their control of the city and the plan to work with the local CLN leaders to govern newly liberated Florence. It would take weeks to fully see an end to all danger. But by then the city was largely free of

Germans, paid for with the lives of the many fallen Resistance members.

Teresa and her family were finally able to return to their home on the outskirts of the city, where she heard Nino's final story of battle. The Youth Front and the GDD would continue to help support the partisan fight in the north in what ways they could. But for them the fighting was over. Florentines could start to rebuild and move on with their lives.

In these moments of quiet, a luxury she hadn't had in almost a year, Teresa was able to begin processing what she had endured. During the chaotic final fight for freedom, Teresa had watched her comrades murdered by Nazis wielding a flamethrower and sat comforting a friend who died from his wounds, his head on her lap. Her time in battle had ended, but she knew the war was not decided. It was then that she dedicated herself to working for change in a new Italy.

"War is a terrible thing," Teresa later reflected. "That is why I am concerned with peace, so that no boy or girl should ever take up arms or carry bombs."

CHAPTER 79

ANITA

EMILIA-ROMAGNA
AUTUMN 1944

Anita had been in the camps for a few weeks, charged with making connections with their allies in the villages, gathering information, and continuing to relay messages and arms as needed between the camps. And then she received word that she had a visitor. She should go to a safe house in Ceresola where he was waiting for her.

ANITA ARRIVED TO find her fiancé. As soon as she saw his face, Anita understood that a "real storm was brewing," as she later described. The result of more staffette joining the brigades in the mountains was the gossip whispered among those remaining in the towns and cities—these were loose women, sleeping among men.

"You're leaving with me right now," Anita's fiancé told her. They hadn't seen each other in over a month.

"Why do you think I would do such a thing? I came here in order to *not* be executed," she replied with her usual fire.

"We'll get married. You'll come to Varese with me, and no one will look for you there," he answered.

"You think I'll be safe in Varese?" she retorted. Varese was a small city north of Milan, about 130 miles away. "Would you be happier if I was tortured? You must be joking." She paused and added, "I made this decision. Why should I leave now?" Her decision was more than saving herself from the Nazi-Fascists. She had found freedom in the mountains as well, despite the risks.

He sneered at her. "If you stay here, you're not worthy of raising my children!"

"You go home and be the man of the house there," she said in return. "I'm staying." Anita turned her back on him and walked back into the forest.

CHAPTER 80

ON EMPTY

Through the summer of 1944, the Germans had faced numerous losses in battle—and were closing in on four million soldiers killed to date. The Soviet army tore through the Axis front in Ukraine and obliterated sixteen German divisions in Romania. These losses, along with a number of defections from the Axis powers—Romania, Bulgaria, and Finland all would align themselves with the Allied nations as the German front faltered—put Germany at a severe disadvantage. Then Paris was liberated at the end of August, and Brussels and the port of Antwerp by early September. Since the Allied landing in Normandy in June, the British- and American-led forces had been marching across Western Europe with relative speed and success.

Hitler had done what he could to increase wartime production despite his army's heavy losses. He changed the age of conscription to all men between sixteen and sixty and decreed a mandatory sixty-hour workweek. Universities and other nonessential industries were shuttered, with all available workers redirected to the war effort. The Germans were at their highest level of production, but still were coming out on the losing end, particularly vulnerable to the Allies' superior airpower.

But then the Allied forces ran out of gas—quite literally. A supply failure hampered their advance in Western Europe, in some instances within sight of the German border. This forced pause allowed Germany to regroup, and Hitler to imagine an audacious surprise attack that he envisioned bringing the Allied forces to their knees. Injured from an assassination attempt and increasingly paranoid, Hitler summoned his best generals in mid-September—some pulled back from forced retirement—and outlined his latest plan. His new orders seemed, to his military advisers, unrealistic and rash. But, after various suggestions about paring back his objectives over the following weeks, Hitler gave a last directive—with NOT TO BE ALTERED! stamped on the top in bold writing. His officers had no choice but to set about gathering and training the soldiers they would need for their secret December operation. Germany refused to give up.

CHAPTER 81

BIANCA

TURIN
AUTUMN 1944

With the Axis retreat after the liberation of Florence, Bianca and her team had much to report in the underground newspapers they were writing. But every location for their printshop seemed more tenuous than the last. After leaving the apartment, they were next offered the back room of a pasta shop. It was an ideal spot to hide the printer—its bulk and noise not that different from those of the pasta-cutting machine—and a perfect excuse for women to arrive and leave with bundles. But that solution was short-lived.

Finally they were offered something more permanent. They carried their heavy load—the typewriter and mimeograph machine and paper, again hidden among washing and groceries—to the house of a group member's cousin, where Bianca and her team could focus on planning the first issue of *La Difesa della Lavoratrice,* the name similar to that of a Socialist paper that had been published in the early years of Mussolini's rule, until it was shut down along with all the other non-state-sanctioned publications. This paper, they dreamed, would be the voice of the local women's groups, representing news important to the workers and housewives, who continued to meet in small groups, gather donations for the partisan army, and fight in what ways they could.

Like her giornalino *Il Proletario,* this would be a single mimeographed sheet with printing on both sides, the articles born from the news of the Resistance, both local to Piedmont and from the front line farther south. But just as important, Bianca wanted to publish stories about the demands and experiences from the women in the war. As she often did, Bianca stayed up late with Ada or other GDD members, writing and editing, before they set up the printer. This being the first issue, Bianca worked to get the tone right. It might have been based on a past publication, but she wanted this newspaper to speak directly to the women of the Resistance. And so the first article was published in October 1944 and shared widely among the women around Turin:

> The continuous development of the "Defense Groups" and the constant demand for the press has determined the initiative to publish a provincial newspaper. The title of the newspaper, for the pre–1914/18 war generation, is not new. In Italy it was the only newspaper written by women, for women, at that time. It was an educational newspaper, well written and technically well-edited—but it was not a fighting newspaper. Worker collaboration was almost nil, the problems of social reform and those concerning the excessive exploitation of women workers were treated with a few abstract articles. . . .
>
> The newspaper that comes back to life after more than twenty years finds a situation with the working class as the vanguard, finds a mass of women fighting alongside men in all the battles that will lead us to victory. . . . It is a newspaper of agitation and battle, suitable for the moments in which we live.

BIANCA AND HER friend Ada Gobetti were riding their bicycles into the Alpine valleys again, bags as large as they could manage on their backs, stuffed with any kind of supplies they might be able to bring for the partisans. Bianca, with her strong legs, was standing on her pedals to make it up a particularly steep incline, Ada, more petite and two decades older, falling a bit behind.

"When this war is over," Ada joked, "I don't ever want to touch a bicycle again!"

To keep their minds occupied while they passed the waning autumn greenery of the areas they knew were now held by the partisans, they recounted the stories from their favorite books and shared anecdotes from their pasts. Another favorite topic was the parties they would throw when the war was over: whom they would invite, the succulent dishes they would prepare, the games they would play. And so the miles went by.

But they would fall silent, too, as they rode through areas that were being fought over, passing burned-out buildings that had recently seen German retaliation for the actions the women knew Alberto and Paolo were taking part in. Since the summer, the men's battalion had been responsible for sabotage of communications and transport infrastructure, attacks on Nazi-Fascist soldiers, and stealing supplies and arms. They saw blackened houses, some still smoking. The Nazis had burned entire neighborhoods that housed people they suspected were supporting the partisans. Sometimes, they burned houses with no provocation at all. The women would pedal quietly for a while, hoping their loved ones would be waiting for them, to receive the bags packed with such care, at the end of these long rides.

CHAPTER 82

ANITA

EMILIA-ROMAGNA
AUTUMN 1944

I t's not a small choice; it's a difficult choice," Giambattista told Anita. "You can't make a choice and then all your life suffer because you have made a mistake." She had returned from the meeting with her fiancé and was agonizing over whether she had done the right thing by calling off their engagement.

Anita and Giambattista had become close, working together as members of the same detachment of partisans. He had approached her one day when she had been sitting quietly by herself, looking out into the vast green expanse of trees that surrounded their camp. The two soon became friends, often chatting late into the nights when there were no actions. They would talk and debate, Anita astounded that a man would be interested in her perspective on the world and even acknowledge that perhaps she was right and he was wrong at times. They had formed a deep mutual respect in the few months they had known each other.

I won't regret ending things, she told him. *This is what I want.*

They sat at the edge of the camp, Anita realizing that her engagement was truly over, and that she was comfortable with her decision. She was finally free of any expectation or duty other than what she owed her fellow partisans. Anita leaned into Giambattista, their shoulders touching, closing the physical distance between them for the first time since they had become friends.

THAT AUTUMN IN the mountains, one of Anita's tasks was reconnaissance, heading out beyond their camp alone, as if she was merely a young woman on a walk, to take note of any Fascist or Nazi camps or checkpoints. If she found anything useful—food, weapons, blankets—she brought those back along with the information she had gathered. No matter if she had walked a dozen or more miles in a day—up and down inclined roads or steep ridges, sometimes sleeping in the woods—she was expected to wear a knee-length dress and nice shoes in case these walks took her into German-controlled territory where the conservative clothing would help her blend in among the women there.

Other times she, perhaps with fellow staffette, was sent with information to share with other battalions, bringing back their own intel. They couldn't use the radios in the mountains in the same way they had in the cities, so the women were the partisans' telephones. She and the other staffette hiked down from the camp, delivering weapons, detailed maps of current German encampments, or what Anita had gleaned from her connections in the towns. Her network was made up of the local women who had counted the numbers of trucks and noted their insignia, and even the children might innocently ask the Germans questions about their impressive guns or next destination. She would gather this information and then relay what they found out to the staffette.

Anita liked being sent out with Tatiana, who had spent her entire life as a shepherd in the same small town and didn't know how to read or write. She had never ridden a train before or been to the cinema. Anita promised her they would do these things once the war was over. But Tatiana knew how to forage and could create a meal for them from the wild roots and plants that she found on their walks. The women came to know the partisan paths through the forested ridges and valleys of the Apennines intimately, because they traversed them all. But at night, darkness would envelop them. When the paths became impassable, the women would curl up together for a few hours of sleep until dawn, often with just the clothes on their backs and, if they were lucky, a foraged dinner in their bellies. In the quiet of the dark forest, sounds became amplified. Anita had become much more comfortable with these noises since her first time on watch, but she was still acutely aware of how even the sound of leaves blowing in the wind or a twig cracking from an animal heightened their sense of danger.

ANITA HAD JUST returned from camp, having walked close to thirty miles in the previous days to check in with all of the local encampments. The nights were getting colder as autumn deepened. The leaves were starting to change and fall, providing less protection from the wind—and from being seen—and the sun set earlier, necessitating more walking in the dark. Once back at camp, they couldn't even light a fire or their location would be discovered.

Anita sat down to remove the shoes from her blistered feet. Darkness was falling and she hadn't eaten all day. She had to wear her heeled shoes again and was shivering in her dress. Giambattista came up next to her, perhaps covering her shoulders with a musty blanket and offering a plate with some cheese and a hunk of stale bread. It wasn't much, but Anita devoured it, sitting close to her friend to enjoy his warmth.

When she was done, they sat for a bit, maybe recounting what had transpired since they last saw each other—news from other camps, or Nazi sightings from the binoculars they used for surveillance, enjoying having someone to share the mundanities of the day with, even during war.

Suddenly he blurted, "Let's get engaged."

"Oh, Giam," Anita said with a sigh. She did feel that she loved him—for seeing her for who she really was, and not just some young woman who might keep his home or bear him children. "Thank you, really. You are so important to me," she said, still leaning close to him as they both looked into the black of the forest. "But I'm just coming out of this dramatic experience. Let me get through this. But please stay close to me."

"You're right," he said, "I understand you. But I'm twenty-two years old and I've only worked. I've never had a girlfriend—I never had anything! Now I've met a girl with whom I can build something. Let's seize the day."

"And he was right, of course," Anita would say years later. "You would go to bed at night and thank God you were alive. You didn't know if tomorrow morning would bring the same thing. . . . I loved him dearly."

CHAPTER 83

NOT A SUMMER SPORT

Anyone with a radio—and that was most people, Fascist, anti-Fascist, or otherwise—could hear it. It was announced around the world on the evening of November 13, 1944. Most Italians listened to the state-sanctioned radio nightly, to hear what new edicts the Nazi-Fascists announced or at least some version of the events of the war. Many also sought information, much more quietly, from Radio London for yet another version of events. There was little else to do in the interminable hours after curfew. Certainly that evening, the partisans in the mountains would be crowding around whatever radio they had—some were homemade, or connected to a scavenged battery—knowing that whatever was said would have a direct and immediate effect on what transpired the next day.

Huddled together in chilly houses or partisan camps or requisitioned regal homes or war-planning rooms, everyone around Italy heard the same thing. British general Harold Alexander publicly announced that the Allies would pause their engagement in Italy because of the brutal winter weather expected. He suggested that the partisans return home until the Allies resumed fighting again in the spring.

Every partisan would have wondered the same thing: Where could they go?

THE PARTISANS WERE not alone in their shock and dismay at this announcement. A few days later, on November 17, even *The New York Times* seemed to question the logic of this decision by the Allied forces. The article notes that the reaction to General Alexander's announcement "has not been enthusiastic," citing partisans quoted in the underground newspaper *Italia Libera* as saying that "the war against the Nazis is not 'a summer sport.'"

The *Times* article continued:

> The simple fact is that Italians who have been fighting the Germans and the "black brigades" of Fascists ever since the Allies launched their spring offensive would, in many cases, in effect, commit suicide by attempting to filter back to their villages and resume their normal activities.

The partisans already knew this. So did the Nazis and Fascists. Now the world did, too. But would it make a difference?

CHAPTER 84

BIANCA

TURIN

AUTUMN 1944

Even after they settled into their new safe printing shop that autumn, Bianca and her team knew that their struggles were not over. The weather became quite cold as winter neared, which made printing more difficult. Their space wasn't heated, and the ink had a tendency to thicken in low temperatures, making it hard to pass through the fine mesh of the filler net on the mimeograph. The young women had to warm the ink in a saucepan on the stove, returning it to the machine to quickly pass the roller before the ink refroze, printing sheets one by one. Invariably their hands would be stained blue with ink, a telling sign of potentially illicit activity. The women tried to keep their gloves on as much as they could when out in public to avoid suspicion.

BIANCA FINALLY RAISED enough money for a more advanced mimeograph machine that would increase their printing abilities. She and her comrade Maria went to make the purchase, and after Bianca paid, the salesman asked where he could deliver it.

Of course she couldn't give him the address, so Bianca answered, as if it were obvious, "I'll carry it now, of course."

Maria helped wrap it in a large cloth that they had brought for this purpose, and the salesman helped load the heavy machine on Bianca's shoulders. She made every effort to walk out the door as naturally as she could to catch the tram, with Maria following at a safe distance to allow her to escape if Bianca was stopped.

On the tram, Bianca, so focused on her heavy load and already prone to letting her mind wander, didn't pay attention to the route. As they neared their print shop, Maria announced loudly from across the tram car, "Miss, isn't this your stop?"

Bianca's attention snapped back to the present and she carried her load off the tram, Maria exiting as well, keeping watch as Bianca heaved the machine to its new home.

BIANCA'S WAS FAR from the only clandestine paper published by women around Turin. *Noi Donne*—"We Women"—was the official publication of the GDD, which could be found in Turin and around occupied Italy, and among others, there was the paper *In Marzo*—"In March," referring to the month of International Women's Day and the worker strikes Bianca had helped plan—published by the Christian Democratic Women starting in November 1944. *In Marzo* was written and printed in the back of the church of Nostra Signora della Salute, and then brought to a safe space accessed from the chapel where the Shroud of Turin is displayed. From there, parcels of papers made their way around the city, hidden in shopping bags and under other items by the women who distributed them.

In addition to papers that focused on more general topics, some skilled tradesmen published their own as well. There were newspapers published by anti-Fascist metalworkers and chemists, among others. All of these publications would help fill the vacuum of information left by the Nazi-Fascist-sanctioned propaganda press and serve to inspire millions of Italians to support the Resistance in what ways they could, reminding them that they were not alone. Bianca and her team were only a small but influential part of a movement to free information.

Through her late-night talks with Ada, and her own experiences as well, Bianca came to understand how important the underground press had become to the Resistance. It was the main form of news about the war and communication from their CLN government, with directives and encouragement from Resistance leadership. But more so their articles helped put words to the feelings and desires of those who wanted change, uniting a country long fractured by oppressive politics and war. The words Bianca and her team wrote were never signed by the author, as they were certain the Nazi-Fascists would see many of these publications after they had been passed hand to hand, perhaps discarded, their readers in fear of being discovered. But the women wrote their messages of fierce defiance to not only bolster their intended readers but also communicate with the enemy. *We will not be daunted.*

ONE DAY, A young woman came to the door of Bianca's family's apartment. "I heard that you could help in various subjects," she said. "I'm here to take lessons."

Bianca was confused—she certainly had not given any lessons on any topics other than the political, where she was still learning herself. But she knew she couldn't trust a stranger with this knowledge.

"Carla sometimes gives drawing lessons if that is what you mean. Otherwise, I think you have the wrong people."

"Yes, drawing. Learning to draw is fine," she insisted, and they arranged a time for her to return for lessons. Despite the request being strange, the young woman seemed harmless and the money was welcome.

The young woman returned a few times to draw with Carla, the two of them meeting in the kitchen—the only heated room of the house, where Bianca joined them as well, reading in the corner. Nothing seemed out of the ordinary.

The last time they met, the woman paused close to the door, her coat and bag in her hand as she prepared to exit. "I'm not coming back," she said quietly. "I wanted to let you know that I was sent by others." And with that warning, she slipped out the door, never to return.

And so Bianca was reminded of, as she described, the "uncertain border between trust and suspicion, confidence and distrust that could creep into relations between people . . . a wrong encounter, a word more or less, that could decide one's fate."

Bianca wouldn't know what happened to this young woman until after the war when she was accused of collaborating with the Nazi-Fascists. The woman found Bianca and her family to ask for a statement saying that she had warned them of danger, in hopes of leniency. Remembering her actions, Bianca obliged.

CHAPTER 85

ANITA

APENNINE MOUNTAINS
NOVEMBER 1944

Castelnovo ne'Monti is situated atop a low mountain at the northern edge of the long Apennine Mountains, best known for the dramatic plateau Pietra di Bismantova—a rock that juts up from the peak of the mountain, marking this town perched in the skyline. One of the partisan paths that Anita and her fellow staffette often took traced its way up the mountain ridge to the fields below the pietra, just above the main street. They could hear the sounds of life below them and perhaps they sat for a moment, making a soft seat among the fallen leaves. They were higher than anyone else for miles around and well hidden. But Anita felt exposed among the newly naked trees. It was such a different feeling walking among them in the last few weeks since they had lost their leaves than when she could hide amid their lushness when she had first arrived in the summer.

They had left two days earlier from a neighboring partisan camp, stopping to spend the first night at a friendly farmer's house along the way before reaching Castelnovo. And now they were almost at the home of a fellow partisan's father, a man who would shelter and feed them until a relay from Reggio Emilia arrived with news. Then they would set off again to share the information the relay brought.

The partisan bands had grown in size and number since the summer, even briefly liberating full towns and areas, where they could walk with impunity, with a stationed sentry keeping watch along the perimeter for Nazi-Fascists. But with the ongoing German retreat from the south, there were a greater number of the enemy in a smaller geographic area. Once the defeated armies regrouped and rested their battered forces, the autumn was bringing a renewed German effort to make the Resistance pay for their role in their losses in Rome and Florence. And now, without the Allied forces to worry about, the Germans could focus entirely on destroying their remaining partisan foes.

Anita had become the commander of the new Information Office at the start of that month, which brought all of the staffette of the brigade together in a single formation. It was her role to organize receiving information from the brigades in the plains around the city of Parma or the gappisti in Reggio Emilia, and then disseminate it to all the battalions around her valley. Anita coordinated all this information, and then sent women couriers out to share the intel they received. It was often she who would take the most difficult routes or deliver the most sensitive information.

By midafternoon the staffetta from Reggio Emilia had arrived and handed over that day's documents. Perhaps she took a moment to rest from the long uphill trek, sharing some of the food the farmer had offered the women. It was harvesttime, so there were often potatoes along with chunks of locally made Parmegiano Reggiano cheese.

Anita looked at the documents she was given and became alarmed. They had known an attack was coming, but the scale was staggering. Imminently, the Nazis were sending troops to fan out along the valley floor, where the Enza River provides the boundary between the provinces of Parma and Reggio Emilia. Then their plan was to move upward to the ridges. With their sheer advantages in number, they could canvass the entire area from Reggio Emilia to Monte Caio—one of the highest peaks of the Apennines, and the one from which these valleys and lower ridges descended—finding every partisan camp along the way.

We have to leave now! she told her fellow staffetta, who was enjoying the rare warmth of the farmhouse's small fire. They had to let their comrades know what was coming.

BY MIDNIGHT ANITA had reached the first camp, a dozen miles west of the farmhouse. The walk had been difficult, starting off with a few hundred feet straight downhill from Castelnovo's ridge and then a similar distance back up toward their destination, high above the Enza Valley. The day had been cold and damp, with low clouds filtering any sunlight into gray. In the last few hours, it had also started to lightly rain.

"I have to get back to my camp," she told the officer in charge after she delivered her messages. She wanted to warn the women and men who had become like family to her these last few months— especially Giambattista.

"But they've already left for the battle," he informed her. Exhausted and wet, Anita sank to the ground. In the silence of the forest, they could hear the first shots fired of what would be known as the Battle of Monte Caio.

AT DAYLIGHT, THE officer sent Anita and her staffetta with a group of armed fighters to the valley floor, where many of the local detachments were meeting to form larger armies to engage the Germans.

As she neared the next camp Anita saw a familiar silhouette in the distance. It was Giambattista—but she didn't recognize the men he was with.

Anita ran up to him. "What are you doing here?" she asked.

"The commander asked me to form a new detachment," he told her. "One of them is a kid, only seventeen years old. I need to watch out for him."

"Please be careful," she told him. She stood close and buried her face in his chest at the next round of machine-gun fire in the distance. He pulled her into an embrace and tilted her face toward his.

"I love you," he whispered, and kissed her. Anita returned his affections and they held each other close.

This first kiss would also be their last.

ANITA MET UP with other staffette from her camp, who were now ordered to move with a new detachment. In the chaos of escaping the roundups in the valley and with partisans gathering from various regions to face the Germans, there were groups of varying sizes, many with inadequate weapons. These bands were being reorganized and sent to strategic places around the valley. Anita was among a group of about twenty who were tasked with keeping up the connections between the groups. The few with guns would help to protect the others.

The group moved across the Enza River, Anita carrying a staffetta who was weak with fever on her shoulders. They climbed up the next ridge until long after dark, the drilling of machine-gun fire and blasts of grenades coming from all corners of the valley. The group eventually paused for a few hours of sleep, huddled together on the ground. Their only cover from the cold, now-insistent rain was a silk parachute one of them carried in their backpack.

They awoke at dawn and Anita found a clearing where she could see the opposite ridge. She trained her binoculars at some movement among the trees and gasped. It was Giambattista, now wearing civilian clothes and a priest's hat. He had a machine gun in one hand and a chain of ammunition in the other. Anita watched him, followed by a few other members of his detachment, move across the ridge, and then duck back into the trees out of view.

THE GROUP SPLINTERED—Anita and four other staffette were now to connect with the remaining detachments and then report back to the brigade command in the southern town of Miscoso.

For days, the women moved up onto the ridges and down into the valleys, as the Battle of Monte Caio raged around them. As they walked, the sounds of war echoing off the mountainsides, they passed otherworldly sights. Discarded weapons, burned houses, trails of blood, signs of a battle often waged just hours before, sometimes arriving when bullets were still flying. When they found their comrades, they heard stories of those who had fallen, of the weapons and number and tactics of the enemy. They shared what intel the other battalions had told them, and then the women took their leave.

It had been more than a week since Anita had changed clothes, and she and her team of staffette had long been out of food, eating what scraps they could find on their way, sleeping a few hours on the ground when they could walk no more. The battle had moved northward and they had finally made it to the brigade command in the south.

Anita was hoping to wash herself and change her clothes—she was still wearing a knee-length dress, with only a light coat on top, her gun stuffed in its pocket, always at hand. Her leather-soled shoes were caked with mud and coming apart where the top was stitched to the sole. This stop promised a moment of respite, perhaps a meal.

As soon as the women were in sight of the base, she saw her cousin Sandra running toward her.

"I have to give you bad news," she said, crying. "They have been desperately looking for Giambattista for three days and they can't find him." Anita fell to her knees.

What no one would know for months was that his body lay among the trees on the ridge, his life cut short by a Nazi bullet.

CHAPTER 86

ANITA

APENNINE MOUNTAINS
NOVEMBER 1944

In her state of mind, grieving Giambattista, the freezing rain seemed to seep deeper through her skin and into her soul. But Anita wasn't the only one bereft. There had been more than a hundred partisan casualties during the battle, and few knew then whether their loved ones had survived. At the camp she found that there was no change of clothes and few supplies—everything had been destroyed or lost. But nearby was a farm whose owners the partisans knew to be friendly.

The woman who answered the door welcomed Anita inside and began heating up a tub of water for her. She gathered the dirty clothes and promised to wash them as well, giving Anita a clean outfit when she emerged from the tub: a red silk dress and a raincoat, with a cloth rag she could possibly use as underwear. It wasn't much, especially with the rain coming down harder now, but it was something. Using these small kindnesses to steel herself, Anita returned to camp for the night.

EARLY THE NEXT morning, Anita and a partisan officer named Gianni were ordered to lead around a hundred partisans—most of them unarmed and in a state of shock—over the next ridge of the Apennine Mountains toward safety in liberated Tuscany. They had to move quickly as the Germans were preparing to encircle the partisans, soon to block the way to the south now that they had time and resources to spare.

The entire day it rained. A cold, bone-chilling rain—"water that God sent," as a flood-like deluge is called in Italian. It ran down Anita's skin and filled her shoes. The hike had the group climbing straight up, into the mountains, and traversing the Lagastrello Pass, an area prized by nature lovers and hikers in peaceful times.

As she had so many times before, Anita acted as relay—traveling ahead alone and then back and then forward again with the larger group when the coast was clear. Anita was always visible, even in the fog, shivering in her red silk dress.

Near their destination, Anita had gone ahead once again to gather intel from a partisan encampment, climbing farther up the mountain to hear whether they had seen any Germans.

"They passed through," she was told, "but there's none up ahead."

She hurried back down to share the news, clutching her thin coat over her dress as the wind whipped up.

"Oh, what we make our women do!" her fellow officer Gianni called out as she descended, only to climb back up with the men once again.

It was half past one in the morning when the group arrived at Castello di Comano, welcomed by the partisans, who helped them dry off and warm up, sharing what food they had. The women there, too, prepared a hot tub for Anita, who peeled her soaked dress off and rubbed her raw skin, dyed pink from the silk, to help warm herself.

ANITA

———

WHEN ANITA RETURNED to her camp after this trek, she fell sick with rheumatic fever and spent the next two weeks recovering, a few inches of straw as her only mattress.

"There was no doctor, no medicine, nothing. Not even milk to drink," she later remembered. "This was the life you had to live, you had no escape."

CHAPTER 87

BATTLE OF THE BULGE

In early December, Hitler called his top military commanders for final meetings in preparation of an audacious attack. Commanders were disarmed and searched before being led into a meeting where they were shocked at the condition of their leader. Hitler had a stooped back, so unlike his usual rod-straight posture, and his left arm shook. One attendee later recalled, "He looked like he was about to collapse." But his oratory skills were still present, and he lectured for more than an hour about the assured success of this action. It would cause, he boomed, the Allied forces to "suddenly collapse with a huge clap of thunder." His lackeys, mesmerized by their Führer's performance, returned to their men and continued preparations for the Battle of the Bulge.

On the afternoon of December 15, as sunset neared at the early winter hour of four P.M., more than 200,000 German soldiers moved into position, along with nearly 1,000 vehicles, 2,000 cannon, 16,000 tons of ammunition, 4,500,000 gallons of fuel, and 50,000 horses. They were hiding among the rolling wooded hills of the Ardennes, primarily in Belgium but edging over the Luxembourg, French, and German borders, near where the American forces had stopped en route to Germany. It was an area with peat bogs near its lowest point, with hills rising more than a thousand feet over rounded peaks, steep valleys, and dense woods along the way—with unpredictable weather in the winter. Surprise was on the Nazis' side—the Allied forces could not imagine that Germany would wage battle in such an inhospitable area. Before dawn on December 16, German armed forces began to attack the Americans along eighty-five miles of the Ardennes, in what would be one of the bloodiest actions of the war. Swaths were cut through the forest from mortars and bullets—like a tornado, one Midwesterner recalled. Another American soldier, from Buffalo, New York, said, "I thought I knew cold, but I didn't really know cold until the Battle of the Bulge."

The Germans dropped English-speaking paratroopers behind enemy lines, wearing American uniforms and trained to speak without an accent, who helped wreak havoc on the battle-weary Allies. They changed road signs and were meant to infiltrate the ranks and create confusion. American soldiers attempted to weed out these saboteurs with American trivia questions, like asking to name the capital of Illinois, or questions about positions on the line of scrimmage in American football.

For six weeks the Germans poured reinforcements into the Battle of the Bulge, taxing the Americans, who were forced to redirect resources as well. There would be around 19,000 Allied soldiers killed in action there, 47,000 wounded, and more than 12,000 taken prisoner or missing. About 100,000 Germans would also be killed, wounded, or captured. The Americans would emerge victorious on January 25, 1945, and begin their march toward Berlin, but their success had been paid for with the lives of many.

CHAPTER 88

BIANCA

TURIN
WINTER 1945

The winter of 1945 was the coldest in recent memory, making the already precarious existence of the hiding partisans even more challenging. After the Allies' announced pause in late autumn, the Germans had redoubled their efforts to subdue and arrest the partisan army in Piedmont as well, reclaiming some of the areas the partisans had briefly liberated. From her frequent trips northward, and from the news gathered from other staffette, Bianca and her team reported on those murdered in the mountains, along with the heroic acts of sabotage that the partisans had conducted. It was through these stories that the GDD helped encourage donations and showed the dedication of those fighting for the future of all Italians. They detailed:

It's rough in Punta Novosa. The wind blows. The fire from the bivouacs keeps blowing out. . . . The freezing air lashes their bodies and makes them shiver in their miserable blankets, then again tomorrow and tomorrow again. In the feverish expectations that create wrinkles on youth, they desire, they want, they believe in the dawn of freedom.

—*Difesa della Lavoratrice,* December 1944

It was Bianca and her team's goal to tell the stories of the atrocities of the Nazi-Fascists, to highlight their callous disregard for life. The enemy didn't care about the young men and women they killed, or the families they ripped apart. These accounts, which would have gone unreported without the underground press, countered the propaganda in the state-sanctioned newspapers about the Nazi-Fascists' desire to keep the peace and blame the partisans for aggression. They wrote:

They arrested them, a circle of danger closed them in
without trials, no accusations, condemned like this
without responsibility for misdeeds. On the square of
a small town three boys: three Heroes! . . . And they left them,
corpses united in sleep like brothers in the supreme hour
of death.

—*Difesa della Lavoratrice,* December 1944

Bianca and her publishing comrades reminded their readers of their larger political goals as well—a new, more capable, and just government. They wrote:

The Fascist government is allegedly incapable of carrying out
any function of simple control. . . . Its henchmen are made up of
the worst gang, vile and dishonest. THE FASCIST
GOVERNMENT IS INCAPABLE OF PROVIDING FOR OUR

CHILDREN.... THE MASSES ARE SUFFERING FROM
HUNGER.

—*Difesa della Lavoratrice,* January 1945

In a section titled "Correspondence" the women covered reports from the local factories—which groups of women workers went on strike, or threatened to, because of lack of pay or rations; promises kept or ignored; workers who were fired or factory managers who told lies. In their pages, they advocated for better pay and treatment of substitute teachers at their children's schools, and amplified calls for more work stoppages to increase rations and wages. And they had messages for the Fascist factory owners who clung to power in these waning days of war as well:

It seems that the warnings you have received are not enough to
stop you in your actions.... Be careful. The workers see very well
what is rightful and wrongful in your company. Why did he fire
two women while the others have seen an increase in hours?
Therefore, it is not entirely true that there is a lack of materials.

—*Difesa della Lavoratrice,* January 1945

Bianca and her team reported news from the presumed postwar government, the CLN, which finally allowed women in its ranks, declaring:

THE SECRETARY OF THE WOMEN'S DEFENSE AND
ASSISTANCE TO FREEDOM FIGHTER GROUPS HAS
LEARNED WITH GREAT SATISFACTION THAT IN
LIBERATED ITALY THE ADMINISTRATION HAS GRANTED
WOMEN THE RIGHT TO VOTE.

—*Difesa della Lavoratrice,* February 1945

They shared news from around Italy—occupied and liberated—and from the front line. And finally, the newspaper's calls for insurrection began. Liberation felt near. These single-sheet newspapers, never signed by their authors, always using every inch of space on both sides of the page, became a lifeline, a signal, a sign of hope for the future.

> The Red Army is at the gates of Berlin while the Anglo-Americans' offensive is pressing the Nazis from the west. The oppressed populations feel the hour of liberation is near.
>
> —*Difesa della Lavoratrice,* February 1945

As the end of winter neared, Bianca and her team reminded their women readers that this fight was as much for the liberation of Italians as it was for women's rights:

> Our Piedmont sharpens its weapons and tempers its people in the intensified clandestine struggle of every day and is directed toward a goal: POPULAR INSURRECTION! To save what can be saved, people will rise up.
>
> —*Difesa della Lavoratrice,* February 1945

> All women must fight to the point of extreme sacrifice to accelerate liberation of the Homeland and the destruction of the Nazi-Fascists. . . . In this fight Italian women claim their political and social rights.
>
> —*Difesa della Lavoratrice,* March 1945

CHAPTER 89

ANITA

APENNINE MOUNTAINS
WINTER 1945

Snow covered the ground, making walking the paths more difficult. But at least now Anita wore boots and pants for these missions. A deputy commissioner had tried to ban women from wearing
pants in any weather, but Anita and other staffette had refused
this edict, finally recognizing and pushing back on these sexist
inequities—"frightening sectarianism," as Anita described it—that
she and the other women might have accepted just a few years
before.

They were headed to Ceresola to blow up a bridge. The area was
still controlled by the Nazi-Fascists but was actively contested.
Anita was asked, as she often was, to be the relay—to travel ahead
as lookout, returning to lead her men forward toward the action.
She took the smallest revolver she could find and hid it in her pants
pocket, taking special care as she grew closer to the town where her
face was known.

"If I can't make it back, I'll fire a shot to signify danger," she told
the men.

"But you're crazy," said Gianni, the same officer with whom she
had led a hundred men to safety in Tuscany after the Monte Caio

battle. He knew that for her to fire a shot meant to start a battle between the Nazi-Fascists and the partisans, both lying in wait for provocation. "You would be in the middle of two fires!"

"I know," she responded. "But you have given me the task, and the minute I accepted the responsibility of being your outrider I understood that something like this can happen. At least let it be a German bullet and not a partisan killing me!"

Close to the bridge, Anita was spotted as she went ahead to scout. But before she was even able to fire her gun, bullets began whizzing past her from both sides. She felt the familiar electric shock of fear that started in her feet and blazed through her body, making her hyperaware of her actions, knowing that to make a mistake would mean death. She dropped to the ground and, not for the first time, crawled under the flying bullets toward safety.

THE PROCESS OF women's emancipation was taking place every day, in mundane moments when the partisans shared the work of cooking and cleaning and keeping watch equally, with no regard to gender roles. Or in the times of battle, when dozens of men put their lives in the hands of Anita or other women, trusting them to guide the partisans toward their next action. Anita was sent on missions or given orders not because she was a woman, who might be able to better blend in among the locals, but because she had proven herself the most capable person for the job.

Anita was also sent on some of the most delicate missions, such as meeting with British command as the front line grew nearer. The way she held the respect of so many of her comrades only highlighted the constant underestimation by others. That winter, in a mission to the plains, she was given a German prisoner to escort to another camp. She took her Sten submachine gun, pointed it into the prisoner's back, and began to march him forward. He was a big man, six feet tall and broad-shouldered. They began the trek along the paths, perhaps slipping on the icy snow that had melted and re-frozen in the warming days of late winter.

Every few hundred yards the prisoner would stop and turn back toward Anita, his face incredulous at her raised gun. "But you women, you are born to make love!" he would say.

"Stop this nonsense!" Anita ordered. "Keep on walking!"

They stopped at a camp along the way, Anita finding the officer in charge there to ask him to watch the prisoner so she could take a brief break.

"Who gave you orders to come armed?" he demanded when he saw her with the Sten.

Anita's fire blazed. "Do you realize what you are saying? Do you see this one here? This is a German prisoner, with military rank. I took him in because I got the order, and I am taking him to the bri-gade command. But to get there alive I have to be armed."

There had been some debate among partisan leaders whether women should be allowed to carry arms—an idea Anita had disre-garded as sexist—"We're not rabbits!" she had said. It would have been foolish, she argued, for them to be traveling through contested territory unable to defend themselves.

To this partisan commander she said, "This is my gun. If you want it, come and get it!"

CHAPTER 90

BIANCA

PIEDMONT
WINTER 1945

Bianca and Alberto sometimes met at Ada's house in Meana, a few valleys over from Alberto and Paolo's camp at La Gianna. It would not have been an easy trip, although the partisans traveled between the valleys often. Perhaps Alberto volunteered to go this distance to help bring back information or supplies, knowing that it might offer him a few fleeting moments with his fiancée. The promise of a warm meal and a bath, perhaps even a night spent in a real bed—often not alone—would also be a draw. But being a partisan in a village, even a friendly one, was also a risk. Neighbors were close by; there were patrols.

During one of these trysts, Alberto and Bianca were in a bedroom when they heard a Nazi-Fascist patrol knock at the front door. There was no opportunity for escape—so as the officer went from room to room, they pretended they were having sex and didn't hear the door open. The patrol just laughed and let them be.

FOR THE FIRST time in Italian culture, young men and women spent time alone together before marriage—much of it after dark.

Bianca's mother rarely knew when or if to expect her home. Whether sleeping outside or locked in for curfew, Bianca and many others often found themselves spending the night with someone with whom they might have a mutual attraction that they acted upon. Couples disappeared together to find what privacy they could, and hearing amorous sounds in the darkness was common, especially as the partisans felt more united by their shared work and passion.

There were reports of partisan commanders holding unofficial weddings, or small-town parish priests performing ceremonies with only a few comrades present, sometimes to cement bonds made among circumstances of life and death, other times to assuage the guilt of having sex outside marriage.

"We made love—a lot," Bianca said about the Resistance years later. "Sometimes the feminist movement, twenty years later, acts like they discovered everything, but perhaps they forgot that others had similar experiences, too."

CHAPTER 91

THE FINAL MARCH

The Gothic Line was the last German stronghold in Italy, and like the previous fortifications in the south, it consisted of dug-in trenches and artillery garrisons installed at strategic positions spanning Italy from east to west, many of these points along the ridges of the Apennine Mountains.

After pausing for the first months of winter—and largely leaving the partisans to fend for themselves—the Allied forces returned in late February, this time with help from allies from around the globe. While the Gothic Line had technically been breached in autumn 1944, it had not fallen. It would be Brazilian soldiers who broke through the German defensive line at Monte Castello in the Apennine Mountains, opening the door to the Po Valley and finally cracking the Gothic Line for good. Other Allies soon joined them.

Elsewhere in Europe, the Nazis were pulling back their forces to defend Germany while the Allied forces marched eastward after their difficult victory at the Battle of the Bulge, as well as other strategic wins. There were final, desperate offenses—like the last V-2 rockets the Germans launched, killing almost two hundred civilians in England and Belgium. Yet the end of the war seemed truly, enticingly near. But the question in occupied Italy would be: How painful would the Nazis make these final weeks?

CHAPTER 92

BIANCA

TURIN

MARCH 1945

On March 8, Bianca and her team released an issue of *La Difesa della Lavoratrice* with the leading article titled: "A Day of Struggle for Women," compelling women to see this year's International Women's Day as a "cry of protest launched by thousands and thousands of women united so that the horrors and massacres would never happen again in the world."

The leaders of the GDD told women to "create a schism . . . in every workshop, in every home, in every office." Past actions by specific factories were detailed: stories of successfully demanding—often through work stoppages—higher wages or rations. They wrote: "And in this unrest we must recognize that the defense groups receive some credit. We must recognize that the women in our organization are always on the forefront and we are proud of that."

Other articles honored women who were killed in the Resistance:

From the liberated lands, the name of a female victim frequently comes, discovered after the expulsion of the Nazi-Fascists. . . .

And why was she killed? Because asylum was given to a patriot, the wounded were helped, a very important connection was maintained, dangerous documents were transported, press was spread to keep the morale of the fighters and the population high, to wake up the women still asleep in their strange lethargy and make them live these last hours of struggle, prepare them for the world tomorrow that awaits them.

These articles supported one of Bianca's key roles as she helped plan the insurrection—organizing the many smaller groups of agitators, particularly in the factories, so they could contribute to the Resistance effort with greater impact. While they had encouraged strikes to coincide with International Women's Day and the anniversary of the strikes from the previous two years, Bianca and her team were also well aware of the possible repercussions. "We did not want to send anyone to the slaughterhouse," as another organizer said, the Resistance learning lessons from the bloody insurrection in Florence. Rather these actions were meant to be largely symbolic of worker power, with the real focus on the coming insurrection since the Germans were expected to further retreat as the Allied forces advanced.

The agitation committees specified that their charge was to represent all workers—no matter their role, political affiliation, gender, or religion—and they began meeting often to decide their course of action. Bianca's charge in *La Difesa della Lavoratrice* from the previous autumn, of helping women workers realize their power, was coming to fruition. The next step was to put plans in place for the final battle. For that they would need their staffette and the partisans within Turin and from the Alpine region beyond.

ON THE NIGHT of March 12, Fascist officers banged on the door of the working-class Arduino family's home, looking for the sisters

Vera and Libera, nineteen and sixteen. The young women had been active in the Resistance—Vera as a staffetta, often making treks to the mountains and around Turin, while Libera helped organize workers in the city. They were also both members of the GDD and had participated in workers' rights actions.

At gunpoint, the Fascists took the sisters, as well as their father and Libera's boyfriend, leaving behind their mother and younger siblings. Beyond the house, the men and the sisters were separated. The officers marched the teens through the cold night to a bridge, where they were shot, their bodies left as a warning to other partisans. Women were rarely executed in this manner, and the execution of girls was rarer still. Their bodies would be found the next day when curfew lifted. The men had also been killed, their bodies left elsewhere in the city.

The murder of the sisters galvanized Turin, provoking fervent protests tied to their funeral. Even those who had strived for political neutrality asked: *What kind of people would kill unarmed teenagers?* The GDD encouraged their members to attend the burial wearing "something red" to signify their commitment to the Resistance. Leadership forbade Bianca and a few other important members to attend, not wanting them to risk arrest at this critical moment. So Bianca spent the day locked in the library of the Legal Institute, leafing through magazines, upset and tormented about not being able to take part in something about which she felt so strongly.

Hundreds of people protested at the entrance to the cemetery—most of them women, and most carrying red bouquets of flowers or wearing red ribbons and crowns—awaiting the arrival of the bodies. As soon as the procession arrived, so did three large empty trucks helmed by soldiers. The mourners immediately tried to run to safety, but still a hundred people were arrested—mostly women—among them Bianca's sister, Carla.

In her fear, their mother blamed Bianca for her sister's arrest, the only time she expressed anger at her work in the Resistance. "You'll be the ruin of our family," Bianca's mother yelled.

And Bianca was awash with guilt. She felt responsible that Carla had been arrested—and mad at herself that she hadn't disobeyed the leadership and been there as well to protect her sister. She had heard too many stories, had in fact helped write and publish many of them as news and warnings, to keep her fear at bay. After a year and a half of harrowing tales of the torture that the Nazis and Fascists inflicted on those arrested, Bianca tried not to allow herself to imagine what her sister was enduring in prison at the hands of desperate men.

OVER THE NEXT few days, a few women at a time would be quietly released from the prison where the protesters were housed, so as not to attract a crowd. Carla would soon be home, telling Bianca that they had been held without being questioned. She explained that she had calmed herself in the overcrowded cells by reciting poetry. The wait for Carla's freedom had been interminable; that she was home, alive and unharmed, felt like a miracle.

AS MARCH TURNED toward April, Bianca and others planned numerous "flying rallies" around the city.

At a crossroads in the middle of the city center, a tram car was overturned—just one of many moments of civil disobedience meant to prove the strength of the people to their detested Nazi-Fascist oppressors. Workers came out of the nearby factories and gathered around the tram when one of Bianca's comrades arrived. She jumped up on the tram car's side, gave a short speech about readying for the insurrection, flashed a red flag, and then made her escape.

At Microtecnica, a comrade named Vittoria snuck into the cafeteria at lunchtime, climbed up on a table, and made a similar, brief speech, encouraging everyone to participate in the coming fight.

Other women arrived at the factories when it was time to leave, and sitting astride their bicycles to enable a quick getaway, they incited workers to join the insurrection. They threw leaflets into the air and rode off.

Bianca, though not drawn to public performance, committed herself to dozens of these rallies, climbing upon lampposts or standing with her bicycle in front of markets or on street corners, invoking the latest rallying cry: "We have conquered the squares, we must not lose them!" In front of groups sometimes comprised of four or five people, at other times a dozen or more, Bianca overcame her hesitancy for public speaking as she, and so many others, rallied the people of Turin to ready themselves to fight for their freedom.

CHAPTER 93

ANITA

EMILIA-ROMAGNA
APRIL 1945

S top!" the Fascist officers at the checkpoint commanded. Anita was coming from her camp on a relay mission, using the roads because she had no weapons or illicit documents on her. Perhaps the first signs of spring were in the air—birds chirping, crocuses popping up their purple heads. Maybe Anita was too tired to even be concerned that she might be questioned. She was dirty, her hair, once meticulously styled, full of lice. Her gums bled from malnutrition, and she, and most of the other staffette, had long ago stopped menstruating.

"Do you know this woman?" the officer asked Anita, thrusting a photograph toward her. Anita started as she recognized the round face, the scoop-necked dress, white with a dainty flower print. Her thoughts went back to the day this photograph was taken by the Fascist police when they had come to her house to question her—the day she fled to the hills. It had been months, but it felt like a lifetime ago.

"She's a partisan called Laila." The officer looked at Anita for a long moment. "Have you seen her?"

Anita just shook her head and walked on.

So changed was her appearance thanks to the brutal winter that she and her comrades had endured in the mountains, the Germans hadn't recognized her from the photo they held in their hands.

WHILE THE LARGER northern cities had not been liberated, by the beginning of April the partisans had conquered smaller cities like Ciano and San Polo d'Enza, which were in the Apennine foothills, as the Resistance extended its reach toward the plains. There was still a Nazi-Fascist presence, but the checkpoints were fewer and farther between, the contested areas moving north as they retreated toward Germany. But the partisans' role was still necessary.

Anita had just returned to camp from a mission in the Parmigiano area when one of her comrades ran up to her with a message.

"Your father is waiting for you in San Polo," the partisan told her. "He brought you supplies." She desperately wanted to see him but was exhausted from her mission. She hadn't seen anyone from her family since she had left for the mountains the previous summer, although she had given a fellow staffetta from a different city, who would go to Reggio Emilia to buy supplies, her home address, sending and receiving messages through her. As much as she wanted to start walking toward her father, she didn't have the energy. The lack of nutrition left her constantly exhausted, and she had to warm up her muscles just to get moving.

But she wouldn't have to walk. She looked up in awe: Her father had sent a horse. She climbed on its back and began to ride.

Astride the horse, she could see her father from a distance, smiling widely, bags of food and clean clothes by his sides. When Anita dismounted, she nearly collapsed in his arms. He held her tightly and told her, "I am so proud of you."

CHAPTER 94

TOWARD THE PO

The Allied forces in Italy, with soldiers from six continents, outnumbered and outresourced their battered Axis foe. But the Führer, and others, would be delusional about their now assured loss—even as they retreated, there was talk among their ranks of an unspecified weapon that would end the war in Germany's favor. Many Nazi soldiers, who themselves had given so much for their misguided beliefs, desperately wanted to believe this was true.

In the first week of April, the Allies had begun a large, coordinated assault on the Gothic Line and elsewhere, which they hoped would break through the last Axis strongholds. Diversionary battles distracted Axis soldiers as the Allied forces focused on breaking into the Po Valley, which separated the Apennines from the Alps. Extensive damage to supply routes from Allied bombing and partisan sabotage meant that the remaining Axis forces were running out of food, weapons, and equipment.

Finally, on April 13, Allied forces pushed over the Santerno River, between the Adriatic Sea on Italy's east coast and Bologna, beginning their multiphase plan of attack to enter the Po Valley from the east. This was the last area of Italy occupied by the Germans before the imposing Alps. Over the following days, the Allies made much progress, wearing down the stubborn Axis forces, who continued to retreat north and west, sowing destruction as they went.

CHAPTER 95

BIANCA

TURIN

APRIL 1945

Everyone felt the change—the power in the air. Bianca was on a tram on April 18, standing, as usual, close to the door to make a quick exit should she need to escape. The tram neared its next stop, Bianca pulled from her thoughts by the sound of the brakes screeching on the track.

"Everyone, we're getting off. It's the insurrection!" the driver announced. The general strike had begun. Bianca and the other riders looked around in surprise, and then delight, as they disembarked to walk the rest of their journey.

As the end of war grew more certain, their committees worked with the partisans to coordinate a work stoppage that was seen by many as practice for the coming insurrection. The "strike against hunger and terror" commenced on April 18, across almost all industries in Turin and beyond. Among their demands were a higher wage, firewood, and a steep increase in rations. To communicate with the people of Turin, clandestine publishers like Bianca printed tens of thousands of newspapers and pamphlets, detailing their demands and the calls to strike and join the insurrection.

But there would also be another audience that day. There was a publication aimed at Fascists, too. SURRENDER OR PERISH! the flyers said, reminding them of the fate of others who had been caught and paid with their lives.

Along with these publications there were posters, plastered at night after curfew on walls around the city by women of the GDD who prepared jam jars with glue and paintbrushes for members to use. Others threw flyers off bridges. Graffiti was painted on walls around the city, including drawings of the hammer and sickle or sayings like LONG LIVE CLN! One of the signs that the Fascists were losing their hold on power: These posters and markings stayed up, no one daring to tear them down or paint over them.

CHAPTER 96

ANITA

REGGIO EMILIA
APRIL 1945

Anita would spend the days before the final insurrection in Reggio Emilia in the mountains, anticipating the need to send her relays to spread information as the Germans retreated and the Allied forces advanced. She had seen many battles in her nearly nine months in the mountains, but, for Anita at least, it seemed like the fighting might be over.

But not so for her longtime friend Maria Montanari, who had first met the German soldiers on the same day as Anita in early September 1943. Maria had become active in the Resistance alongside Anita. Yet while Anita had escaped to the mountains, Maria's work remained undetected in Reggio Emilia, where she gathered supplies and information from her job at a Nazi-Fascist hospital.

Reggio Emilia looked to liberated cities like Rome and Florence and, as the Allies advanced, ordered armed partisans to descend from the mountains toward the cities, ready to help drive out the Nazis in a final battle and save their infrastructure from the destruction and plundering that had occurred in the south. It was late April, and the remaining German troops were told to withdraw, their defeat now certain. But there were still more than one hundred and fifty miles to go to the Austrian border. The Nazi army was demoralized—they wanted someone to pay for their suffering.

Maria had been stationed near the hospital, which was just beyond the central city walls, monitoring the German retreat. She stood in front of a green door at a curve in the road, across from the church of San Pellegrino. From her vantage point she could see what those in either direction on the main road could not: a group of partisans advancing from the hills were about to meet the retreating Germans.

She ran into the middle of the road, toward a small piazza with a fountain that she could climb for better visibility. Maria, her back to the Germans, began waving her arms and yelling to the partisans, alerting them of the danger around the bend. A shot rang out from the Germans crossing the bridge behind her and Maria fell to the ground. The partisans she warned hid themselves amid the alleys and doorways along the road as the Nazis advanced, and the massacre that might have been was averted.

Watching this murder unfold from the hospital windows, a friend in nurse's whites ran to Maria through the scrum of soldiers, but it was too late. Blood stained both of their clothes. The bullet had severed Maria's femoral artery and killed her instantly.

CHAPTER 97

BIANCA

TURIN

APRIL 1945

When Bianca and her comrade arrived at the tire factory where they had been assigned, two beefy men in blue suits met them at the door, clearly armed. "Don't worry," one told her conspiratorially, "we're here to protect you."

It was April 22—a day after the Allies had reached Bologna, two hundred miles to the east. Bianca and another Resistance member were among the women sent to the factories in the days leading up to the fight for Turin's liberation to rally the workers for the final battles in the streets.

The bodyguards led them across two deserted courtyards to the refectory, where hundreds of workers—many women, as well as men and even factory managers, Bianca was pleased to note—were cheering their arrival. Bianca hoisted herself onto a table from a chair, so she could be heard and seen by the crowd below.

"Comrades!" she yelled to the crowd. "The Allies are advancing, the glorious Soviet armies are at the gates of Berlin." There was thunderous applause, and an older worker near the front began to cry tears of joy, causing Bianca to tear up as well. Even as Bianca had emerged as a capable leader over the last year, she wasn't one for big speeches, always preferring to lead quietly. Her loudest words had most often been on the page during the flurry of publishing—and now she was struggling to say out loud the things she had long refined in her mind and at the typewriter.

Her partner sensed her emotion and encouraged her, "Come on, go ahead!" But Bianca couldn't finish. So her comrade climbed onto the table as well, grabbing Bianca's hand with her own and holding them up together. "Let's get ready for the insurrection!" she yelled to a swell of cheers from the crowd below.

LEARNING LESSONS FROM Florence, the well-organized insurrection included groups of factory workers who barricaded themselves at their places of work to keep the Germans from destroying them in their retreat. Partisans in their dirt-caked fatigues came down from the Alps to fight alongside Turinese men in suits and ties. Women picked up guns when they had them and joined the men in the streets. Members of the GDD organized into groups of medics, hoping to keep themselves from being targets by carrying a red cross flag, dressing in white, or wearing an armband.

In the days leading up to the final battle, staffette were tasked with hiding partisans who were sneaking back into the city. Others had brazenly biked around Turin and its outskirts as spies, noting locations and details of Nazi battlements. More and more women agreed to fight or help—even those who had spent much of the war claiming neutrality. For some, this was their last chance to contribute to a cause they believed in. For others, they wanted to end the war on the winning side.

This was the culmination of the final insurrection that the CLN and local Resistance leadership had been planning for weeks. As a leader representing the city center, Bianca was calling to action the women and factory workers whom she had been organizing for a year and a half—encouraging them to fight for their neighborhoods; secure local infrastructure, public works, and works of art; and protect their factories and places of business.

ON THE EARLY morning of April 26, the telegram was sent to all of the partisan formations: ALDO DICE 26 X 1 ("Aldo says 26 times 1")—the signal to start the insurrection. There were around thirteen thousand Nazi and Fascist soldiers in Turin, though many of the Fascists were only holding their position because of the rations and paychecks or threat of retaliation. They had been offered a date of April 25 to give up their weapons and stand down, and many had done so, weakening their ranks. But the remaining soldiers were much better armed than the partisans who returned to the city. Still, the citizens' army had comparable numbers, and took up what weapons they could find.

Like in Florence and elsewhere, at the signal, the partisans began attacking the remaining Nazi and Fascist soldiers in the city, with a goal for them to surrender or retreat. As the fighting began on the streets of Turin, staffette hid in doorways with guns, pulled injured partisans to safety, and stood shoulder to shoulder with male partisans to keep retreating Nazis from destroying historic buildings. There was no telephone service, so staffette were also charged with facilitating communication among the bands engaged in battle.

Bianca moved around the city on foot and by bicycle, wearing a red cross armband. Avoiding firefights and grenades, she brought messages from one area to another, sharing information about what was happening in battle with the other sector leaders and partisan commanders. Despite the detailed plans from the Resistance, who used their intel to map out where enemy strongholds remained, the city was in chaos. Small battles erupted on narrow blocks, separated by wide, empty piazzas. It was difficult to know whether areas were truly liberated, or if dozens of soldiers lay in wait behind closed shutters to begin fighting anew. As she often was during her many missions since the start of the occupation, Bianca was alone, unarmed, with only her sharpened senses to keep her safe.

Bianca was crossing through Piazza Carlina alone, to deliver information to another partisan commander. She knew the neighborhood well—it was close to the university and to her home—but the square had few shadowy doorways and no porticoes in which to hide.

The sounds of gunshots rang out around the city, but the fighting did not seem perilously close, so she decided it was safe to slip through the square rather than move along the perimeter. Moments after she emerged into the seemingly abandoned piazza, Bianca heard shouting and the sound of leather soles running toward her—she was spotted by a group of teen boys. Bianca recognized them, although she did not know them personally. Recruited by the Fascists from the local Ferranti Aporti reform school, these boys were recently deputized to roam the city in search of partisans, to arrest them—or worse. She had written about them in her graduate school thesis just a few years prior: She knew intimately how many had lost parents to poverty or war, had turned to criminal behavior in desperation, had been indoctrinated by the Fascist government, which saw them as pawns to help entrench their own power.

The boys surrounded her, yelling, excited at their catch. Bianca insisted she was a nurse, pointing to her armband. Perhaps they debated why she was all alone, and in this part of the city—not in the midst of the fighting where the injured would be. Maybe they didn't care, eager to exercise their ill-gotten power in these last few hours of the war.

In the moment, none of them likely considered the statue of the Count of Cavour that loomed over them from the center of the piazza. It had been there for more than seventy-five years, honoring the unification of Italy and the young country's strength and resilience. Beneath the white marble sculpture of the count at its apex, the monument included a sculpture of a woman holding children in her arms, one representing a government by the people and the other, revolution. On the opposite side was a sculpture of a woman in a helmet, representing independence. She is throwing a broken chain to the ground next to sculptures of two children representing freedom and unity. The founding fathers of Italy had foreseen women's role in the birth of freedom, of a nation, even if it had taken more than eighty years for them to truly exercise this power.

Long minutes later the boys' commander caught up with them. Bianca's heart was beating fast as she feared that, after so many close encounters with the enemy, her life might end at the hands of these young thugs in the war's final hours. Assessing the situation, the commander saw Bianca's armband. *Of course women aren't partisans.* He underestimated Bianca, like so many of the enemy before him. The commander told the boys to set her free.

On April 25, 1945, Anita was sitting on a rock outside the mountain town of Gottano, a few dozen miles from Reggio Emilia. She could hear the last firefights happening in the valley below, but after the long, cold months in the mountains, she finally felt certain that the war was over and that she would live to see a free Italy. A great sadness overtook her, in part because she was thinking about all of her comrades who had not lived to see the end of the war. She had only recently heard that they had found Giambattista's body, uncovered once the winter snow had melted. He had a gunshot wound to his arm and had died from blood loss and exposure. She had accepted that he was gone since the autumn, but this news dashed whatever hope she might have held on to for their reunion.

But she was also starting to mourn the freedom she had experienced among the partisans. She didn't know how she could return to the life she had before the occupation. "I didn't want to listen to my brothers or father telling me what to do," she said. "I had broken what I had built and I did not intend to rebuild it." She began to imagine a different reality for herself, one she couldn't have had under Fascism.

Anita's experience echoed that of many women returning to domestic life. No matter that so many risked everything for this victory, women's contributions to the partisan effort during the war would not be more widely recognized until decades later. But for so many women—tens of thousands were known to have taken part in armed resistance and more than a hundred thousand were members of women's groups and provided material support—the freedom they had to make their own decisions and feel like an integral part of a larger movement was hard to replicate even in the more progressive post-war Italian culture. Yet still, so many worked to create the change for which they had risked their lives.

Anita Malavasi would never marry or have children of her own, but she dedicated herself to continuing the work for justice—particularly for women and for workers—that she believed her comrades had given their lives for. And she would, for the rest of her life, bring flowers to Giambattista's grave.

Both Carla Capponi and Teresa Mattei would be elected to national parliament roles a few short years after the war with a platform focusing on women's rights. Teresa helped to write the new Italian constitution, earning her the lifelong moniker "the mother of the constitution." Carla would marry Rosario and Teresa would marry Bruno, both couples realizing that their time in battle created a bond that they could never hope to find with another. Although these paths were not easy. Bruno died just a few years after his and Teresa's union, leaving her with two young children: Gianfranco and Antonella. Carla and Rosario would divorce decades later.

Bianca Guidetti Serra would finally find work as a lawyer and spend her career fighting for the rights of women and children. She married Alberto Salmoni in the first civil wedding in Turin after the war, and the first officiated by a woman—her friend and mentor

Ada Gobetti, who was appointed the first female deputy mayor of Turin. She would also work with her friend Primo Levi, who was one of the very few who returned from Auschwitz, to educate people about the atrocities of the Holocaust.

These women's experiences are dramatic and brave—and I chose to amplify their stories because I do believe they represent the breadth of the work women performed in the Resistance. Yet there are as many stories as there are women. Widely published estimates point to women making up about 10 percent of the three hundred thousand partisans who took part in armed actions—or around thirty-five thousand. But the definition of what should be considered resistance is still evolving. Hundreds of thousands of women actively supported in other ways. These women helped lead a nation and turn the tide of dual fronts of war, both what is considered by many to be the Italian civil war and World War II. In this history, I don't mean to subjugate other mundane but integral material support to the background, and I have strived to acknowledge these stories throughout. Giving up rations, sending desperately needed money, making food, knitting socks, tending to the bodies of the deceased, refusing to join Fascist events—all could result in arrest, torture, or death. Historians calculate that for every armed partisan fighter, there were fifteen people supporting them in various ways—the vast majority of this support system being women. I also want to value the everyday acts of *le maternage,* as the feminist Italian scholar Anna Bravo coined activist works of mothering and nurturing, that upward of a hundred thousand women performed at great risk to themselves. This term echoes the concept of "activist mothering" popularized by Dr. Françoise Hamlin, a scholar of American activism.

So much of the Resistance was actually led by the working class, by mothers, by caretakers. Many of these women *had* to work, or their families would not eat. They *had* to figure out childcare, as often their husbands were dead or deported or in the mountains or on the front line, not to mention that this was also generally the woman's role, even if a partner was around. They might not have wielded a gun or slept on the ground in fear of Nazis stumbling over them, but they endured great suffering in service for revolution. I want us to be inspired by them as well. The Resistance would not have existed without these women, and their sacrifices are just as important.

Many consider the expanding roles of women during the war as ushering in a new wave of Italian feminism. And women did enjoy vastly more opportunities after the war than they had during the prior two decades of Fascist rule—or beforehand. But the deeply seated conservative beliefs around gender roles and xenophobia have been hard to overcome—in the decades after the war and continuing to the present day. Yet there are still many ways that these women of war led to great change in post-war Italy, even as there is much work that remains to be done, as evidenced in the recent political victories of neo-Fascist candidates and ideologies.

I read early in my research that in the victory parades after liberation, very few women marched with the partisans—a detail that shocked me. How could these men, who knew the contributions of the women among them, allow them to return to the sidelines? And then I read the account from a woman who said that her male comrades suggested she not be among them in the parades, anticipating the reaction from the onlookers. She watched with the crowds on the sidewalk as her all-male battalion went by, followed by another battalion whose women also marched.

"Mamma mia," she said, "thank goodness I wasn't [marching with them]. People were saying they were whores." Was she excluded or protected? Perhaps both—by her partisan comrades, but also by the Italian people, men and women, whom she helped to free. Among the rolling liberation parades as the Nazis moved northward, there are reports similar to these, as well as others where women were asked to wear red cross armbands to imply they were nurses. In some places these women were celebrated, in others, where women walked confidently, many still wearing pants, some in the crowd gasped, *What have we done to our country?* Much changed with the fall of Fascism, but many social norms and beliefs were deeply embedded, some still unmoved to this day.

In the past decade or so in Italy, there has been a renewed interest in telling the stories of these partisan women, with a handful of new biographies and documentaries available, of course with Benedetta Tobagi's well-received book *La Resistenza delle Donne,* which was published in Italy midway through the research for this book, among the most prominent. And as recently as spring 2022, the Tuscan regional government compiled a document with resources on female partisans for the first time, continuing to reconcile the vast underrepresentation of female contributors in the archives dedicated to documenting the partisans of World War II. Although there are clearly many smaller archives that have long been working hard to preserve the memories, and acknowledge the contributions, of women during the war.

It is clear there is power in telling these stories. Readers can see how the women partisans themselves became empowered during the war and throughout their lives as they told their truth, with some finally getting their due for their contributions only late in their lives. And, of course, we can be inspired today by the work of these activist mothers (and sisters and friends), who fought against Fascist tyranny and for women's rights.

Anita said she started writing in those last days of war from atop her mountain ridge in the Apennines.

"I said goodbye to the plants, the trees that had protected me.... Then I said goodbye to the mountains, and for the first time from the mountain I saw a corner toward La Spezia where there was a stormy sea. You could just see the wave breaking, and it was a sunny, white light kind of day. You felt like you could reach out and catch the sea.

"When I got home, with this new reality in front of me, I said, 'Well, now I'm going to get to work on building what these guys, like Giambattista, fell for, those guys we left behind in the mountains, and who had so much hope.'"

I am sad to say goodbye to these women, whose lives I became so immersed in as I sought to share their stories. But I am also inspired to work on building—like Carla, Teresa, Anita, Bianca, and so many others did—a better tomorrow. As the stories of these women are amplified, a new narrative emerges, one of bravery and agency in the face of oppression—and of the true costs of freedom. The stormy seas are out there—these women have shown them to us. And they have also shown us how we can chart a path forward.

ACKNOWLEDGMENTS

Women of War would not exist without the support of so many people. Thank you, Monika Woods, for your rigorous feedback to help shape this book from my earliest ideas, and thank you to your team at Triangle House for years of advocating for my work. Deepest appreciation to Brent Howard for first seeing the potential of *Women of War,* and Cassidy Sachs for such thoughtful feedback and continual guidance through writing, production, and beyond. So many librarians, archivists, experts, and assistants were essential support throughout the research process. Thank you to the excellent research intern Zoya Rehman, whose work helped organize enough information on Italian female partisans to write five more books. And *tante grazie* to Giaime Spina, who provided research and translation help, as well as his vital perspective.

Much appreciation to Chiara Torcianti, Davide Cillo, Massimo Storchi, Michele Bellelli, Giacomo Prencipe, and others at IS-TORECO in Reggio Emilia, who not only pulled out every interesting source and artifact to help tell Anita's story, but shared deep expertise about the resistance in Reggio Emilia, the Apennines, and beyond; to Francesco Campobello, and the folks at the Centro

Studi Piero Gobetti, who supported my research across three visits; to Cristina Sara and Andrea D'Arrigo and other archivists and librarians at ISTORETO, who pulled out many books and boxes from the archives, helping me fill in details about the Resistance in and around Turin across three visits, as well as track down obscure sources only alluded to in other publications. I appreciate the time spent at the UDI library and the Via Tasso archive, and the librarians at Istituto Storico Toscano della Resistenza who unearthed more boxes from the archives and newly published links about women in the local resistance over multiple visits. And much appreciation to Mayara Pereira and Cristina Bellini at the Ulivi Library, and Bruce Edelstein at NYU Florence, who gave advice on local resources and helped track down other hard-to-find resources in the city and beyond. And there are many folks whom I have not met, but who found dusty tomes from the off-site storage at NYU Bobst Library, or tracked down interlibrary loans for other rare books, who deserve my appreciation as well.

I would also like to thank Santina Mobiglia and Fabrizio Salmoni, who provided details about the life of, respectively, their friend and mother, Bianca Guidetti Serra. I also acknowledge the time Simonetta Soldani spent talking about the life and legacy of Teresa Mattei. Thank you to Serena Balestracci for sharing your expertise in Florence.

The writing of this book required a village as well. Sarah DiGregorio and Luisa Tucker both gave the most careful and kind suggestions and cheerleading. NYU professors Mark Braley, Michelle McSwiggan Kelly, Noelle Molé Liston, Nate Mickelson, Jenni Quilter, Avia Tadmore, Natasha Zaretsky, and other esteemed colleagues all supported this project in some crucial way. The Global Research Initiative at NYU provided funding and research opportunities in Florence in the summer of 2023, with support from people met during that time lasting far beyond.

But I would be nowhere without the support of my family. *Grazie mille* to my mother, who watched the kids, made the food, read an early draft, and sent the preorder link to all her friends. She is the daughter of my Nani, our last direct link to our Italian heritage, who would be the exact age of these women I spent so much time with on the page. *Grazie infinite a mio marito*, Steve Mayone: from driving us into the rural countryside in search of an archive (and then entertaining the kids in the piazza while I worked), to encouraging me to take whatever time I needed to make every deadline and refine every sentence, to the celebratory wine and your vocal championing to friends, family, and beyond—my success is your success. And to Rocco and Lucian, who gamely tagged along to libraries and waited for dozens of tardy Italian buses in the scorching summer heat, *grazie di cuore* for your love and support.

And, finally, this book is dedicated to the memory of Pattra Wirojratana Mattox, whose acute sense of justice helped me understand these women in a deeper way, and who was supportive of this project from its earliest days. You are greatly missed.

Allpersonal details, inner thoughts, and dialogue in scenes with Carla, Teresa, Bianca, and Anita were quoted and re-created from the following personal writing, interviews, biographies, and testimonies, except where noted. These are all also cited in the bibliography.

Carla's experiences were taken primarily from her memoir, *Con Cuore di Donna,* and other noted interviews (see "In Via Rasella Carla Capponi Spiega i Momenti dell'Attacco Partigiano del 23 Marzo 1944" and "Carla Capponi 3 Le Motivazioni della Lotta Partigiana"), with additional insight provided by the authors Katz, Kurzman, and Portelli, who integrated previously unpublished details and interviews into their histories of Rome under occupation. I always deferred to Carla's words when information differed that could not be confirmed elsewhere.

Teresa's experiences were taken from biographical publications by Pacini, Soldani, and Panichi, and from interviews (see Teresa Mattei, *Dall'Antifascismo Attivo all'Assemblea Costituente,* interview with B. Enriotti and I. Paulucci and "Teresa Mattei, Una Vita Partigiana," interview with G. Minà).

Bianca's experiences were taken from her memoir, *Bianca la Rossa;* an unpublished interview from the ISTORETO archives in Turin; an interview I had with her memoir's co-writer, Santina Mobiglia, as well as her other written and cited works about Bianca; an interview with her son, Fabrizio Salmoni; and the other writings by her cited in the bibliography.

Anita's experiences were taken from written and oral testimonies from archives at the University of Bologna, the ISTORECO archives in Reggio Emilia, and La Fondazione Archivio Diaristico Nazionale in Pieve Santo Stefano.

If not otherwise noted, all of these sources were consulted to provide various perspectives on each scene, as most scenes were discussed in multiple resources, often with collaborating—and occasionally conflicting—information, which is not unexpected when working from memory, and the recounting of experiences many years later. For the rare details in each of these women's stories that did not align with history as I understand it from scholars, or that conflicted with other accounts, I used my best judgment about when to place it in the story and what might be considered truth, trusting the women's own experiences over the remembered experiences of others while using the work of scholars and historians to fact-check.

Other details about historical context of their experiences and that of those who were with them at the time were also added from various testimonies, written and oral, and scholarly and historical accounts. Some of these sources were audio or video, and others were printed, but unpublished, testimonies; of the memoirs I read, I often used the e-books since the sources are difficult to find in print outside Italy, thus there are rarely page numbers. Likewise much of the printed archival material was found by sorting through thick stacks of material provided by the librarians when I gave them the topics I was researching, without a detailed finding aid. If future scholars are interested in referencing specific information, please reach out and I am happy to point you in the right direction or share my images. Everything in quotations is a direct quote. The very few scenes with italicized English dialogue include words re-created from conversations referenced in accounts, allowing for a more seamless reading experience. Every scene, interaction, and emotion noted comes directly from the written or spoken words of the women themselves.

Nearly all of these primary sources are in Italian, and I have translated most of the written sources myself, checking meaning at times from native speakers. Most audio transcriptions were done by native speakers of Italian, with Giaime Spina doing the vast majority of this work.

For the historical and military background, I read copious books that covered overlapping periods and subjects. For the brief chapters that offer a broader context of the war, I consulted numerous sources and did not cite what was widely available, nor did I note sweeping histories of World War II in this bibliography, as there are many. For histories that focus on the war in Italy, I often did not cite the source of a quote or detail if the same information was presented in two or more books, which happened often since this topic is also well-trodden, but I have listed all sources used in the bibliography. These books were mostly in English. I also consulted detailed histories of the Resistance in each region as noted (see Calamandrei, Francovich, Padovani, Paterlini, Storchi) as well as other primarily Italian sources that helped put these women's stories into the larger context of Fascism, war, and the Resistance (see Alano, Antonelli, Bravo and Bruzzone, D'Amelio, De Grazia, Gasco, Saba, Slaughter, Tobagi) with an Italian bias and a more granular focus than many of the mainstream English histories.

NOTE ON SOURCES

I am very lucky that New York University—my home institution—has one of the best Italian-language libraries covering this period in the United States. I was able to request some books that are otherwise difficult to find in the United States from deep storage or access them on the circulating shelves. A few others I was able to get through interlibrary loan. However, there were still numerous texts that I could only read in an archive or library in Italy, taking many photos to reference later. All of the sources I consulted are in the bibliography, but if they are not noted in the endnotes, it is because they were used to provide corroboration of details or a broader overview of this time.

I welcome sharing my research with future writers and scholars!

BIBLIOGRAPHY

Adduci, Nicola. *Gli Altri: Fascismo Repubblicano e Comunità nel Torinese (1943–1945)*. FrancoAngeli, 2014.

Alano, Jomarie. "Armed with a Yellow Mimosa: Women's Defense and Assistance Groups in Italy, 1943–45." *Journal of Contemporary History*, vol 38, no 4, 2003.

Antonelli, Laura. *Voci dalla Storia: Le Donne della Resistenza in Toscana tra Storie di Vita e Percorsi di Emancipazione*. Pentalinea, 2006.

Artom, Emanuele. *Diari di un Partigiani Ebreo*. Bollati Boringhieri, 2022, e-book.

Atkinson, Rick. *The Day of Battle: The War in Sicily and Italy, 1943–1944*. Little, Brown, 2007.

Averett, Matthew Knox. "'Redditus Orbis Erat': The Political Rhetoric of Bernini's Fountains in Piazza Barberini." *Sixteenth Century Journal*, vol 45, no 1, 2014, 3–24. JSTOR, http://www.jstor.org/stable/24247470.

Baldoli, Claudia. "Spring 1943: The Fiat Strikes and the Collapse of the Italian Home Front." *History Workshop Journal*, no 72, 2011, 181–89, JSTOR, http://www.jstor.org/stable/41306844.

"Battle of the Bulge." History.com, July 20, 2020, https://www.history.com/topics/world-war-ii/battle-of-the-bulge.

The Battle of the Bulge: An Allied Victory and the Road to Liberation. Lemaitre Publishing, 2016.

Baxa, Paul. "Capturing the Fascist Moment: Hitler's Visit to Italy in 1938 and the Radicalization of Fascist Italy." *Journal of Contemporary History*, vol 42, no 2, 2007, 227–42. JSTOR, http://www.jstor.org/stable/30036443.

Behan, Tom. *The Italian Resistance: Fascists, Guerrillas and the Allies*. Pluto Press, 2009.

Benito Mussolini speech, Rome, March 26, 1939, YouTube.com, April 12, 2012, https://www.youtube.com/watch?v=Hpn9iPLbNDc.

"Benito Mussolini: What Is Fascism, 1932." *Internet Modern History Sourcebook*, Fordham University, Aug 1997.

Bentivegna, Rosario. *Achtung Banditen! Prima e Dopo Via Rasella.* Gruppo Ugo Murisa Editore, 2004.

Bentivegna, Rosario. *Operazione Via Rasella.* Editori Riuniti, 1996.

Bentivegna, Rosario. *Senza Fare di Necessità Virtù: Memorie di un Anti-fascista.* Einaudi, 2011.

Bracker, Milton. "Italian Partisans Resent Allies' Ban." *New York Times,* Nov 17, 1944, https://www.nytimes.com/1944/11/18/archives/italian-partisans -resent-allies-ban-protest-alexanders-order.html.

Bravo, Anna, and Anna Maria Bruzzone. *In Guerra Senza Armi: Storie di Donne (1940–1945).* Lazterza, 2000.

Brigham, Daniel T. "North Italy Idle in Wide Protest," *New York Times,* March 4, 1944, https://www.nytimes.com/1944/03/04/archives/north-italy-idle -in-wide-protests-6000000-are-locked-out-or-on.html.

Brunelli, Camilla. "A Short Introduction of the Strike in March 1944 and of Political Deportation from Prato," Museo della Deportazione, http://www.mu seodelladeportazione.it/en/political-deportation-from-prato/.

Calamandrei, Piero. *Uomini e Città della Resistenza.* Linea D'Ombra, 1994.

Capponi, Carla. *Con Cuore di Donna.* Il Saggiatore, 2000.

"Carla Capponi 3 Le Motivazioni della Lotta Partigiana," Banca della Memoria Roma. YouTube.com, Feb 12, 2014, https://www.youtube.com/watch?v =eYJE46a8KC0.

Chaisson, Patrick J. "Was Hitler's Ardennes Offensive Brilliant or Delusional?" Warfare History Network, https://warfarehistorynetwork.com/was-hitlers -ardennes-offensive-brilliant-or-delusional/.

Clark, Lloyd. *Anzio: Italy and the Battle for Rome—1944.* Atlantic Monthly Press, 2006.

Corner, Paul. *Mussolini in Myth and Memory: The First Totalitarian Dictator.* Cambridge University Press, 2022, e-book.

D'Amelio, Dan A. "Italian Women in the Resistance, World War II." *Italian Americana,* vol 19, no 2, Summer 2001, http://www.jstor.org/stable/29776690.

De Grazia, Victoria. *How Fascism Ruled Women: Italy, 1922–1945.* University of California Press, 1992.

De Lazzari, Primo. *Storia del Fronte della Gioventù nella Resistenza.* Gruppo Ugo Murisa Editore, 1996.

De Vito, Christian G. "Paradoxical Outcomes? Incarceration, War and Regime Changes in Italy, 1943–54." In *Incarceration and Regime Change: European Prisons during and after the Second World War,* edited by Christian G. De Vito, Ralf Futselaar, and Helen Grevers. Berghahn Books, 2017.

Dominici, Daniele. "Supporting the Radio CORA: Memoirs of Michele Della Corte." *Il Colle di Galileo,* vols. 2 and 4. Firenze University Press, 2015.

Edsel, Robert M. *Saving Italy: The Race to Rescue a Nation's Treasures from the Nazis.* W. W. Norton, 2013.

Fisher, Ernest F. *Cassino to the Alps: U.S. Army in World War II,* vol. 6-4-1. Center of Military History, United States Army, 1993.

Francovich, Carlo. *La Resistenza a Firenze.* La Nuova Italia, 1962.

Gagliarducci, Stefano, Massimiliano Gaetano Onorato, Francesco Sobbrio, and Guido Tabellini. "War of the Waves: Radio and Resistance during World War

II." IZA Institute of Labor Economics, Discussion Paper Series, Dec 2017, https://docs.iza.org/dp11244.pdf.

Garvin, Diana. "The Italian Coffee Triangle: From Brazilian Colonos to Ethiopian Colonialisti." *Modern Italy,* vol 26, no 3, 2021, 291–312.

Gasco, Anna, ed. *La Guerra alla Guerra: Storie di Donne a Torino e in Piemonte tra il 1940–1945.* Laissez Passer, 2007.

"Gilda La Rocca: Una Radio-Partigiana Leale e Invisible." Radio d'Epoca Umberto Alunni, Aug 15, 2019, https://www.umbertoalunni.it/gilda-la-rocca-una-radio-partigiana-leale-e-invisibile/.

Gli Scioperi del Marzo 1944. Città di Torino, 2004.

Gobetti, Ada. *Partisan Diary: A Woman's Life in the Italian Resistance.* Translated and edited by Jomarie Alano. Oxford University Press, 2014.

Guidetti Serra, Bianca. *Bianca la Rossa.* Einaudi, 2021, e-book.

Guidetti Serra, Bianca. *Compagne: Testimonianze di Partecipazione Politica Femminile,* vol. 1. Einaudi, 1977.

Guidetti Serra, Bianca. "Minima Personalia." *Belfagor: Rassenga di Varie Umanità.* Casa Editrice Leo. S Olschki, 1991.

Guidetti Serra, Bianca. *Primo Levi, the Friend.* CPL Editions, 2014.

Guidetti Serra, Bianca. "Quello Che Scrivevano le Donne Della Resistenza Sui Loro Giornali." *Il Voto Alle Donne.* FrancoAngeli, 1998.

Guidetti Serra, Bianca. "Una Donna, Una Persona." Fondazione Nuto Rivelli, http://www.resistenzauominiedonne.org/, n.d.

Hapgood, David, and David Richardson. *Monte Cassino.* Congdon & Weed, 1984.

Hibbert, Christopher. *Mussolini: The Rise and Fall of Il Duce.* Griffin, 2008.

"Il Monte Caio: Vero Parco UNESCO degli Apennini." Parks.it, June 24, 2019, https://www.parks.it/news/dettaglio.php?id=54858.

"In Via Rasella Carla Capponi Spiega i Momenti dell'Attacco Partigiano del 23 Marzo 1944." ERODOTO TV di Enzo Antonio Cicchino, YouTube.com, Jan 6, 2021, https://www.youtube.com/watch?v=I8D1eSOsyfw.

"Italy Surrenders Unconditionally." *Guardian,* Sep 9, 1943, https://www.theguardian.com/world/1943/sep/09/secondworldwar.italy.

Jackson, W. G. F. *The Battle for Italy.* B. T. Batsford, 1967.

Katz, Robert. *The Battle for Rome.* Simon and Schuster, 2003.

Kurzman, Dan. *The Race for Rome: How the Eternal City Was Saved from Nazi Destruction.* Doubleday, 1975.

Lamb, Richard. *War in Italy: 1943–1945.* St. Martin's Press, 1993.

López, Óscar González. *Freeing Mussolini: Dismantling the Skorzeny Myth in the Gran Sasso Raid.* Pen & Sword Books, 2018.

Lucas, Richard. *Axis Sally: The American Voice of Nazi Germany.* Casemate, 2010.

Luzzatto, Sergio. *Primo Levi's Resistance.* Henry Holt, 2013.

Mattei, Teresa. Interviewed by Antonio Carioti. "Così Abbiamo Ucciso Gentile." *Corriere della Sera,* Aug 6, 2004.

Mattei, Teresa. Interviewed by Bruno Enriotti and Ibio Paolucci. "Testimoni del 900." *Triangolo Rosso,* https://deportati.it/static/pdf/TR/2004/maggio/10.pdf.

McConnon, Aili, and Andres McConnon. *Road to Valor: A True Story of World War II Italy, the Nazis, and the Cyclist Who Inspired a Nation.* Crown, 2013, e-book.

BIBLIOGRAPHY

"Military Police Find Rita Louisa Zucca in Turin—Relatives in New York Deny She Served Foe Willingly; Family Denies Voluntary Talks." *New York Times,* June 8, 1945, https://www.nytimes.com/1945/06/08/archives/americans-seize-axis-sally-in-italy-fascist-broadcaster-born-here.html.

Mobiglia, Santina. "Bianca Guidetti Serra e le Domeniche a Reaglie." *Ada e le Altre: Legami Femminili tra Educazione e Valore della Differenza.* Biblion International Monographs, 2015.

"Noi, Compagne di Combattimento . . . : I Gruppi di Difesa della Donna, 1943—1945." ANPI, 2017, https://www.anpi.it/media/uploads/files/2017/11/Noi_compagne_di_combattimento_-_testi.pdf.

Origo, Iris. *A Chill in the Air: An Italian War Diary, 1939–1940.* Pushkin Press, 2017.

Origo, Iris. *War in Val d'Orcia: An Italian War Diary, 1943–1944.* David R. Godine, 1984.

Orlandini, Laura. *La Democrazia delle Donne: I Gruppi dei Difesa della Donna nella Costruzione della Repubblica (1943–1945).* BraDypUs, 2018.

Pacini, Patrizia. *La Costituente: Storia di Teresa Mattei.* Altre Economica, 1999.

Padovani, Gigi. *La Liberazione di Torino: Aprile 1945: Le Sette Giornate dell'Insurreczione.* Edizioni del Capricorno, 2022.

Panichi, Silvia. *Teresa Mattei.* Pacini '900 Ritratti, 2014.

Paoletti, Paolo. *Il Delitto Gentile: Esecutori e Mandanti.* Le Lettere, 2005.

Paterlini, Avvenire. *Partigiane e Patriote della Provincia di Reggio Emilia.* Libreria Rinascita, 1977.

Patriarca, Carlo, et al. "Jewish Anatomic Pathologists in the Time of Italian Racial Laws." *Pathologica,* vol 114, no 2, Apr 2022, 179–84, doi:10.32074/1591-951X-713.

Pavone, Claudio. *A Civil War: A History of the Italian Resistance.* Verso, 2013.

Pesce, Giovanni. *Senza Tregua: La Guerra dei GAP.* Feltrinelli Editore Milano, 1967.

Portelli, Alessandro. *The Order Has Been Carried Out: History, Memory, and Meaning of a Nazi Massacre in Rome.* Palgrave Macmillan, 2003.

Pugliese, Stanislao G. *Fascism, Anti-Fascism, and the Resistance in Italy: 1919 to the Present.* Rowman and Littlefield, 2004.

"Reggio Emilia, Italy. 3 March 1944. An aircraft factory was put out of production in two attacks . . ." Australian War Memorial, https://www.awm.gov.au/collection/C367725.

Rodano, Marisa. *Memorie di Una Che C'era: Una Storia dell' UDI.* Il Saggiatore, 2010.

Rosengarten, Frank. *The Italian Anti-Fascist Press (1919–1945).* Press of Case Western Reserve University, 1968.

Saba, Marina Addis. *Partigiane: Tutte le Donne della Resistenza.* Gruppo Ugo Murisa Editore, 1998.

Saba, Marina Addis. *La Scelta: Ragazze Partigiane, Ragazze di Salò.* Editori Riuniti, 2005.

Sanguinetti, Paola. *La Storia di Bruno.* Vangelista, 1997.

Slaughter, Jane. *Women and the Italian Resistance, 1943–1945.* Arden Press, 1997.

Soldani, Simonetta. "Teresa Mattei." *I Deputati Toscani All'Assemblea Costituente: Profili Biografici.* Edited by P. L. Ballini. Consiglio Regionale della Toscana, 2018, 415–27.

BIBLIOGRAPHY

Spriano, Carla Guidetti Serra. "Un'Esperienza al Femminile: Diario 1939–1945." *Torino in Guerra.* Gribaudo, 1995.

Storchi, Massimo, ed. *20 Mesi per la Libertà: La Guerra di Liberazione dal Cusna al Po.* Edizioni Bertani, 2005.

"Targa Memorial Partigiana 'Mimma.'" ANPIReggioEmilia.it, https://www.anpireggioemilia.it/targa-memoriale-partigiana-mimma/.

"Teresa Mattei. Dall'Antifascismo Attivo all'Assemblea Costituente." Interview with B. Enriotti and I. Paulucci. *Triangolo Rosso,* May 2004.

"Teresa Mattei, Una Vita Partigiana." Interview with G. Minà, Mar 7, 1997.

"Teresa Mattei—Wikiradio del 08/03/2017: Raccontata da Simonetta Soldani." RaiRadio, Mar 8, 2017.

Tobagi, Benedetta. *La Resistenza delle Donne.* Einaudi, 2022.

Toland, John. *Battle: The Story of the Bulge.* University of Nebraska Press, 1999.

Torino in Guerra 1940–1945. Gribaudo Editore, 1995.

United Press. "Text of Mussolini Speech; Rumors Laid to 'Riffraff' Mere Discussions Barred Allies' 'Wise Intention.'" *New York Times,* Sept 24, 1939, https://www.nytimes.com/1939/09/24/archives/text-of-mussolini-speech-rumors-laid-to-riffraff-mere-discussions.html.

Wilhelm, Maria de Blasio. *The Other Italy: Italian Resistance in World War II.* W. W. Norton, 1988.

Willson, Perry. *Women in Twentieth-Century Italy.* Palgrave Macmillan, 2010.

Whitlock, Flint. *Desperate Valour: Triumph at Anzio.* Da Capo Press, 2018.

Zuccotti, Susan. *Italians and the Holocaust.* University of Nebraska Press, 1987.

The location of Casa Internazionale della Donna in Rome is also home to the headquarters of UDI (Unione Donne in Italia), the feminist organization that grew out of the GDD after the war, and there I accessed books that are unavailable in the United States that helped add understanding and context to the experience of women under Fascism and during the war.

Centro Studi Piero Gobetti in Turin, over three visits, provided archival and historical information about Ada Gobetti and Bianca Guidetti Serra. Here I also spoke with the director of Bianca's archive, Francesco Campobello, and her close friend and co-writer of *Bianca la Rossa,* Santina Mobiglia. Both provided greater context and detail into Bianca's work, and Santina in particular answered many questions about Bianca and her experiences and elaborated on stories from her memoir, adding additional recollections as well. In my first visits here I also accessed artifacts from Ada Gobetti and books that provided more information about the Resistance movement during the war.

La Fondazione Archivio Diaristico Nazionale, Archives of Pieve

Santo Stefano, allowed me to read a testimony of Anita Malavasi that is unavailable elsewhere.

The Fosse Ardeatine Memorial is located at the site of the Ardeatine cave murders, committed by the Nazis in retribution for the Via Rasella attacks. Not only did their resources help me re-create this painful moment but there is also an extensive museum about the experience of the Resistance in Rome during the occupation, with artifacts, primary sources, and historical context. There is also copious information about the Via Rasella attacks, and I also spoke with a guide who shared his perspective and expertise on this event and its aftermath.

The Istituto Storico Toscana della Resistenza library and archive in Florence provided information about the Resistance in Florence, as well as details about many women and men who were active in the Resistance. I visited here twice, once at the start of my research when their information gave me a solid grounding of the Resistance and offered books unavailable elsewhere, and then near the end of my research to help fill in details about the history of the Resistance in Florence, including details about Radio CORA and information about Teresa Mattei.

ISTORECO (Historical Institute of the Resistance) Reggio Emilia provided video testimony of Anita Malavasi, as well as other archival and historical material chosen by the librarians about this time. Over two visits, with additional correspondence, I also spoke with archivists Massimo Storchi and Chiara Torcianti, who provided more detail and contextual information about the lives of the partisans during the occupation and answered specific questions. Davide Cillo, Giacomo Prencipe, and others at the Institute provided additional information and assistance.

ISTORETO (Historical Institute of the Resistance) Turin provided a deep trove of primary and secondary research over three visits, primarily focused on the resistance in the Piedmont region, but also extending to clandestine publications and the life and experiences of Bianca Guidetti Serra. Here I also accessed an unpublished interview with Bianca that added detail to her published experiences in *Bianca la Rossa*. The archived primary documents found here were chosen by the librarians when I inquired about information concerning the March 1944 worker strikes, the GDD, and any documentation about Bianca Guidetti Serra and the Resistance in Turin and around the region.

The Museo Diffuso della Resistenza in Turin helps make the experience of the occupation come alive for visitors. Over three visits, it also provided historical background on the war and occupation with a focus on the city of Turin and the Piedmont region, interviews with survivors and partisans, including Bianca Guidetti Serra, as well as artifacts, virtual reality experiences, and more, both in the main museum space and in the walking tour around the city, which takes visitors to key locations of the local Resistance.

The Museo Storico della Liberazione at Via Tasso is a museum and archive situated in the former Nazi-Fascist prison and includes primary and secondary sources within the cells and offices, including graffiti and other writing and artifacts from prisoners that recreate the time and experiences of partisans during the war and occupation, both within the prison and beyond. There is also an archive and library that provided historical texts unavailable in the United States and news clippings and personal writings and ephemera from gappisti in Rome, which helped give shape to Carla's story and many of the incidents she described.

The University of Bologna provided access to hours of audio testimonies of Anita Malavasi as well as books unavailable in the United States that gave broader context to the lives and experiences of partisans and women during the occupation.

Resistance-Archive.org has edited videos of partisan testimony, including from Anita Malavasi and Lidia Valeriani. Anita's testimony here is an edited version of what I accessed from ISTORECO (Historical Institute of the Resistance) Reggio Emilia.

Stampaclandestina.it is an archive of searchable digitized clandestine newspapers from around Italy and provided images of multiple publications referenced here.

Professional tour guide and historian Serena Balestracci provided background on the history of Florence before and during World War II and Hitler's visit to Florence in 1938, through a private walking tour and interview in July 2023.

I interviewed Santina Mobiglia, co-writer and friend of Bianca Guidetti Serra, in March 2024, asking about Bianca and for additional information beyond what was on the pages of Bianca's memoir. She continued to answer follow-up questions via email.

I interviewed Fabrizio Salmoni, Bianca Guidetti Serra's son, in September 2024. He confirmed details of many stories recounted by his mother over the years and provided added context to the lives and experiences of both his mother and his father.

I interviewed Simonetta Soldani, a feminist scholar who has also researched the life of Teresa Mattei, in July 2022. She also wrote a scholarly biography as cited.

I interviewed Massimo Storchi at ISTORECO (Historical Institute of the Resistance) Reggio Emilia in March 2024 for broader context, asking specific questions about the Battle of Monte Caio, the Resistance in Reggio Emilia and the Apennine Mountains, the experiences of Anita Malavasi, and other related topics.

I also spoke informally with many librarians and archivists and museum workers during my research, and some contextual details can be attributed to these conversations.

NOTES

PROLOGUE: CARLA

In this chapter and others telling Carla's story, quotations and scene details are taken from her memoir, *Con Cuore di Donna,* which I accessed as an e-book. All dialogue and other direct quotes are from her memoir unless otherwise noted. I often cross-referenced scenes she detailed with Bentivegna, *Senza Fare di Necessità Virtù,* as well as the other texts written by Bentivegna as cited; Katz, *The Battle for Rome;* Kurzman, *The Race for Rome;* and Portelli, *The Order Has Been Carried Out.* Bentivegna was Carla's fellow partisan and former husband and was present for many of these moments. Katz, Kurzman, and Portelli interviewed Carla for their books and include never-before-published details. I never superseded her assertions with theirs.

Robert Katz's *The Battle for Rome* provided a lively and granular dive into the experience of the resistance in Rome. I primarily consulted this book in this chapter and others for details about the German occupation in and around Rome and the experiences of the people of Rome. I will note direct quotes or specifics from his work that I only found here, but I also used this source as a broader reference. When he quotes other sources, I strived to go to the original for broader context, but this was not always possible. He does re-create some scenes taken from Carla's memoir, but I did not use his translations, preferring to consult this primary source myself.

Atkinson, *The Day of Battle,* provides a detailed account of the Allied landing in Italy.

10 **"Today we choose to drop":** Katz, *The Battle for Rome,* 11.
10 **"If the enemy were to":** Katz, *The Battle for Rome,* 12.

1: TERESA, MILAN AND FLORENCE, 1929–1938

In this chapter and others telling Teresa's story, scene details are taken from Pacini, Panichi, Soldani, and various interviews with Teresa as noted in the bibliography.

17 **trajectory of Benito Mussolini:** For further details about Benito Mussolini's life, see Hibbert, *Mussolini.*

19 **ideologist and philosopher Giovanni Gentile:** "Benito Mussolini: What Is Fascism, 1932."

19 **Unlike the ideals:** This is, of course, a simplistic comparison of these governing and economic philosophies. I strived to give a brief, concise comparison for those who are not familiar with these terms, or only understand them through an (often biased) historical context.

20 **the new media of film:** Corner, *Mussolini in Myth and Memory.* Corner also provided additional details and context of Italian life under Fascism.

21 **Decades later a defense:** Corner, *Mussolini in Myth and Memory.*

24 **Il Duce met Adolf Hitler's:** This and other details and analysis of Hitler's visit to Italy are primarily from Baxa, "Capturing the Fascist Moment."

Additional reference photos about Hitler's visit to Florence come from Maxim Chornyi's website https://war-documentary.info/hitler-goes-florence/, with additional details coming from a private tour and personal interview with Florence tour guide and historian Serena Balestracci.

25 **Mussolini had, just weeks earlier:** This refers to the Easter Accords. See Baxa, "Capturing the Fascist Moment," for more analysis.

26 **The most notable protest:** Balestracci's tour and interview brought me to this and other key locations that helped me imagine these moments while walking through present-day Florence.

26 **blaming them for high rent:** See Zuccotti, *Italians and the Holocaust,* chapters 1 and 13, for more context and information specifically about this topic. The entire book is useful for the larger story of the experience of Jewish people in Italy during this time.

27 **composed the *Manifesto*:** See Patriarca et al., "Jewish Anatomic Pathologists in the Time of Italian Racial Laws."

27 **Mussolini surely recognized how farcical:** See Zuccotti, *Italians and the Holocaust,* 34–42, for more context about the racial laws during this time.

28 **where barely 20 percent of seats:** Behan, *The Italian Resistance,* 161.

2: BIANCA, TURIN, 1938

In this chapter and others telling Bianca's story, scene details are taken from her memoir, *Bianca la Rossa,* which I accessed as an e-book, other writing by Bianca as noted in the bibliography, and an unpublished interview transcribed and accessed from the ISTORETO (Historical Institute of the Resistance) Turin archives. I also interviewed Bianca's friend and memoir co-writer Santina Mobiglia, who added more detail and answered questions about Bianca and her experiences; and her son, Fabrizio Salmoni, who did the same. At times her friend Ada Gobetti referenced activities they did together, and her diary was also consulted. Most scenes were recounted in multiple places, and my re-creation is a combination of details from various sources.

32 **As Gentile said:** Willson, *Women in Twentieth-Century Italy,* 70.
32 **Fascist propaganda had long discouraged:** Willson, *Women in Twentieth-Century Italy,* 71.

3: ON THE BRINK

34 **In late March 1939:** Benito Mussolini speech, Rome, March 26, 1939.
35 **"peace and justice":** Origo, *A Chill in the Air,* 37–39. This book and Origo's diary of wartime, *War in Val D'Orcia,* both provided contextual details in this chapter and others.
35 **Even as a million:** Origo, *A Chill in the Air,* 35.
36 **A letter written:** Origo, *A Chill in the Air,* 74.
36 **Of course there were many:** Corner, *Mussolini in Myth and Memory.*
36 **As summer began to wane:** See Origo, *A Chill in the Air,* 73–82, for these details and more about Italy during this time.
36 **response to an international embargo:** Garvin, "The Italian Coffee Triangle: From Brazilian Colonos to Ethiopian Colonialisti."
37 **Thus was the distillation:** United Press, "Text of Mussolini Speech; Rumors Laid to 'Riffraff' Mere Discussions Barred Allies' 'Wise Intention.'"
37 **On June 3, 1940:** Origo, *A Chill in the Air,* 144.

4: BIANCA, TURIN, 1940–1942

See note in chapter 2 on sources informing Bianca's personal story.

40 **whether or not Bianca:** Tobagi's excellent book *La Resistenza delle Donne* covers many stories of Italian women in the Resistance, and from pre-Fascism through the war.
40 **Once the war began:** Taken from stories from Tobagi, *La Resistenza delle Donne,* and Guidetti Serra's *Compagne.*
42 **The city had been under increasing:** Baldoli, "Spring 1943: The Fiat Strikes and the Collapse of the Italian Home Front."
44 **Soon more than half:** Behan, *The Italian Resistance,* 78.

5: ANITA, EMILIA-ROMAGNA, MARCH 3, 1943

In this chapter and others telling Anita's story, details are taken from her various interviews and testimonies, accessed from ISTORECO (Historical Institute of the Resistance) Reggio Emilia (video); La Fondazione Archivio Diaristico Nazionale, Archives of Pieve Santo Stefano (written); and University of Bologna (audio).

NOTES

The experiences of women under Fascism are also informed by De Grazia, *How Fascism Ruled Women*, and Willson, *Women in Twentieth-Century Italy*.

45 **In early March:** "Reggio Emilia, Italy. 3 March 1944..."

6: BIANCA, TURIN, SPRING 1943

See note in chapter 2 on sources informing Bianca's personal story.

Additional strike details from Baldoli, "Spring 1943: The Fiat Strikes and the Collapse of the Italian Home Front," and Behan, *The Italian Resistance*, chapter 3.

54 **which had caused some workers:** Behan, *The Italian Resistance*, 40.
55 **"something about the Communist Party":** As noted, the Communist Party was founded in Italy with a primary focus on workers' rights and a higher standard of living for Italy's many impoverished citizens. Because of a broad lack of news and transparency from the 1920s until after the war, the main information Italians had about Communism came through a handful of books, such as works by Marx and Trotsky. Like in the United States, politicians and factory and landowners often sought to vilify Communism in Italy because an embrace of this idealized philosophy would mean lower profits, greater wealth distribution, and a less concentrated political power structure.

7: CARLA, ROME, JULY AND AUGUST 1943

See note in the prologue on sources informing Carla's personal story.

59 **At school, a British:** Kurzman, *The Race for Rome*, 98.
60 **The fifteen hundred prisoners:** De Vito, "Paradoxical Outcomes?"
60 **which carried a typical sentence:** Behan, *The Italian Resistance*, 161.
62 **Years later, historians would ask:** Lamb, *War in Italy*, 2, 13.

8: TERESA, FLORENCE, SUMMER 1943

See note in chapter 1 on sources informing Teresa's personal story. Additional details taken from *La Storia di Bruno,* a biography of Bruno Sanguinetti written by his daughter Paola.

64 **She trusted Teresa:** Sanguinetti, *La Storia di Bruno*, 235–36.
66 **been in Piazza Vittorio Emanuele II:** Piazza Vittorio was renamed Piazza della Repubblica after the war.
66 **organize into the Fronte della Gioventù:** See De Lazzari, *Storia del Fronte della Gioventù nella Resistenza*, which informed the history of Fronte della Gioventù, adding context to the stories from Bruno and Teresa.
66 **Bruno then found some:** Sanguinetti, *La Storia di Bruno*, 231.
67 **"Pay attention," he told them:** Sanguinetti, *La Storia di Bruno*, 234.
67 **Bruno asked her to convene:** Sanguinetti, *La Storia di Bruno*, 238.

NOTES

67 **The group drafted an official:** De Lazzari, *Storia del Fronte della Gioventù nella Resistenza*, 40.

9: OCCUPATION

69 **On August 18, 1943:** Details in this chapter are informed by Lamb, *War in Italy*, 14–19.

10: CARLA, ROME, AUGUST AND EARLY SEPTEMBER 1943

See note in the prologue on sources informing Carla's personal story.

74 **when driving private cars became:** Origo, *A Chill in the Air*, 73–75.

11: SEPTEMBER 7, 1943

Quotes and details in this chapter are informed by Lamb, *War in Italy*, 14–19.

12: BIANCA, TURIN, SEPTEMBER 8, 1943

See note in chapter 2 on sources informing Bianca's personal story.

13: CARLA, ROME, SEPTEMBER 8–9, 1943

See note in the prologue on sources informing Carla's personal story. Further details about these days are informed by Katz, *The Battle for Rome*; Kurzman, *The Race for Rome*; and Lamb, *War in Italy*.

79 **He intoned: "Italy Surrenders Unconditionally."**
80 **There were plenty of Italian:** Lamb, *War in Italy*, 20–21.

14: SURRENDER

87 **instructed his soldiers to:** This and other quotes by Badoglio from Lamb, *War in Italy*, 20–22.

15: ANITA, REGGIO EMILIA, SEPTEMBER 1943

See note in chapter 5 on sources informing Anita's personal story.

16: DVX

Note that for the remainder of the book, "Nazi-Fascist" will often be the default descriptor used for groups of soldiers operating in occupied Italy, as research notes that there was often some combination of Republic of Salò soldiers and Axis soldiers working together at prisons, at roadblocks, on actions, and so on. "Fascist" will refer to Republic of Salò soldiers, possessions, or leadership (as well as the Italian ruling philosophy), and the term "Nazi" will refer to non-

Republic of Salò "Axis" soldiers, possessions, or leadership. If "Nazi" or "Fascist" is used as a descriptor it is because this is explicitly known. The term "German" will be used if speaking explicitly about soldiers, possessions, or leadership that is known, and is often, but not always, synonymous with Nazi, and used to be more specific when this information is known.

91 **On September 11, Field Marshal Kesselring:** Lamb, *War in Italy*, 34.
91 **In a blow to worker:** Lamb, *War in Italy*, 22.
91 **The next day, a German:** The details of this rescue are recounted from López, *Freeing Mussolini*.
92 **Yet while Mussolini was grateful:** Lamb, *War in Italy*, 23.
92 **There, Il Duce was under:** Lamb, *War in Italy*, 25–28.
93 **a dual war:** Others, notably the historian and former partisan Claudio Pavone, would assert that there was a third front of war as well—a class war.

17: BIANCA, TURIN, SEPTEMBER 1943

See note in chapter 2 on sources informing Bianca's personal story.

95 **Germany demanded that sixty thousand:** Katz, *The Battle for Rome*, 68.
95 **Young men with backpacks headed:** Luzzatto, *Primo Levi's Resistance*, 14.
96 **When, after September 8:** For these and other details about Primo Levi's experience, see Luzzatto, *Primo Levi's Resistance*, 14–18.

18: CARLA, ROME, SEPTEMBER AND OCTOBER 1943

See note in the prologue on sources informing Carla's personal story.
Details about life in Rome during this time are informed by Katz, *The Battle for Rome*; Kurzman, *The Race for Rome*; and Bentivegna, *Senza Fare di Necessità Virtù*.

98 **Dead partisans would soon:** Behan, *The Italian Resistance*, 195.

19: ANITA, REGGIO EMILIA, SEPTEMBER AND OCTOBER 1943

See note in chapter 5 on sources informing Anita's personal story.
Also informed by Storchi interview and Storchi, *20 Mesi per la Libertà*.

20: CARLA, ROME, AUTUMN 1943

See note in the prologue on sources informing Carla's personal story.

105 **Carla learned that the GAP:** Katz, *The Battle for Rome*, 71; for more information about GAP, see Pesce, *Senza Tregua: La Guerra dei GAP*.
106 **Like Carla, he had run:** Details about Rosario Bentivegna's feelings and experience are from his memoir *Senza Fare di Necessità Virtù*, 95, 102.

NOTES

21: BIANCA, PIEDMONT REGION, AUTUMN 1943

See note in chapter 2 on sources informing Bianca's personal story.

108 **Women and men, young and old:** Gobetti, *Partisan Diary,* 80–81.

110 **As one partisan described it:** Gobetti, *Partisan Diary,* 61.

110 **There would be more than:** Rosengarten, *The Italian Anti-Fascist Press,* 96–97.

111 **Germans issued terrifying local edicts:** Rosengarten, *The Italian Anti-Fascist Press,* 99.

112 **What emerged were words:** This primary document, and others cited as being from the ISTORETO archive, were found among the folders of documents the archive librarians chose for the author, who also translated them. As described in more detail in the note on sources, these do not have a detailed finding aid or digital footprint. The author has digital photos of every source quoted and a record of the correspondence with the librarians should future researchers be interested in learning more about these sources.

113 **But she soon familiarized herself:** Mobiglia, "Bianca Guidetti Serra e le Domeniche a Reaglie," 131–34.

22: CARLA, ROME, OCTOBER 16, 1943

See note in the prologue on sources informing Carla's personal story. Bentivegna, *Senza Fare di Necessità Virtù,* was also consulted.

114 **it explains the "Revolutionary Organization":** This issue of *Voce Operaia* was first published on October 4, 1943. The Stampa Clandestina (https://www.stampaclandestina.it) digital archive has images of many underground publications from Italy during this time, searchable by location, title, and date. For the image of this issue, see https://www.stampaclandestina.it/wp-content/uploads/numeri/VOCE_OPERAIA_A1_N1.pdf.

115 **At five-thirty that morning, the SS:** Zuccotti, *Italians and the Holocaust,* chapter 6.

116 **"understand that they were not":** Quoting Mario Fiorentini from Katz, *The Battle for Rome,* 87.

117 **only compounded the recent murder:** Bentivegna, *Senza Fare di Necessità Virtù,* 90.

23: TERESA, ROME AND FLORENCE, AUTUMN 1943

See note in chapter 1 on sources informing Teresa's personal story.

118 **With Bruno, he had also:** Sanguinetti, *La Storia di Bruno,* 242–43.

119 **or face "immediate death":** Zuccotti, *Italians and the Holocaust,* chapter 8, photo insert.

120 **who had gone into hiding:** Lamb, *War in Italy,* 55.

121 **There had been some stories:** Zuccotti, *Italians and the Holocaust,* 105.

122 **There were five hundred Jewish:** Zuccotti, *Italians and the Holocaust,* chapter 7.

24: CARLA, ROME, NOVEMBER 7–8, 1943

See note in the prologue on sources informing Carla's personal story. Bentivegna's *Senza Fare di Necessità Virtù* was also consulted.

123 **The revolution, they were taught:** This first Women's Day was celebrated on March 8, 1917, which was February 23 on the Julian calendar.

25: RULES OF PARTISAN WARFARE

129 **As more men escaped:** Behan, *The Italian Resistance,* chapter 4.
129 **printed "Rules of Partisan Warfare":** Katz, *The Battle for Rome,* 59–60.

26: TERESA, FLORENCE, AUTUMN 1943

See note in chapter 1 on sources informing Teresa's personal story.
The role of staffette has been widely discussed in Bravo, Saba, and Slaughter, among other sources detailing the experiences of women in the Resistance.

27: ANITA, EMILIA-ROMAGNA, AUTUMN 1943

See note in chapter 5 on sources informing Anita's personal story.

28: BIANCA, PIEDMONT, NOVEMBER AND DECEMBER 1943

See note in chapter 2 on sources informing Bianca's personal story. Gobetti, *Partisan Diary,* was also consulted.
For details on the birth of the GDD, see Alano, "Armed with a Yellow Mimosa"; Behan, *The Italian Resistance,* chapter 9; Orlandini, *La Democrazia delle Donne,* preface and chapter 1; and Rodano, *Memorie di Una Che C'era,* chapter 1.

140 **"Call to Italians":** Document from the ISTORETO archive. For more information, see the note on sources and the citation in chapter 21.
140 **"Italian women who have always":** Alano, "Armed with a Yellow Mimosa," 618.
141 **"Program of Action":** Document from the ISTORETO archive. For more information, see the note on sources and the citation in chapter 21.
142 **Others were instructions:** Documents from the ISTORETO archive. For more information, see the note on sources and the citation in chapter 21.
143 **as the first military draft:** Luzzatto, *Primo Levi's Resistance,* 37–38.
144 **Ada's son, Paolo, would turn:** Gobetti, *Partisan Diary,* 67.
145 **The anti-Fascists were also:** Luzzatto, *Primo Levi's Resistance,* 40.
145 **Then on November 30:** Informed by Luzzatto, *Primo Levi's Resistance*; Lamb, *War in Italy.*
145 **For young Jewish men:** Luzzatto, *Primo Levi's Resistance,* 34–35.

NOTES

146 **On December 13:** Luzzatto, *Primo Levi's Resistance*, 75–77. Details of this experience were later included in fiction written by Levi. Luzzatto is asserting here their basis in truth.

29: THE FIRST WINTER AT WAR

This chapter is informed by numerous historical accounts and analysis, including Clark, *Anzio*; Behan, *The Italian Resistance*; Kurzman, *The Race for Rome*; and Lamb, *War in Italy*.

30: CARLA, ROME, DECEMBER 1943

See note in the prologue on sources informing Carla's personal story. Bentivegna's *Senza Fare di Necessità Virtù* was also consulted.

154 **A major part of:** Pacini, *La Costituente*.
159 **When first erected:** Averett, "'Redditus Orbis Erat.'"
163 **Giovanni Gentile would answer:** Bentivegna, *Senza Fare di Necessità Virtù*, 92.

31: TERESA, FLORENCE, DECEMBER 1943

See note in chapter 1 on sources informing Teresa's personal story. Also informed by Sanguinetti, *La Storia di Bruno*.

32: ANITA, REGGIO EMILIA, WINTER 1944

See note in chapter 5 on sources informing Anita's personal story.

33: TO THE LAST MAN

168 **Radio London was believed:** Gagliarducci et al., "War of the Waves."
169 **German commander Kesselring understood:** Behan, *The Italian Resistance*, 198.
169 **Pope Pius XII would have:** Lamb, *War in Italy*, 42.
170 **On January 12, 1944:** Sanguinetti, *La Storia di Bruno*, 291.

34: TERESA, FLORENCE, JANUARY 1944

See note in chapter 1 on sources informing Teresa's personal story.

171 **The Florentine gappisti ended:** Francovich, *La Resistenza a Firenze*, 161.
172 **The first message was *L'Arno*:** Details from documents found at the Istituto Storico Toscana della Resistenza and from "Gilda La Rocca."
173 **And so began one of:** Francovich, *La Resistenza a Firenze*, 154–57.

35: ANZIO

Atkinson, Clark, Katz, Lamb, and Whitlock were also consulted.

NOTES

175 **A British newspaper headline announced:** Clark, *Anzio*, 123.

36: CARLA, ROME, JANUARY 1944

See note in the prologue on sources informing Carla's personal story. Also informed by Bentivegna, *Senza Fare di Necessità Virtù.*

37: HELLO, SUCKERS

179 **"Hello, Suckers":** Most of the broadcasts by "Axis Sally" in Italy were by Rita Zucca, who emulated the more popular American Mildred Gillars, originally from Maine, who moved to Germany after failing to get her stage career off the ground. Mildred was later caught by Americans, tried, and convicted of treason. After the war Rita would also be arrested by the Allies, but she could not be tried for treason because she had renounced her American citizenship. She would be returned to Italy and tried as a collaborator there, serving nine months in jail, and living the rest of her life in Italy, barred from returning to the United States.

For more information about Axis Sally, see also Lucas, *Axis Sally*, and "Military Police Find Rita Louisa Zucca in Turin—Relatives in New York Deny She Served Foe Willingly; Family Denies Voluntary Talks."
Further details from the Museo Storico della Liberazione at Via Tasso.
Clark, Kurzman, and Portelli were also consulted.

38: BIANCA, PIEDMONT, WINTER 1944

See note in chapter 2 on sources informing Bianca's personal story. Gobetti, *Partisan Diary*, also helped inform this chapter.

183 **even as the temperature dipped:** Luzzatto, *Primo Levi's Resistance,* 96–97.
184 **The trip to this part:** Spriano, "Un'Esperienza al Femminile."

39: FLORENCE UNDER OCCUPATION

186 **For many people in Florence:** Francovich, *La Resistenza a Firenze,* 138.
186 **But for others, this was:** Francovich, *La Resistenza a Firenze,* 125–26.
187 **By the end of 1943:** Behan, *The Italian Resistance,* 79.

40: TERESA, FEBRUARY 1944, ROME

See note in chapter 1 on sources informing Teresa's personal story.
Teresa has told this story numerous times in interviews and recounted it in biographies. Some minor details in these various accounts differ, but this account seems like the most logical and consistent explanation of what happened, taking into account what Teresa has said in her own words as well as how other researched accounts, including those by Pacini, Soldani, and Sanguinetti, have written about this.

41: DESTRUCTION OF MONTE CASSINO

Informed by Atkinson, Fisher, Hapgood and Richardson, Katz, and Whitlock.

42: BIANCA, TURIN, FEBRUARY 1944

See note in chapter 2 on sources informing Bianca's personal story.
The story of Bianca and Primo's friendship is recounted from Bianca's various testimonies with additional information from Luzzatto, *Primo Levi's Resistance.*

196 **on February 18:** Luzzatto, *Primo Levi's Resistance,* 97.

43: TERESA, ROME AND FLORENCE, FEBRUARY 1944

See note in chapter 1 on sources informing Teresa's personal story. Also informed by Sanguinetti, *La Storia di Bruno,* and information from the Museo Storico della Liberazione at Via Tasso.

44: CARLA, ROME, MARCH 1944

See note in the prologue on sources informing Carla's personal story. Bentivegna's memoirs were also consulted.

201 **The stalled Allied effort:** Katz, *The Battle for Rome,* 182–83.
201 **fellow partisans Caterina and Cesare:** These are their battle names; their real names were Laura Garroni and Giulio Cortini.

45: BIANCA, TURIN, MARCH 1944

See note in chapter 2 on sources informing Bianca's personal story.
Other details from the strike come from *Gli Scioperi del Marzo 1944*; Guidetti Serra, *Compagne*; Bianca's testimonies; Behan, *The Italian Resistance;* and the ISTORETO archives.

202 **"Turin workers!":** *Gli Scioperi del Marzo 1944,* 75.
203 **They read:** "Workers, Technicians, Employees! . . ." and "Stop the machines, close . . .": Printed matter from the ISTORETO archives. For more information, see the note on sources and the citation in chapter 21.
203 **A woman named Fiorina:** Fiorina Friziero, from Guidetti Serra, *Compagne,* 284.
204 **Bianca and her staffette would:** Gobetti, *Partisan Diary,* 25.

46: CARLA: ROME, MARCH 3, 1944

See note in the prologue on sources informing Carla's personal story.

NOTES

47: TERESA, FLORENCE, MARCH 3, 1944

See note in chapter 1 on sources informing Teresa's personal story.
Also informed by Francovich, *La Resistenza a Firenze,* 142–45; and Guidetti Serra, *Compagne.*

48: CARLA, ROME, MARCH 3, 1944

See note in the prologue on sources informing Carla's personal story.

49: NAZIS STRIKE BACK

215 **Women like Lidia Valeriani:** Lidia's story is recounted from her testimony at Resistance-archive.org.
217 **Anna Anselmo was among:** Anna's story is recounted from Guidetti Serra, *Compagne,* 74–77.
218 **On March 4, *The New York Times*:** Brigham, "North Italy Idle in Wide Protests."
218 **Twenty thousand workers from factories:** Brunelli, "A Short Introduction of the Strike in March 1944 and of Political Deportation from Prato."
218 **In and around Florence:** All following details about the strikes and their aftermath in Florence are from Francovich, *La Resistenza a Firenze,* 142–45.

50: CARLA, ROME, EARLY MARCH 1944

See note in the prologue on sources informing Carla's personal story.
Also informed by Bentivegna, *Senza Fare di Necessità Virtù,* 133–35.

222 **Carla's commander informed:** Bentivegna, *Operazione,* 55–56.

51: SURGICAL STRIKES

224 **Before dawn on March 11:** The details of this bombing run are recounted from Edsel, *Saving Italy,* 106–11.
224 **outside the city center:** Edsel notes that the marshaling yards of Campo di Marte as well as the outskirts of Florence had been bombed prior, with limited accuracy, causing more than two hundred casualties.
227 **A *New York Times* correspondent:** Katz, *The Battle for Rome,* 190.
227 **One gappista questioned why:** Said by Marisa Musu as quoted in Katz, *The Battle for Rome,* 182.

52: CARLA, ROME, MARCH 1944

See note in the prologue on sources informing Carla's personal story.
This chapter is also informed by Bentivegna's memoirs; Portelli, *The Order Has Been Carried Out,* chapter 6; Katz, *The Battle for Rome,* chapters 13–14; and the Fosse Ardeatine monument and museum.

229 **Nearly every day that winter:** These soldiers were from an Alpine region of Italy that voluntarily joined Germany in 1939; the people chose to obtain German citizenship and fight alongside the Nazis prior to the occupation.

229 **"rotten green":** Portelli, *The Order Has Been Carried Out,* 134.

231 **nome di battaglia was Spartaco:** His real name was Carlo Salinari; Cola's real name was Franco Calamandrei; Giovanni's real name was Mario Fiorentini. Guglielmo's full name was Guglielmo Blasi. His nome di battaglia is never noted, perhaps as commentary on his betrayal.

53: BIANCA, PIEDMONT, MARCH 1944

See note in chapter 2 on sources informing Bianca's personal story. This chapter is also informed by Gobetti, *Partisan Diary,* 84–85, and Artom, *Diari di un Partigiani Ebreo.*

233 **This position was one:** Behan, *The Italian Resistance,* 70–71.

54: TERESA, FLORENCE, MARCH 1944

See note in chapter 1 on sources informing Teresa's personal story. This chapter is also informed by Sanguinetti, *La Storia di Bruno.*

235 **On March 22, five young men:** The entirety of this scene is re-created from various primary accounts quoted and cited in Francovich, *La Resistenza a Firenze,* 176–79.

55: CARLA, ROME, MARCH 22–23, 1944

See note in the prologue on sources informing Carla's personal story.

Also informed by Bentivegna's memoirs; Portelli, *The Order Has Been Carried Out,* chapter 6; Katz, *The Battle for Rome,* chapters 13–14; and the Fosse Ardeatine monument and museum.

246 **Among the insults:** Quoted from Pasquale Balsamo in Portelli, *The Order Has Been Carried Out,* 136.

247 **"created a ceiling of glass":** Quoted from Pasquale Balsamo in Portelli, *The Order Has Been Carried Out,* 137.

247 **The platoon's commander:** Quoted from Joseph Praxmarer in Portelli, *The Order Has Been Carried Out,* 137.

56: REPRISAL

Informed by Katz, *The Battle for Rome,* chapters 14–16; Portelli, *The Order Has Been Carried Out,* chapters 6–7; and the Fosse Ardeatine monument and museum.

249 **"make the world tremble":** Katz, *The Battle for Rome,* 229.

NOTES

57: BIANCA, TURIN, MARCH 23, 1944

See note in chapter 2 on sources informing Bianca's personal story.

251 **Bianca, Ada, and a few other:** Gobetti, *Partisan Diary*, 85–86.

58: CARLA, ROME, MARCH 24, 1944

See note in the prologue on sources informing Carla's personal story.
The story of the Via Rasella attacks and the Nazi retribution has been written about in numerous places. The details here, of which many are overlapping, have been informed by Katz, *The Battle for Rome*, chapters 14–16; Portelli, *The Order Has Been Carried Out*, chapters 6–7; and the Fosse Ardeatine monument and museum.

254 **the state press agency issued:** This has been quoted in Katz, Portelli, and elsewhere. The author translated it here from the original Italian.
256 **Kesselring finally acknowledged the danger:** Katz, *The Battle for Rome*, 270.

59: BIANCA, PIEDMONT, LATE MARCH 1944

257 **The serene, almost festive rhythms:** Gobetti, *Partisan Diary*, 87.
258 **The stories Paolo and Alberto:** Gobetti, *Partisan Diary*, 101.

60: TERESA, FLORENCE, APRIL 1944

See note in chapter 1 on sources informing Teresa's personal story. This chapter is also informed by Sanguinetti, *La Storia di Bruno*, and Paoletti, *Il Delitto Gentile*.

261 **"We were at war":** Paoletti, *Il Delitto Gentile*, 139.

61: CARLA, ROME, APRIL 1944

See note in the prologue on sources informing Carla's personal story. This chapter is also informed by Bentivegna, *Senza Fare di Necessità Virtù*.
Additional details about the women's bread riots from Katz, *The Battle for Rome*, 275.

264 **"Rome must starve till freed":** Katz, *The Battle for Rome*, 284.

62: CAPTURING MONTE CASSINO

Informed by Fisher, *Cassino to the Alps*; Katz, *The Battle for Rome*; Kurzman, *The Race for Rome*; Lamb, *War in Italy*; and Whitlock, *Desperate Valour*.

271 **"At 11 o'clock about a thousand":** Katz, *The Battle for Rome*, 286.
272 **"The first blow for the":** Katz, *The Battle for Rome*, 286.

NOTES

63: TERESA, FLORENCE, MAY 1944

See note in chapter 1 on sources informing Teresa's personal story.

273 **In the first weeks of:** Francovich, *La Resistenza a Firenze*, 138–39.
273 **Bruno had been arrested:** Sanguinetti, *La Storia di Bruno*, 313.
273 **taken directly to Villa Triste:** Various buildings around occupied Italy were called this colloquially, indicating a place where the Nazi-Fascists tortured prisoners—*triste* means "sad." In Florence it referred to a building on Via Bolognese where the Banda Carità had cells and tortured prisoners in the basement and lower floors.

64: ANITA, REGGIO EMILIA, SPRING 1944

See note in chapter 5 on sources informing Anita's personal story.

65: CARLA, ROME AND THE HILLS NEAR PALESTRINA, MAY 1944

See note in the prologue on sources informing Carla's personal story. This chapter is also informed by Bentivegna, *Senza Fare di Necessità Virtù.*

66: CROSSROADS

This chapter is informed by details and analysis from Fisher, *Cassino to the Alps,* chapter 11, and Kurzman, *The Race for Rome.*

284 **"as militarily stupid":** D'Este as quoted in Katz, *The Battle for Rome,* 301.

67: CARLA, ROME, JUNE 1944

See note in the prologue on sources informing Carla's personal story. This chapter is also informed by Bentivegna, *Senza Fare di Necessità Virtù,* and Katz, *The Battle for Rome;* Kurzman, *The Race for Rome,* is also referenced.

287 **Rosario approached warily:** Katz, *The Battle for Rome,* 317–18.

68: TERESA, FLORENCE, JUNE 1944

See note in chapter 1 on sources informing Teresa's personal story.

69: BIANCA, PIEDMONT, SUMMER 1944

See previous note on sources informing Bianca's personal story.

297 **Despite the losses:** Informed by documents from the ISTORETO archive. For more information, see the note on sources and the citation in chapter 21.
300 **Lina told her:** This story was re-created from Bianca's memoir and interview and a historical placard posted by the Comune di Fenestrelle that

NOTES

recounts the same event. An interview with her son, Fabrizio Salmoni, confirmed the details of the events as she had told him as well.

70: RADIO CORA

Informed by Francovich's *La Resistenza a Firenze.*

303 **The Radio CORA operators:** Much of the detail here about how Radio CORA operated came from Dominici, "Supporting the Radio CORA."
305 **But this fear was quickly:** McConnon and McConnon, *Road to Valor.*
306 **"I fooled that pig":** Sanguinetti, *La Storia di Bruno,* 327–29.

71: ANITA, EMILIA-ROMAGNA, SUMMER 1944

See note in chapter 5 on sources informing Anita's personal story.
Also informed by Paterlini, *Partigiane e Patriote della Provincia di Reggio Emilia.*

72: TERESA, FLORENCE, JULY 1944

See note in chapter 1 on sources informing Teresa's personal story. This chapter is also informed by Sanguinetti, *La Storia di Bruno.*

311 **the Resistance circulated a manifesto:** From Enzo Enriques Agnoletti, cited in Francovich, *La Resistenza a Firenze,* 209.
314 **"It is not possible to change":** Sanguinetti, *La Storia di Bruno,* 330–31.
314 **On July 8:** Francovich, *La Resistenza a Firenze,* 253.

73: A DESPERATE FLORENCE AWAITS

Informed by Francovich's *La Resistenza a Firenze,* chapter 6, and Calamandrei, *Uomini e Città della Resistenza.*

316 **would disappear in the looting:** Francovich, *La Resistenza a Firenze,* 253.
317 **More than half of the:** Behan, *The Italian Resistance,* 87–88.

74: BIANCA, PIEDMONT, JULY 1944

See note in chapter 2 on sources informing Bianca's personal story.

320 **Their call to arms read:** Printed material accessed through the ISTORETO archive. For more information, see the note on sources and the citation in chapter 21.

75: ANITA, REGGIO EMILIA, AUGUST 1944

See note in chapter 5 on sources informing Anita's personal story.

The scenes in this chapter are re-created from Anita's detailed recollection in various testimonies. While the dialogue in italics is slightly rephrased, it is accurate to her retelling.

76: FALLING BRIDGES, FLORENCE, AUGUST 1944

Informed by Francovich, *La Resistenza a Firenze*; Calamandrei, *Uomini e Città della Resistenza*; and an interview with Serena Balestracci in Florence.

329 **After watching the other bridges:** There are a few different, overlapping stories about how the Ponte Vecchio was saved. This version is the most credible based on numerous accounts and is the story that local historian and tour guide Serena Balestracci asserts is true.

77: ANITA, EMILIA-ROMAGNA, AUGUST 1944

See note in chapter 5 on sources informing Anita's personal story.

Also informed by Paterlini, *Partigiane e Patriote della Provincia di Reggio Emilia*, and Storchi, *20 Mesi per la Libertà*.

78: TERESA, FLORENCE, AUGUST 1944

See note in chapter 1 on sources informing Teresa's personal story. This chapter is also informed by Francovich, *La Resistenza a Firenze*, and Fisher, *Cassino to the Alps*, chapter 16.

337 **The Germans were retreating:** Francovich, *La Resistenza a Firenze*, 278.
337 **To bolster the population:** Behan, *The Italian Resistance*, 90.
340 **Finally, on August 15:** Francovich, *La Resistenza a Firenze*, 286–88; Fisher, *Cassino to the Alps*, 294.

79: ANITA, EMILIA-ROMAGNA, AUTUMN 1944

See note in chapter 5 on sources informing Anita's personal story.

80: ON EMPTY

Informed by Chaisson, "Was Hitler's Ardennes Offensive Brilliant or Delusional?"; Toland, *Battle;* and *The Battle of the Bulge,* with other accounts of this genesis of the Battle of the Bulge widely available.

81: BIANCA, TURIN, AUTUMN 1944

See note in chapter 2 on sources informing Bianca's personal story.

347 **And so the first article:** The Stampa Clandestina (https://www.stampa clandestina.it) digital archive has images of many underground publications from Italy during this time, searchable by location, title, and date. For

the image of this issue, see https://www.stampaclandestina.it/wp-content /uploads/numeri/110-LaDifesaDellaLavoratrice_N1.pdf.

348 **Since the summer, the men's:** A detailed log of the actions of the La Gianna partisan band was found in the ISTORETO archives. For more information, see the note on sources and the citation in chapter 21.

82: ANITA, EMILIA-ROMAGNA, AUTUMN 1944

See note in chapter 5 on sources informing Anita's personal story.
This chapter is also informed by Storchi, *20 Mesi per la Libertà*, and interview with Storchi.

83: NOT A SUMMER SPORT

354 even *The New York Times*: Bracker, "Italian Partisans Resent Allies' Ban."

84: BIANCA, TURIN, AUTUMN 1944

See note in chapter 2 on sources informing Bianca's personal story.

356 **Bianca's was far from:** Information about other clandestine newspapers is informed by Bianca's recounting from Guidetti Serra, *Bianca la Rossa*, primary documents viewed at the ISTORETO archive (for more information, see the note on sources and the citation in chapter 21), and Rosengarten, *The Italian Anti-Fascist Press*.

85: ANITA, APENNINE MOUNTAINS, NOVEMBER 1944

See note in chapter 5 on sources informing Anita's personal story.
Additional details about the Monte Caio battle from Paterlini, *Partigiane e Patriote della Provincia di Reggio Emilia*, Storchi, Storchi interview, and documents from the ISTORECO archive.

86: ANITA, APENNINE MOUNTAINS, NOVEMBER 1944

See note in chapter 5 on sources informing Anita's personal story.

365 **more than a hundred partisan:** "Il Monte Caio: Vero Parco UNESCO degli Apennini."

87: BATTLE OF THE BULGE

Statistics and analysis informed by *The Battle of the Bulge* and Toland, *Battle*.

368 **"suddenly collapse with a huge":** Chaisson, "Was Hitler's Ardennes Offensive Brilliant or Delusional?"

369 **Swaths were cut:** "Battle of the Bulge." These details have also been corroborated by multiple other published accounts.
369 **American soldiers attempted to weed:** "Battle of the Bulge"; Toland, *Battle*.

88: BIANCA, TURIN, WINTER 1945

See note in chapter 2 on sources informing Bianca's personal story.
The Stampa Clandestina (https://www.stampaclandestina.it) digital archive has images of many underground publications from Italy during this time, searchable by location, title, and date. Note the links for the images of each issue.

370 **"It's rough in Punta Novosa":** *Difesa della Lavoratrice*, December 11, 1944, https://www.stampaclandestina.it/wp-content/uploads/numeri/DIFESA_LAVORATRICE_11-12-1944.pdf.
371 **"They arrested them":** *Difesa della Lavoratrice*, December 11, 1944, https://www.stampaclandestina.it/wp-content/uploads/numeri/DIFESA_LAVORATRICE_11-12-1944.pdf.
371 **"The Fascist government is allegedly":** *Difesa della Lavoratrice*, January 20, 1945, https://www.stampaclandestina.it/wp-content/uploads/numeri/LaDifesaDellaLavoratrice_A02-N06.pdf.
372 **"It seems that the warnings":** *Difesa della Lavoratrice*, January 20, 1945, https://www.stampaclandestina.it/wp-content/uploads/numeri/LaDifesaDellaLavoratrice_A02-N06.pdf.
372 **"THE SECRETARY OF THE WOMEN'S":** *Difesa della Lavoratrice*, February 20, 1945, https://www.stampaclandestina.it/wp-content/uploads/numeri/LaDifesaDellaLavoratrice_A02-N03_001.pdf.
373 **They shared news from around:** *Difesa della Lavoratrice*, February 20, 1945, https://www.stampaclandestina.it/wp-content/uploads/numeri/LaDifesaDellaLavoratrice_A02-N03_001.pdf.
373 **"Our Piedmont sharpens its weapons":** *Difesa della Lavoratrice*, February 20, 1945, https://www.stampaclandestina.it/wp-content/uploads/numeri/LaDifesaDellaLavoratrice_A02-N03_001.pdf.
373 **"All women must fight":** *Difesa della Lavoratrice*, March 1945, https://www.stampaclandestina.it/wp-content/uploads/numeri/DIFESA_LAVORATRICE_03-1945.pdf.

89: ANITA, APENNINE MOUNTAINS, WINTER 1945

See note in chapter 5 on sources informing Anita's personal story.

90: BIANCA, PIEDMONT, WINTER 1945

See note in chapter 2 on sources informing Bianca's personal story. Also informed by the interview with Santina Mobiglia.

91: THE FINAL MARCH

Informed by Fisher, *Cassino to the Alps;* Lamb, *War in Italy*; and other corroborating accounts.

NOTES

92: BIANCA, TURIN, MARCH 1945

See note in chapter 2 on sources informing Bianca's personal story.

381 **On March 8, Bianca and her team:** *Difesa della Lavoratrice*, March 1945. The Stampa Clandestina (https://www.stampaclandestina.it) digital archive has images of many underground publications from Italy during this time, searchable by location, title, and date. For the image of this issue, see https://www.stampaclandestina.it/wp-content/uploads/numeri/DIFESA_LAVORATRICE_03-1945.pdf.

382 **"We did not want to":** Padovani, *La Liberazione di Torino*, 36–37.

382 **On the night of March 12:** The story of the murder of the Arduino sisters can be read in Guidetti Serra, *Bianca la Rossa*; Alano, "Armed with a Yellow Mimosa"; and Padovani, *La Liberazione di Torino;* and has been widely written about elsewhere as well.

383 **the execution of girls:** At this time, twenty-one was considered the age of adulthood.

93: ANITA, EMILIA-ROMAGNA, APRIL 1945

See note in chapter 5 on sources informing Anita's personal story.
Also informed by Paterlini, *Partigiane e Patriote della Provincia di Reggio Emilia.*

94: TOWARD THE PO

388 **The Allied forces focused on:** These details and the analysis from this chapter are informed by Fisher, *Cassino to the Alps*; Lamb, *War in Italy*; and other corroborating accounts.

95: BIANCA, TURIN, APRIL 1945

See note in chapter 2 on sources informing Bianca's personal story.
Also informed by Padovani, *La Liberazione di Torino.*

391 **"Surrender or perish!":** ISTORETO archive. For more information, see the note on sources and the citation in chapter 21.

391 **Along with these publications:** Behan, *The Italian Resistance,* 166.

96: ANITA, REGGIO EMILIA, APRIL 1945

See note in chapter 5 on sources informing Anita's personal story.
The story of Maria Montanari is recounted from "Targa Memorial Partigiana 'Mimma.'"

97: BIANCA, TURIN, APRIL 1945

See note in chapter 2 on sources informing Bianca's personal story.

396 **early morning of April 26:** Padovani, *La Liberazione di Torino*, chapter 4. This book also provided other contextual details for this chapter.

EPILOGUE

See note in chapter 5 on sources informing Anita's personal story.

401 **But the definition of what:** See Bravo and Bruzzone, Saba, Willson, Slaughter, and Tobagi—both what is cited in the bibliography as well as their broader work.

401 **Historians calculate that for every:** Behan, *The Italian Resistance,* 161.

402 **She watched with the crowds:** Willson, *Women in Twentieth-Century Italy,* 102.

403 **in others, where women walked:** Behan, *The Italian Resistance,* 181.

INDEX

Note: Italicized page numbers indicate material in photographs or illustrations.

abortion laws, 60
Abyssinia. *See* Ethiopia
Action Party, 56, 61
activist mothering, 401–2
air power, Allied
    and Allied advance on Po Valley, 388
    attacks on industrial targets, 10
    attacks on Monte Cassino, 194–95,
        271–72, 279–80
    blackouts in Rome, 57
    damage to roads and railways, 190,
        278–79
    factories targeted, 10, 39–45, 50, 89,
        217, 225
    and Florence city center, 312
    and German retreat, 281–82
    and German wartime production, 345
    and leaflet campaigns, 10, 43, 286
    and onset of war in Italy, 10–14
    and partisan radio broadcasts, 304
    precision raid on Florence,
        224–28
    psychological impact of, 323–24
    at Reggio Emilia, 89
    Resistance information on
        targets, 180
    supply airdrops, 168, 172–74, 294,
        303–4, 307–8
Alban Hills, 180
Albania, 35, 59
Albergo dei Tre Re, 299
Alexander, Harold, 353–54

Allied forces
    agreement with CLN Military
        Command, 285, 287
    assault on Monte Cassino, 194–95,
        271–72, 274, 279–80
    and Battle of Anzio, 151, 175–77, 180,
        194–95, 201, 225, 227–28, 239, 271,
        278, 283, 304
    Calabria landings, 75
    and final insurrection in Reggio
        Emilia, 392
    Gothic Line breached, 379
    Italian volunteers with, 104
    and Normandy invasion, 304
    and surrender negotiations, 69, 76,
        79–80
    variety of forces, 388
    See also air power, Allied
Allied Radio, 286
Alps and Alpine borderlands
    Alpine Musketeers, 196, 297
    and Bianca's factory job, 38
    courier and supply missions in, 297, 348
    and final insurrection in Turin, 395
    German citizens from, 437n229
    and German invasion of Italy, 70
    and Hitler's trip to Italy, 24
    and La Gianna, 233
    military significance of Po Valley,
        388–89
    Nazi-Fascist attacks on partisans,
        251, 297

Alps and Alpine borderlands (*cont.*)
and organization of Resistance groups, 95–97, 113, 145–46
partisan camps and paths in, 129, 183
railroads in, 184
and scope of text, 3
support for Resistance forces in mountains, 108
and underground press, 382
Amay, Italy, 97
amphibious landings, 12–13. *See also* Battle of Anzio
Anna Karenina (Dostoyevsky), 46
Anselmo, Anna, 217
antiaircraft fire, 158
anti-Fascists
and Adele Bei's background, 100
and Carla's political education, 60, 123–24
collaboration among Resistance groups, 93
and Mussolini's rise to power, 20–21
newspapers, 356–57
recruitment, 145
and small Italian towns, 95
and student activism, 66
Anti-Fascist Front for Peace, 18–19
anti-Semitism, 28, 29–30, 120, 145. *See also* Jewish Italians
Apennine Mountains
and Allied air raids, 45–46, 89
and Anita's activities with partisans, 89, 137, 139, 276–77, 332, 374–76, 404
and Battle of Monte Caio, 361–64
German advances into, 359–61, 366
German retreat from Italy, 387
and Gothic Line defenses, 294, 308, 379, 388
partisan camps and paths in, 103, 129, 137, 139, 309, 351, 359
and supply drops to partisans, 307–8
"arcangelo" password, 63, 100
Archives of Pieve Santo Stefano, 419–20
Ardeatine cave murders, 254, 256, 420
Ardennes forest, 368–69
Arduino, Libera, 382–83
Arduino, Vera, 382–83
Arno Hotel, 261
Arno River, 312, 318, 328, 329–30
Artom, Emanuele, 233, 258
Aryanism, 27, 28
assassination, 157–58, 160, 237, 260, 274, 314, 345. *See also* executions
Atkinson, Rick, 425n
Auschwitz death camp, 122, 197, 401
Austria, 24, 70, 161, 393

Aventine Hill, 82
"Axis Sally," 179–80, 434n179

B-26 Marauders, 224
Badoglio, Pietro
and formation of the CLN, 93
and German invasion of Italy, 70
and German rescue of Mussolini, 92
and Italy's surrender, 79–80, 87
and Mussolini's deposition, 61–62, 65
and reprisals for Via Rasella bombing, 255
surrender negotiations with Allies, 69, 76
Balkans, 35
Balsamo, Pasquale, 243, 246, 247
Bandiera Rossa ("The Red Flag"), 155
bandits (*bandite*), 240, 255, 281, 332
Barducci, Aligi (partisan leader), 331
battistrada, 334
The Battle for Rome (Katz), 425n
Battle of Anzio
Allied breakthrough, 283
and Axis propaganda, 179
beach landings, 175–76
and German occupation of Rome, 227
and raids of railroads, 278
and the Roman Resistance, 177, 228, 239, 304
stalemate, 180, 195, 201, 225, 228, 271
and surrender negotiations, 151
Battle of Monte Caio, 361–64, 365, 374–75
Battle of the Bulge, 368–69, 379–80
BBC radio, 35–36. *See also* Radio London
Bei, Adele, 100, 106, 123–24
Bentivegna, Rosario
and Allied landings at Anzio, 177
battle name, 232
bombmaking and bombing missions, 152–54, 159–61, 201, 222–23, 230, 232, 240–47
and Carla's activities with GAP, 105–7, 115–17
and civilian support for Resistance, 252
and German retreat, 281–82
graffiti mission in Rome, 124–27
living conditions in Rome, 200
marriage after war, 400
memoirs, 425n
and provisional government of Rome, 285, 286–88
and Trastevere roundups, 115–17
Berlin, Germany, 150

INDEX

Bianca la Rossa (Serra and Mobiglia), 419,
    421, 426n
bicycle uses and restrictions, 131, 137,
    160–63, 171, 183, 318, 396
black market, 98, 132, 187
blackouts, 13, 57
Blackshirts, 21
Blasi, Guglielmo, 231, 244–45, 264–66
blockades, 132–33. *See also* roadblocks
Boboli Gardens, 328–29
Bocci, Enrico, 172, 304
Bologna, Italy, 46, 121, 143, 294, 388, 394
bombs and bomb making
    and Anita's activities with partisans,
        138–39
    and arrests of Resistance members,
        188–89
    attack on Fascist parade, 223
    and bombing missions in Rome, 162
    bridge targets, 374
    Carla's activities in Rome, 152–58,
        161–63, 221–22, 280
    and the Florentine Resistance, 171
    and general strike of 1944, 206, 218
    and Gianfranco Mattei, 118
    incendiary bombs, 45
    and Piazza Barberini bombing, 157–61
    of railroad tunnels, 293
    reprisals for partisan attacks, 249–50
    safe houses for bomb making, 201, 239,
        267–68
    Teatro Comunale bombing, 273
    Teresa's activities in Florence, 261, 293,
        295, 341
    transport of bombs, 133, 138, 139, 152,
        162, 276
    Via Rasella bomb attack, 230–31,
        240–48, 253–56, 265–66, 420
Braibanti, Aldo, 67
Bravo, Anna, 401
Brazil, 379
Brenner Pass, 24, 70
bribery, 305
Bulgaria, 344

Calabria, 75
Calamandrei, Piero, 18
Calvino, Italo, 118
Campobello, Francesco, 419
Campo di Marte massacre, 235–37,
    436n224
Capponi, Carla
    and air raids, 42–43
    and Allied landings at Anzio, 177–78
    arrest and interrogation of, 209, 212–14

battle name, 101
bomb making and bombing missions,
    152–55, 159–63, 201, 221–22, 229–32,
    239–46
elected to parliament, 400
family background, 58–59
and German retreat, 279–80
graffiti mission, 124–28
and Italy's surrender, 79–81
and joining GAP, 105–7, 114–17
and leaflet campaigns aimed at women,
    207–9
and living conditions in Rome, 200
marriage after war, 400
memoir, 425n
and Mussolini's deposition, 57–58,
    60–62
and Nazi worker roundup of Italian
    citizens, 98–100
and onset of Resistance fighting, 81–84
and onset of war in Italy, 9–14
political education, 58–60, 71–75,
    123–24
portrait of, *xiii*
and provisional government of Rome,
    286, 287–89
and recruitment of Resistance
    members, 222–23
return home, 288–89
on run from Nazis, 266, 267–70, 278–79
and scope of text, 1–3
secretarial job, 71
and transport of weapons, 100–101,
    231–32
and underground press, 114–15
and women's political activism, 73–75,
    123–24
Capponi, Flora, 58
carabinieri, 50–51, 53, 205, 264–65,
    320, 333
Carità, Mario, 235–37, 314
Carità gang (Banda Carità), 93, 305,
    439n273
Casa Internazionale della Donna, 419
Cassuto, Rabbi, 120
Castellano, Giuseppe, 69
Castello di Comano, 366
"Caterina" (Laura Garroni), 201, 230, 252
Catholics and Catholic Church
    and Allies' relationship with Italian
        Resistance, 150
    and anti-Semitic propaganda, 30
    Catholic Communists, 59, 114
    and Hitler's trip to Italy, 26
    Jews registering as Catholics, 119
    Pope Pius XII, 54, 169, 207, 227

Catholics and Catholic Church (*cont.*)
and Teresa's family background,
15–16, 28
See also Vatican City
Centocelle neighborhood, 177
Centro Studi Piero Gobetti, 419
Ceresola, Italy, 135–36, 322, 324, 341
"Cesare" (Giulio Cortini), 201, 230, 252
Chamber of Deputies, 125
Chamber of Fasces and Corporations, 125
Christian Democratic Women, 356
Churchill, Winston, 13, 150, 264
Cillo, Davide, 420
Cinciari, Marisa, 60
Cinema Barberini, 1, 159
ciphers, 172
circulation permit cards
(*personalausweis*), 148, 183–84
Circus Maximus, 83
civil disobedience, 52, 384
civilian casualties, 12, 225, 231, 248,
272, 380
Clark, Mark, 271, 283–84
codes and code words, 168–69, 172,
285, 323
"Cola" (Franco Calamandrei), 231,
244–45, 265–66, 437n231
Committee of Agitation, 143, 203, 205
Committee of National Liberation (CLN)
and Allied landings at Anzio, 151
and assassination missions, 158, 260
Bianca's activities with, 94, 183, 185,
298, 357, 372
calls for Resistance action, 140, 170, 177
and final insurrection in Turin, 391, 395
formation of, 93
and German retreat from Rome, 287
and liberation of Florence, 311–12, 340
Military Council, 285
and underground press, 110–12, 357
and women's role in Resistance, 165
Committee of National Liberation of
Northern Italy (CLNAI), 140
communications systems as targets, 13,
109, 151, 172, 196, 203, 206, 227, 312
Communists and Communist Party
and Allies' relationship with Italian
Resistance, 150
and Anita's political education, 48, 166
and Bianca's political education, 55–56
and Carla's political education, 59–60
The Communist Manifesto (Engels and
Marx), 164, 270
and formation of CLN, 93
founding in Italy, 428n55
and labor strikes, 52, 55–56

L'Unità newspaper, 62–63
and Mussolini's deposition, 61
and Mussolini's rise to power, 18, 19
Pugno Chiuso paper, 67
and recruitment of Resistance
members, 75
and reprisals for Via Rasella
bombing, 255
and sabotage efforts, 41
surveillance of, 65
and Teresa's family background, 18
concentration camps, 99, 103, 115,
196–97, 216
Con Cuore di Donna (Capponi), 425n
conscription, 40, 48, 344
conservatism, 402
Count of Cavour, 398
courier missions, 297, 339, 341, 359–60,
361, 370
CTLN, 311, 330
curfews
and daily life of Resistance members,
223, 353, 378
in Emilia-Romagna, 332
in Florence, 171, 318
in Piedmont region, 299, 320
as reprisal for Resistance actions,
216, 314
in Rome, 99, 124, 127, 153–54, 162, 227,
231, 269
in Turin, 111, 113, 383, 391
and Via Rasella bomb attack, 245, 252
and weapons transport, 138, 231–32

Dalla Costa, Elia, 26, 329
The Day of Battle (Atkinson), 425n
death notices, 256
death penalty, 196, 235, 253. *See also*
executions
declarations of war, 37
deportations
and general strike of 1944, 202, 204,
206, 218–19
and German occupation of
Florence, 318
and German occupation of Rome, 99, 188
and Nazi roundups of Jewish Italians,
120, 122
Primo Levi deported, 197
and women's role in Resistance, 402
deserters, 95, 102–3, 280, 333, 344
D'Este, Carlo, 284
disguises, 84, 123, 153
donations to partisans, 370–71. *See also*
GDD

Dostoyevsky, Fyodor, 46
draft (conscription), 48, 129, 144, 196
draft dodgers, 117, 145, 188, 235
Duilio (partisan), 201, 239, 265–66,
    268, 288

82nd Airborne Division (U.S.), 69, 76, 88
Einaudi, Luigi, 41
Eisenhower, Dwight, 69, 76, 79
"Elena." See Capponi, Carla
Eleventh Company (German), 230,
    241, 248
embargoes, 36
Emilia-Romagna region, 46, 215. See also
    Reggio Emilia, Italy; Apennine
    Mountains; Parma
Empoli, Italy, 210, 316
Engels, Friedrich, 55, 142
England, 23, 34, 37, 73, 380. See also Great
    Britain
Enza River, 360–61, 362
Enza Valley, 361
Ethiopia, 22, 23–24, 27, 36, 48
executions
    and Campo di Marte massacre, 235–37
    murder of Arduino sisters, 383
    of partisans in Florence, 336
    of Radio CORA partisans, 305
    reported in underground press, 371
    and reprisals for Via Rasella bombing,
        249–50, 253, 420
explosives. See bombs and bomb making

factories and factory workers
    activism of female factory workers,
        40–41, 141–42, 182–83, 203–4, 372
    activities reported in underground
        press, 372
    and Allied bombing raids, 10, 39–45, 50,
        89, 217, 225, 323–24
    and Bianca's job as a social worker,
        38–39, 77
    and Bianca's political education, 56
    calls for strikes and work stoppages in
        1945, 381–82
    defended against Germans, 118,
        317–18, 395
    factory owners' support of anti-
        Fascists, 145
    and final insurrection in
        Florence, 318
    and final insurrection in Turin, 394,
        395–96
    and Florentine Resistance, 314

"flying rallies" in Turin, 384–85
    and forced labor, 188
    and general strike of 1944, 204–6, 207,
        210, 215–20
    and German retreat from
        Florence, 339
    and labor strikes in Turin in 1943,
        52–54
    and organization of Resistance groups,
        95–96, 113, 182
    and partisan radio broadcasts, 308
Fascism and Fascists
    and Anita's family background, 46,
        47–48
    and Carla's family background, 59, 74
    collaborators with, 187, 200, 357–58,
        434n179
    and cover for Resistance members,
        276, 326
    education reform, 32, 237
    fasces symbol, 20
    founding date of Fascist Party, 230
    and German occupation of Reggio
        Emilia, 104
    and German occupation of Rome,
        99, 223
    and growth in anti-Fascist activism in
        Rome, 75
    and Mussolini's rise to power, 18, 19, 34
    and political education of Italian
        women, 166–67
    and traditional gender roles, 47–49
    and Via Rasella bomb attack,
        230, 241
    See also Nazi-Fascists
feminists and feminism, 32, 123, 378,
    401–2, 423. See also gender norms
    and roles
Fenestrelle, Italy, 299
Ferranti Aporti reform school, 397
Ferrari brothers, 276
Fiat, 38, 52–54, 91, 217
Finland, 344
firing squads, 111, 236. See also executions
flamethrowers, 341
Flaminio Obelisk, 126
Florence, Italy
    Allied advance on, 316–18, 328–31
    Allied bombing of, 224–26
    Allied control established, 340–41
    Allied radio broadcasts, 172
    Allied supply drops, 172–74
    Campo di Marte massacre, 235–37
    and CLN's goals for liberation, 311–12
    conditions under German occupation,
        186–87

Florence, Italy (*cont.*)
  and final insurrection in Turin, 395
  and formation of GDD, 143
  GAP actions in, 218, 260–61, 312–15
  and general strike of 1944, 210–11, 218
  German retreat from, 336–40
  and Hitler's trip to Italy, 24–25
  and Italy's invasion of Ethiopia, 22
  and liberation of Rome, 294
  and Nazi roundups of Jewish Italians,
    118–22
  partisan bomb attacks in, 171
  partisan radio broadcasts, 172–73, 308
  and scope of text, 2
  street battles in, 335–41
  Youth Front actions in, 66, 68, 132,
    312–15
flyers and pamphlets, 141–42, 215. *See also*
  leaflets
"flying rallies," 384–85
food supplies and shortages
  and Allied advance on Florence, 318
  Allied airdrops of, 294, 307–8
  and black market, 181
  in Florence, 273–74, 312
  foraging, 351
  and general strike of 1944, 205, 216
  and German assault on partisan
    camps, 258
  and German occupation of Florence,
    187, 316
  and German occupation of Rome, 227,
    230, 263–64
  and German retreat from
    Florence, 339
  and labor activism, 54, 143, 205,
    372, 381
  and looting of Florence, 316
  in Palestrina, 279
  reported in underground press, 372
  at safe houses, 267, 278
  and women's bread raids in Rome,
    263–64
forced labor, 188, 207, 218, 272, 294
forged documents, 172, 212–14
Foro Traiano
  and bombing missions, 152, 154
  and Carla's relationship with Rosario,
    105–7
  and Carla's return home, 288
  and graffiti missions, 127, 201
  and living conditions of partisans, 222
  and political activism of women,
    123–24
Forty-Five Days, 93
Fosse Ardeatine Memorial, 420

Fossoli concentration camp, 196–97, 206,
  219, 305
four-pointed nail, 155
France
  Allied invasion at Normandy, 150, 304
  declaration of war, 37
  and Fascist rhetoric, 73
  GAP modeled on French
    Resistance, 105
  and general strike of 1944, 217
  German occupation of, 109
  Italian soldiers in, 48
  liberation of Paris, 344
  and Mussolini's support for Hitler, 34
  and Nazi roundups of Jewish
    people, 120
  and Rules of Partisan Warfare, 130
  and Teresa's first missions for
    resistance, 22–23
Franco, Francisco, 22–23, 35
Friziero, Fiorina, 203–4
Fronte della Gioventù, 66, 68. *See also*
  Youth Front
fuel shortages, 36, 39, 44, 267, 337, 345

Galleria Colonna (Rome), 158
GAP Central, 116
gappisti. See Gruppi d'Azione Patriottica
  (GAP)
Garin, Eugenio, 295
Garrone, Sylvia, 60
gender norms and roles
  and Anita's political education, 46,
    48–50
  and Bianca's political education, 31–33
  and calls for insurrection, 373
  dress codes for women partisans,
    41, 374
  and female revolutionaries, 123–24
  and formation of GDD, 140–44
  and general strike of 1944, 210–11, 218
  importance of women to Resistance,
    131–33
  inequities among partisans, 155–56
  leaflet campaigns aimed at women,
    207–8
  and life after war, 402–3
  and marriage, 136
  publications aimed at Italian women,
    166–67, 320–21, 356
  Resistance activities favoring women,
    111–12, 182, 375
  and sexual violence in wartime, 191–93
  and Teresa's activism in Resistance,
    164–65

INDEX

women honored in underground press,
381–82
and women's firearms use, 375–76
women's role in liberating Italy, 398
Gentile, Giovanni, 19, 32, 163, 186, 237–38,
260–61, 274
"Giambattista" (partisan), 349–51,
361–64, 365, 399–400, 404
"Gianni" (partisan), 365–66, 374
Giardino della Gherardesca, 338
Gillars, Mildred, 179, 434n179
Ginzburg, Natalia, 18
"Giovanni" (Mario Fiorentini), 156–57,
158–59, 161–62, 229–31, 437n231
Giunti, Vittoria, 64
Gobetti, Ada
  Bianca's introduction to, 112–13
  and formation of GDD, 141
  and general strike in Turin, 204
  and German assault on partisan camps,
  257–59
  home in Meana, 113, 258, 377
  husband's death, 184–85
  life after war, 401
  and son's evasion of draft, 144
  source materials on, 419, 427n
  and supply missions, 348
  and underground press, 251, 347, 357
Gobetti, Paolo, 112–13, 144, 184–85
Gobetti, Piero, 112–13, 184–85
Gothic Line, 294, 308, 379, 388
Gottano, Italy, 399
graffiti, 124–28, 201, 391, 421
Grand Council, 57
Gran Sasso Mountains, 91–92
Great Britain, 150, 172. *See also* England
Groups for the Defense of Women and for
  the Assistance to Freedom Fighters.
  See Gruppi di Difesa della Donna e
  per l'Assistenza ai Combattenti della
  Libertà (GDD)
Gruppi d'Azione Patriottica (GAP)
  and Allied supply drops, 174
  Anita's activities with, 137, 322
  archival resources on, 421
  and Arno Hotel bombing, 261
  and assassination of Gentile, 237, 260
  and bomb attacks in Florence, 171
  and bomb attacks in Rome, 152–54, 155,
  159, 162
  bomb making, 154–55
  Carla's activities with, 105–7, 115–16,
  152–53
  and Carla's arrest and interrogation,
  212, 214
  and Communist newspapers, 114

and Florentine Resistance, 312
and general strike of 1944, 218
and German occupation of Rome,
  229–30
and intel operations in the
  Apennines, 360
members betrayed, 264–65
modeled on French Resistance, 105–6
and Nazi roundups of Jewish Italians,
  116, 117, 207
and recruitment of Resistance
  members, 222–23
and reprisals for Via Rasella bombing,
  255–56
safe houses, 267
and slow Allied advance in Italy, 181
and stalemate at Anzio, 228
and Teresa's use of weapons, 262
and underground press, 114–15
and Via Rasella bomb attack, 230–31,
  240–41, 246–48, 252
and women's role in Resistance, 165
Gruppi di Difesa della Donna e per
  l'Assistenza ai Combattenti della
  Libertà (GDD)
  Ada's role with, 141
  Bianca's role with, 141–2, 182
  Carla's role with, 152
  donations to, 370
  and factory activism, 381
  and final insurrection in Turin, 395
  formation and activities of, 140–43
  and general strike of 1944, 210, 215
  and German retreat from Florence, 341
  manifesto of, 320–21
  and murder of Arduino sisters, 383
  and political engagement of women, 167
  and support networks for partisans, 146
  Teresa's role with, 165
  and underground press, 251, 347
  and the Unione Donne in Italia, 419
Gruppi Universitari Fascisti (GUF),
  41, 68
Gualdi, Egle, 123–24
"Guglielmo" (Guglielmo Blasi), 231,
  244–45, 264–66
Gullace, Teresa, 208
Gustav Line, 170, 173–74, 194–95, 225,
  271–72

Hamlin, Françoise, 401
hideouts. *See* safe houses
Historical Institute of the Resistance,
  Reggio Emilia (ISTORECO), 405,
  410, 420–22, 423, 427n

Historical Institute of the Resistance, Turin (ISTORETO), 406, 410, 420, 426n, 431n112
Hitler, Adolf
and Allied invasion of Sicily, 13
assassination attempt, 345
and the Battle of the Bulge, 368–69
and Italy's surrender, 80
and liberation of Mussolini, 92
and reprisals for partisan attacks, 249–50
trip to Italy, 24–26
and wartime production measures, 344
and women's political activism, 73
Holocaust, 401
Honor and Combat group, 212–13
Hotel Arno, 261
Hotel Flora, 161
Hotel Majestic, 156
Hotel Ristoro, 146–47
humanitarian principles, 104

identification papers, 148, 172, 183–84
Il Popolo d'Italia, 18
Il Proletario, 321, 347
incendiary bombs, 45
indoctrination campaigns, 20–21, 397
Information Office, 360
In Marzo, 356
insignias of military units, 173, 350
intelligence operations
Anita's leadership of Information Office, 360
Anita's missions, 342, 350
and bomb attacks in Rome, 161
Carla's missions, 158
and food riots in Rome, 263–64
and partisan radio broadcasts, 172–73, 303–5
and Resistance safe houses, 182
and Sanguinetti's arrest, 274–75
and transport of radio transmitters, 308–10
See also scouting and reconnaissance missions
international law, 99
International Women's Day, 124, 356, 381–82
Istituto Storico Toscana della Resistenza, 420
Italia Libera, 354
Italian civil war, 96, 401
Italian Fascist army, 144, 235. See also Nazi-Fascists

Jewish Italians
and Bianca's background, 29
and Carla's motivations, 240
female Jewish revolutionaries, 123–24
and German occupation of Turin, 94
and Hitler's trip to Italy, 26
Jewish neighborhoods, 115, 117
propaganda campaign against, 26–28
and reprisals for Via Rasella bombing, 253
and Resistance fighting in alpine towns, 96–97
roundups of Jewish Italians, 115–17, 118–22, 145, 147, 197
and Teresa's family background, 16
Justice and Liberty movement, 61

Kappler, Herbert, 188, 189
Katz, Robert, 425n
Kesselring, Albert
and conscription efforts, 95
and German invasion of Italy, 70
and German occupation of Italy, 91
and power of the Resistance, 169, 256
and Resistance fighting in Turin, 95
and Youth Front sabotage missions, 314
kidnappings, 188
Kiev, Ukraine, 123, 125
Koch, Pietro, 169
Koch gang (Banda Koch), 93, 169, 265–66, 286
Kuliscioff, Anna, 123
Kurzman, Dan, 425n

Labò, Giorgio, 155, 188–89, 222
L'Accademia d'Italia, 186
La Difesa della Lavoratrice, 346, 370–73, 381–82
La Fondazione Archivio Diaristico Nazionale, 419–20
Lagastrello Pass, 366
La Gianna talc mine (partisan camp), 108, 233, 251, 258
"Laila." See Malavasi, Anita
Lake Garda, 92
la maternage, 401
Lancia, 91
landmines, 10, 12, 176–77, 329, 336–37
La Resistenza della Donne, 403
L'Arno scorre a Firenze, 172
Larocca, Gilda, 172–73, 304–5
La Spezia, 404

INDEX

leaflets
Allied airdrops of, 10, 43, 286
encouraging mass protests, 54
and Fascist raids on Resistance, 147
and "flying rallies" in Turin, 385
and German retreat from Florence, 337
Teresa's authorship of, 67
and women's activism, 207–8
League of Nations, 22
Legal Institute, 383
Le Murate prison, 67, 313, 315
Levi, Carlo, 18
Levi, Primo
and Bianca's background, 29
escape to mountains, 97
life after war, 401
and roundups of Jewish Italians, 119, 145, 146–47
sent to concentration camp, 196–97
looting, 116–17, 267, 287, 316
loyalty pledges, 186
Lucas (General), 175–76, 180
L'Unità, 62–63, 189, 287
Lusana, Luciano, 152–53, 155, 158, 288
Lusana, Rina, 158–59
Luxemburg, Rosa, 123

Maestro, Vanda, 146
Malavasi, Anita
and air raids, 89–90
arrest and interrogation, 324–27
assisting deserters, 102–3
background, 45–47
battle name, 139
and Battle of Monte Caio, 361–66
broken engagement, 349–50
childhood, 46–47
courier missions, 276–77, 322–24
education of, 47–51
and final insurrection in Reggio Emilia, 392–93
illness, 367
and intel operations in the Apennines, 359–61
life after war, 399–400, 404
and living conditions of partisans, 386–87
with partisan band Apennine Mountains, 332–34
and political education of Italian women, 166–67
portrait of, *xiii*
prisoner transport missions, 375–76
reconnaissance missions, 350–52
sabotage missions, 374–75

at safe house in Ceresola, 342–43
and scope of text, 2, 3
source materials on, 420, 422
and Torelli, 103–4
transport of radio transmitters, 308–10
transport of weapons, 134–39, 322–27
Manifesto of the Racial Scientists, 27
martial law, 218
Marx, Karl, 55, 142, 428n55
Marxism, 52
Mattei, Camillo, 315
Mattei, Gianfranco
arrest and torture of, 188–90, 193, 198–99
and assassination of Gentile, 261
and bomb making, 155, 188
death of, 199
and Nazi occupation of Florence, 118–19
partisan band named for, 338
and Teresa's first mission for Resistance, 66
Mattei, Nino, 199, 313–15, 336, 340–41
Mattei, Teresa
and Allied supply drops, 174
and anti-Jewish laws, 28
and Arno Hotel bombing, 261
arrest and torture of, 191–93
and assassination of Gentile, 237–38
bomb attacks in Florence, 171
bombing of railroad tunnel, 293, 294–95
and Bruno's release from prison, 306
and Campo di Marte massacre, 236
education, 28, 64
family background, 15–21
first actions for Resistance, 22–24
first assignment for Florentine Resistance, 65–66
and general strike of 1944, 210–11
and Gianfranco's arrest and death, 189, 198–99
and intelligence operations, 131–33
life after war, 400, 404
and Nino's rescue from prison, 313–15
and partisan radio broadcasts, 172
portrait of, *xiii*
pursued by Germans, 295–96
and roundups of Jewish Italians, 118–22
and Bruno Sanguinetti's arrest, 273–75
and scope of text, 2, 3
and street battles in Florence, 335, 337–41
and underground press, 189–91
and women's role in Resistance, 164–65

Mattei, Ugo, 16–17, 21, 22–23, 24–26, 118
Mauthausen concentration camp, 218, 219
medical supplies
  and living conditions of partisans, 367
  and partisan raids on Germans, 280
  and raids on partisan safe houses, 324
  shortages in Rome, 181, 200
  staffette's distribution of, 130
  stolen from hospitals, 309
Mediterranean corridor, 12
mercenary forces, 93, 265
Messina, Italy, 12
Microtecnica, 385
Milan, Italy
  activism among female factory
    workers, 40
  factory strikes, 53
  Fascist Party newspapers in, 18
  and formation of GDD, 140–43
  and general strike of 1944, 203, 215,
    218, 219
  and onset of war in Italy, 10
  and Teresa's courier missions, 66
  and Teresa's family background, 16
mimeograph machines, 111, 251, 319,
  346–47, 355–56
"Mimmi." See Montanari, Maria
Ministry of War, 156
Mobiglia, Santina, 419, 426–27n
Montale, Eugenio, 153
Montanari, Maria
  assisting deserters, 102–3
  battle name, 308
  and final insurrection in Reggio Emilia,
    392–93
  and German occupation of Reggio
    Emilia, 90
  supply missions in Apennines, 137
Monte Cassino, 194–95, 225, 227–28,
  271–72, 274, 279–80
Monte Castello, 379
Monte Rosa, 95
Moroccan Goumiers, 272
Morse code, 303
Mount Vesuvius, 242
Museo Diffuso della Resistenza, 421
Museo Storico della Liberazione, 421
Mussolini, Benito
  and antiwar sentiment, 54
  and attacks on Italian Jews, 26–27
  deposed, 57–58, 60–61, 66, 69, 77
  and Fascist indoctrination in
    schools, 32
  and Gentile's philosophy, 237
  and Hitler's trip to Italy, 24–26
  and key tenets of Fascism, 19

  liberated by Germans, 91–92
  and military conscription efforts, 196
  and nationalist parades, 82–83
  and onset of war in Italy, 11
  puppet regime under Hitler, 92, 94–95,
    120, 145, 168
  and rise of Italian Fascism, 34–35
  and scope of text, 4
  and Spanish Civil War, 22–23
  and Teatro Reale dell'Opera, 152
  and Teresa's family background, 16–22
  and women's political activism, 73–74
My Life (Trotsky), 30–31

Naples, Italy, 25, 177, 243, 285, 317
nationalism, 19, 20, 24, 82
National Library, 59
Nazi-Fascists
  and Bianca's courier missions, 297
  and bomb attacks in Florence, 171
  and bomb attacks in Rome, 162
  and Bruno's arrest, 274
  and Campo di Marte massacre, 237
  and collaborators, 358
  execution of partisans, 137–38
  and final insurrection in Florence,
    317–18
  and final insurrection in Reggio
    Emilia, 392
  and Florentine Resistance, 311,
    312, 313
  and "flying rallies" in Turin, 384–85
  and general strike of 1944, 202, 205,
    219–20
  and German occupation of Rome,
    115, 227
  and German retreat from Italy, 387
  and organization of Resistance forces,
    168
  partisan attacks on, 109, 257, 297–98,
    348, 374–75
  and partisan intel operations, 360
  patrols in partisan areas, 377
  propaganda press, 357
  and Republic of Salò, 95
  and stalemate at Anzio, 201
  and street battles in Florence, 337
  use of term, 429–30n
  and Via Tasso prison, 421
Nazis
  and Allied invasion strategies, 150
  and German occupation of Reggio
    Emilia, 89–90, 104
  and German occupation of Rome, 99
  and living conditions in Rome, 200

and Resistance bomb-making
  operations, 189
  response to strikes, 216–20
  roadblocks and checkpoints, 190
  roundup of Jewish Italians, 115, 118–22,
    145, 147
  use of term, 429–30n
  See also Nazi-Fascists
Nebbiolo Macchine, 38
neo-Fascists, 3, 92, 402
"Nerina." *See* Serra, Bianca Guidetti
The New York Times, 218, 227, 354
Nissim, Luciana, 146
Noi Donne, 356
Normandy invasion, 150–51, 304, 344
Nostra Signora della Salute, 356
Nuremberg Laws, 22
nurses, 335–36

Office of Demography and Race, 27
Office of Strategic Services (OSS), 180
Olivetti, Adriano, 18
Olivetti, Camillo, 145
Oltrarno neighborhood (Florence), 25, 65,
    312, 328, 330–31, 336, 339–40
Operation Overlord (Normandy invasion),
    150–51, 304, 344
Organization Todt, 272

pacifism, 17
Pact of Steel, 35
Palazzo Barberini, 243–44
Palazzo Montecitorio, 125
Palazzo Pitti, 25, 328, 330
Palazzo Vecchio, 337–38
pamphlets, 167, 182
Panzer Grenadier Division, 76
"Paolo." *See* Bentivegna, Rosario
paratroopers, 317, 369
Parma, Italy, 360–61
partisan warfare, rules of, 129–30
Pasquale (Balsamo), 243, 246–47
passeggiata (evening walks), 75
passeurs (border smugglers), 97
passwords, 63, 100–101, 106. *See also* codes
    and code words
patriarchy, 193. *See also* gender norms and
    roles
personalausweis (circulation permit
    cards), 148, 183–84
Perugia, Italy, 190, 192
Piazza Barberini, 157, 159–60
Piazza Carlina, 397
Piazza del Popolo, 126, 128, 229

Piazza Santo Spirito, 164, 329
Piazza Venezia, 34
Piazza Vittorio Emanuele II, 56, 66–67,
    214, 222, 231
Piccole Italiane, 47
Piedmont region
  and factory strikes, 53
  and general strike of 1944, 146
  and organization of GDD, 143, 146
  and organization of Resistance,
    108–10
  and underground press, 370–73
Pietra di Bismantova, 359
Pirelli (tire company), 17
Pius XII, pope, 54, 169, 207, 227
Poland, 37, 272
Police Directive Number 5, 145
political prisoners, 21, 60, 67, 100,
    197, 205
Ponte alle Grazie, 329
Ponte dell'Industria, 264
Ponte Santa Trinita, 329
Ponte Vecchio, 25, 329, 336
Porta Maggiore, 222
Porta San Paolo, 81–82, 87
Portelli, Alessandro, 425n
posters, 10, 30, 33, 58, 74, 391
Po Valley, 379, 388–89
Prencipe, Giacomo, 420
Prenestini Mountains, 270
Priebke, Erich, 180–81, 189, 254
printing and publishing. *See specific*
    publication names
printing machines, 110–12, 319–20, 355
prisoners of war (POWs), 197, 375
Program of Action, 141–42
propaganda
  Axis Sally broadcasts, 179–80
  Fascist posters, 10
  and Florentine Resistance, 312–14
  and German control of Italy, 98
  and German occupation of
    Rome, 227
  and Italian antisemitism, 26–28
  and Italy's surrender, 87
  and Mussolini's deposition, 58
  and Nazi-Fascist press, 357
  and the Pact of Steel, 35
  and Resistance fighting in alpine
    towns, 96
  and rise of Italian Fascism, 20–21, 36
  tracts against Republic of Salò, 251
  and underground press in Turin, 111
  See also leaflets
Pugno Chiuso, 67
Pyramid of Caius Cestius, 81–82

Quartiere Coppedè, 268
Quirinal Hill, 159

racism
and attacks on Jewish people, 26, 119
race selection theory, 239
racial laws, 22, 27–29, 69, 118–22
radio broadcasting
and Allied advance on
Rome, 286
and Allied airdrops of radios, 172,
303–4, 307–8
Allied Radio, 286
"Axis Sally," 179–80
BBC radio, 35–36. See also Radio
London
and Fascist propaganda, 10
and German control of Italy, 98
and liberation of Rome, 294
and Mussolini's rise to power, 20
Radio CORA, 172–73, 294, 303–5, 420
Radio London, 35–36, 57–58, 78, 79,
123, 127, 168, 285, 307, 353
Radio Munich, 92
and reprisals for Via Rasella
bombing, 255
transport of radio sets, 308–10
and Via Rasella bomb attack,
252–53
railroads, 151, 184, 224–25, 293, 339
"Raoul" (partisan), 265
rape, 191–93
rationalist architecture, 20
rationing, 36, 74. See also food supplies
and shortages
reconnaissance operations. See scouting
and reconnaissance missions
Red Army, 373
red cross symbols, 335–36, 338,
395–96, 403
refugees, 120, 328, 330
Reggiane aircraft factory, 45, 50
Reggio Emilia, Italy
Allied bombing of, 45
and Anita's family background,
47–50
Anita's missions in, 137, 322–23
and formation of GDD, 143
and German retreat from Italy, 387
and movements of Resistance
forces, 103
and partisan radio broadcasts, 308
safe houses in, 360–61
and scope of text, 2

Regina Coeli prison, 100, 162, 253
Republican National Guard, 144
Republic of Salò
and anti-Fascist propaganda, 251
formation of, 92
gappisti actions against, 262
headquarters in Florence, 237
and military conscription, 95,
143, 168
and "Nazi-Fascist" term, 429–30n
and roundups of Jewish Italians,
120, 145
Resistance-Archive.org, 422
roadblocks, 93, 232, 318, 429n
"Rodolfo" (Resistance member),
124–27
Romania, 344
Rome, Italy
and Allied assault on Monte Cassino,
271–72
and Allied bombing raids, 10
and Allied landings at Calabria, 75
and Allied radio broadcasts, 172
and Allied war strategy, 149–50
bomb attacks in, 189–90, 221–23
bomb making in, 188–89
Carla's assassination mission,
159–61
Carla's bombing missions, 152–58,
161–63
Carla's family background, 58–59
Centocelle neighborhood, 177
and formation of GDD, 143
and German mobilization into Italy,
80–83
Hitler's trip to Italy, 25
and Italy's surrender, 80
Jewish citizens, 115
and labor strikes, 53
leaflet campaigns aimed at women,
207–8
liberation of, 294
living conditions in, 200, 263–64
Nazi occupation of, 99
Nazi roundups of Jewish Italians,
118–22
provisional Allied government, 286
and surrender negotiations, 76
and Via Rasella bomb attack, 239–48
See also San Lorenzo neighborhood;
Trastevere neighborhood
Roosevelt, Franklin Delano, 13
"Rosa" (Marisa Musu), 208–9, 212
"Rules of Partisan Warfare," 129–30
Russian Revolution, 123–26, 128

INDEX

sabotage
  activism among female factory workers,
    40–41
  and Ada's son, Paolo, 184
  and Allied advance on Florence, 318
  and Allied airdrops of munitions,
    172–74
  and dangers of partisan activities, 137
  and Florentine Resistance, 312–14
  and general strike of 1944, 206, 218
  and German retreat from Florence, 339
  and German takeover of Italy, 91
  Nazi reprisals for attacks, 151
  Nazi roadblocks and checkpoints, 190
  selection of targets, 109–10
  and supplies stolen from Nazi-Fascists,
    297–98
  and underground press in Turin, 142
  See also bombs and bomb making
"Saetta" (partisan), 333
safe houses
  bomb making at, 201, 239, 267–68
  Calvino's home in Florence, 118
  Carla on the run from police, 269–70
  Carla's activities with GAP, 105–7
  in Ceresola, 342–43
  Foro Traiano, 105–6, 123–24, 127, 152,
    154, 201, 222, 288
  Gobetti's house in Turin, 204
  outside Rome, 278
  radio broadcasts from, 303
  in Reggio Emilia, 360–61
  and underground press in Turin,
    111–12
  and women's participation in
    Resistance, 182
salaries of Resistance members, 148, 187
Salerno, Italy, 69
Salmoni, Alberto
  and anti-Semitic propaganda, 29
  Bianca's political education, 56
  and German assault on partisan
    camps, 258
  and labor strikes, 53
  life after war, 401
  and partisan sabotage missions, 348
  and Resistance fighting in alpine areas,
    96–97, 184–85, 196
  at safe house in Meana, 377–78
  and supplies stolen from Nazi-Fascists,
    297–98
  support for Resistance forces in
    mountains, 108–9
  and underground press, 251
Salmoni, Fabrizio, 427n

Sandra (Anita's cousin), 102, 137, 322,
    324–25, 332, 364
Sanguinetti, Antonella, 400
Sanguinetti, Bruno
  arrested, 273–75
  and assassination of Gentile, 237,
    260–61
  and death of Teresa's brother
    Gianfranco, 199
  and Florentine Resistance, 313–14
  and German retreat from Florence, 339
  and Le Murate protest, 66–67
  life after war, 400
  political discussions with Teresa, 164
  released from prison, 305–6
  and safe houses in Florence, 118
  and Teresa's courier missions, 131–32
  and Teresa's recruitment into
    Resistance, 64–66
  and women's role in Resistance, 164–65
Sanguinetti, Gianfranco, 400
San Lorenzo neighborhood (Rome), 9–14,
    64, 71–72, 81, 106, 226, 240, 286
Santa Cecelia church, 115
Santa Maria Novella, 219, 224
Santerno River, 388
"sardine can" Italian tanks, 82–83
Scampate, Italy, 217
scouting and reconnaissance missions
  Allied reconnaissance of Rome, 176, 177
  Anita's role for partisan in mountains,
    334, 350–52, 374–75
  bomb targets in Rome, 189
  and GAP missions in Rome, 153
  at Palazzo Montecitorio, 125
  selection of sabotage targets, 109
Senza Fare di Necessità Virtù
    (Bentivegna), 425n
Serra, Bianca Guidetti
  background, 29–33
  battle name, 56
  and bombing raids on factories, 39–44
  and CLN leadership, 185
  courier missions, 297–302
  education of, 30–32, 41, 55, 233–34
  and final insurrection in Turin, 390–91,
    394–98
  and the Forty-Five Days, 94
  friendship with Ada Gobetti,
    112–13, 348
  and general strike of 1944, 202–6
  and German assault on partisan camps,
    257–59
  intelligence-gathering missions,
    183–84

Serra, Bianca Guidetti (*cont.*)
  joining Communist Party, 77
  and labor strikes, 53–56
  life after war, 400–401, 404
  and Mussolini's deposition, 77–78
  portrait of, *xiii*
  and Resistance fighting in Turin, 94,
    96–97
  at safe house in Meana, 377–78
  and scope of text, 2–3
  sister, Carla, arrested, 383–85
  social work job, 38–39, 77
  source materials on, 419, 421, 423,
    426–27n
  supply missions, 183–85, 297–302
  support to Resistance forces in
    mountains, 108–10
  and underground press, 110–12, 251,
    319–21, 346–48, 355–58, 370–73,
    381–82
  and women's activism, 182,
    319–21
Serra, Carla, 30, 42–43, 383–84
sexual violence, 191–93
shepherd paths, 309
Sicily, 12–13, 75
Siena, Italy, 121
snipers, 317, 329–30, 335–36, 338
Socialism and Socialists
  and Allied landings at Calabria, 75
  and Anita's political education, 48
  and graffiti missions in Rome, 128
  and Mussolini's deposition, 58, 60–61
  and Mussolini's rise to power, 17–19
  and political education of Italian
    women, 166
  and response to German occupation, 41
  and underground press, 142, 346
social norms, 403. *See also* gender norms
  and roles
social work, 77
Soviet Communism, 150
Soviet Union, 55–56, 150, 344
Spanish Civil War, 22–23, 35
Spanish Steps, 125, 128
"Spartaco" (Carlo Salinari), 231–32, 244,
    265, 288
spezzone, 162
spying and espionage, 172–73, 180, 276,
    303–5, 313. *See also* sabotage;
    scouting and reconnaissance
    missions
squadristi, 18
squadristi (Blackshirts), 18, 20–21, 34, 54,
    58, 61, 101, 112
SS, 115, 119, 132, 169

staffette
  and Allied air-supply missions,
    294, 303
  and the Battle of Monte Caio, 362, 363
  and bomb attacks, 158–59, 162, 230
  capture of, 325
  dissemination of messages and
    publications, 132, 141, 170–71, 174,
    184, 204, 236, 308, 321, 337–39, 345,
    350, 370, 382, 387
  and final insurrection in Florence,
    395, 396
  and formation of GDD, 141
  gossip targeting, 342, 402–3
  importance to Resistance, 131–33
  and leadership roles, 360, 362
  and living conditions of partisans, 386
  and partisan camps in Apennine
    Mountains, 359
  posing as nurses, 335–36
  Resistance activities favoring women,
    111–12, 182, 375
  scope of responsibilities, 130
  and sexism in Resistance, 374
  and support networks for partisans, 146
  term described, 2
  and transport of weapons, 138–39,
    322, 325
  See also specific individuals
Stalin, Joseph, 55
Storchi, Massimo, 420
strikes
  and labor strike of 1943, 52–53
  and general strike of 1944, 202–6,
    207, 210–11, 215–20
  Nazis response to, 216–20
  strike against hunger and terror of
    1945, 390
  women honored in underground
    press, 382
suicide, 198–99
supply lines, 225
surrender negotiations, 69, 76, 79–80
surveillance missions. *See* scouting and
    reconnaissance missions
Switzerland, 95, 97
Synagogue of Florence, 121

Taddei glass factory, 210
tank battles, 82–83
"Tatiana" (partisan), 350–51
Teatro Argentina, 115
Teatro della Pergola, 171
Teatro Reale dell'Opera, 152
Termini station, 118–19

INDEX

Tiber River, 188
Tiger tanks, 82–83
Tivoli, Italy, 80, 88
Tobagi, Benedetta, 403
Torcianti, Chiara, 420
torture
    and Anita's arrest, 325–26
    and capture of radio operators,
        304–5
    and Carla's arrest, 384
    and Carla's motivations, 240
    and death of Gianfranco Mattei,
        191–93, 198
    and Priebke's interrogations, 180–81
    as reprisal for bomb attacks, 222, 254
Trajan's Column, 82
Trastevere neighborhood (Rome), 115, 117,
    118–21, 127, 158, 201
Trinità dei Monti church, 125
Triton Fountain, 159
Trotsky, Leon, 30–31, 59, 428n55
Turin, Italy
    activism among female factory workers,
        40, 141–42, 182–83, 203–4, 372
    air raids, 42–43
    and Allied bombing raids, 39–40,
        41–44
    and anti-Semitic propaganda, 30
    Bianca's factory job, 38–39
    final insurrection in, 394–98
    "flying rallies" in, 384–85
    and formation of GDD, 143
    and general strike of 1944, 202–6, 215,
        217, 390–91
    and German military advance into
        Italy, 80
    and 1943 labor strikes, 52–56
    and murder of Arduino sisters, 383
    and recruitment to anti-fascist
        forces, 145
    and Resistance fighting in alpine
        towns, 96
    and scope of text, 2–3
    and underground press, 110–12, 142,
        321, 381–82
Tuscany
    and Bruno's importance to
        Resistance, 275
    and CTLN government, 311
    and general strike of 1944, 218–19
    and Hitler's trip to Italy, 25
    and Mussolini's rise to power, 18
    and railway bombing, 293
    and resources on female partisans, 403
    retreat of partisan fighters to, 366, 374
typewriters, 96

Ukraine, 344
Unione Donne in Italia (UDI), 419
United Nations, 80
University of Bologna, 421
University of Florence, 64, 295–96
University of Milan, 66, 118

V-2 rockets, 380
Val Germanasca (Valley of the Partisans),
    108–10
Valeriani, Lidia, 215, 216, 422
Valmonte, Italy, 283
Vasari Corridor, 330, 336, 339–40
Vatican City, 9–10, 99, 169, 207, 250
Verona, Italy, 80, 94, 219
Via Bolognese, 439n273
Via Cavour, 1
Via Dalmazia, 50, 323
Via dei Fiori Imperiali, 82
Via del Babuino, 229
Via del Traforo, 246
Via Marco Aurelio, 239
Via Rasella bomb attack, 230–31, 240–48,
    253–56, 265–66, 420
Via Tasso, 180–81, 189, 198, 240, 254, 288
Via Tomacelli, 223, 230
Via XXIII Marzo, 157
Vienna, Austria, 92
Villa Medici, 126
Villa Montalto, 260–61
"Villa Triste," 273, 304–5, 306, 439n273
Vittoria (partisan), 385
The Vittoriano, 124–25, 127
Vittorio Emanuele III, King of Italy, 18,
    57, 80
Voce Operaia ("The Worker's Voice"), 114
Volkbrinkel, 148

wages
    and Bianca's social work, 39
    and general strike of 1944, 205
    labor strikes and work stoppages, 52,
        372, 381, 390
    and power of labor activism, 54
War and Peace (Dostoyevsky), 46
war crimes, 192, 256
water supplies and shortages, 316
weapons caches and transport, 100–101,
    134–39, 172, 307, 322–27
Winter Line, 149, 170
Wolf, Gerhard, 329
Wolf's Lair, 92
World War I, 16–18, 22–23, 81, 90,
    121, 197

INDEX

xenophobia, 27, 402

Youth Front, 164
Youth Front (Fronte della Gioventù)
    arrested members freed, 336
    arrests of members, 313–15
    attack on GUF offices, 68
    and Bruno's involvement with
        Resistance, 132, 274, 306
    and liberation of Florence, 341
    origins of, 66
    sabotage missions, 312–15
    Teresa's connection with, 132
Yugoslavia, 130

Zetkin, Clara, 123
Zucca, Rita Louisa, 179–80,
    434n179

ABOUT THE AUTHOR

Suzanne Cope is a scholar and narrative journalist and the author of *Power Hungry: Women of the Black Panther Party and Freedom Summer and Their Fight to Feed a Movement.* Her work on themes of political and social change, feminism, food, history, and culture has appeared in *The New York Times, The Atlantic, Los Angeles Review of Books, Food & Wine,* The BBC, *The Washington Post, Aeon,* and other popular and scholarly publications. She also speaks frequently on these topics. Dr. Cope is a professor at New York University. She lives in Brooklyn with her husband, the musician Steve Mayone, and her children, Rocco and Lucian.